PREFACE

THERE is a wild and lonely solitude of sand where the sad cry of the sea-bird and the unceasing lap of the tireless tide are almost the only sounds that meet the ear of the wanderer who tracks along the Glamorgan beach over the site of the buried town—Kenfig—formerly the pride of its possessors, content and happy in its castle, its lands arable and pasture, its corporate and domestic life, its residents and denizens—"in fortune's varying colours drest." This once active centre lies deep below the all-devouring sand which has engulphed everything but one solitary fragment of a wall yet left, in cruel irony, to mark the actual spot where clash of sword and buckler, clatter of hoofs, and clang of arms were heard half a thousand years ago. But the history of the place remains scattered in ancient manuscripts; and to Mr. Thomas Gray, of Port Talbot, we all owe a debt of praise, for he has gleaned the scattered aftermath of its annals, reconstructed to the eye of fancy its edifices, clothed anew with vitality the dry bones of its antiquity, and with the true art of the archæologist caused us to feel, as it were, that we live in the very times which he has so eloquently depicted. And this depicting is not set in the high-sounding phrases of conventional rhetoric, but in a style bred of pure naturalness and keen observation—qualities which endow this book with a grace that cannot fail to charm its readers. The sand-girt town of Kenfig, like many another town in similar plight set on the Wirral of Cheshire, has had its day of fame and glory, its long array of noble owners, its active populace, its trade and its commerce, but these have fled, and it has been left to the author to recover from the veiled past a multitude of interesting records of facts which throw light on the history of Glamorgan.

WALTER DE GRAY BIRCH.

THE BURIED CITY
OF KENFIG

BY

THOMAS GRAY, V.D., J.P., M.Inst.C.E.

ILLUSTRATED

NEW YORK

D APPLETON & COMPANY

1909

To

MISS EMILY CHARLOTTE TALBOT,

OF MARGAM,

WHOSE GENEROUS ASSISTANCE TO THE CAUSE OF

ARCHÆOLOGY, BY PUBLISHING HER EXTENSIVE COLLECTION

OF PRIVATE RECORDS, HAS SO MUCH ADVANCED THE KNOWLEDGE

OF THE ANCIENT HISTORY OF GLAMORGAN, AND HAS IN GREAT

DEGREE ENABLED THIS WORK TO BE PREPARED,

THE AUTHOR GRATEFULLY DEDICATES, WITH

PERMISSION, THIS STORY OF HIS

RESEARCHES INTO THE PAST

HISTORY OF THE BURIED

CITY OF KENFIG.

February, 1909.

CONTENTS

LIST OF ILLUSTRATIONS

THE

BURIED CITY OF KENFIG

CHAPTER I

THE SITE OF KENFIG[1]

OVERHEAD birds are singing with heartfelt joy of life this glorious summer morning. All around me are hillocks of golden sand, tipped with pleasing contrast of colour by the green of the sea-sedge,[2] with which they are clad in part. The soft summer wind whispers its sad note through the waving rushes as it comes from over the great waste of triumphant sand which seems as it were out of place so far from sound of murmuring sea. There are in nature sounds which seem to me to bring

[1] As the traveller proceeds by the Great Western Railway along the coast of South Wales from Pyle to Port Talbot, on his left between the railway and the sea-shore sleeps the lost town to the history of which these pages are devoted.

[2] Sea-sedge : Ammophila arundinacea.

back to mind memories of childhood; so the sighing of the wind in lonely places somehow recalls thoughts and memories of the past, and thus I say the wind's note is sad.

The sand dunes now appear so restful that it is difficult to realise how ruthlessly the sand drove man from home and lands in far-off days. Here and there are still clear spaces of meadow, as if to keep in memory the green fields which once smiled in the face of the sun.

Gazing seaward, all seems a dreary, desolate waste; but if you walk among the dunes and take notice, wild flowers, and many, greet you here and there in brilliant clusters of varied colours. Sweetest of them all, I think, the little burnet rose,[1] which cowers low because the sea-wind has at times so little kindness. Wild mint[2] in patches gives pleasing glint of blue. Sea-holly,[3] with leaves of glaucous green and purple flower. The gold and the purple iris[4] with sword-like leaf. Viper's bugloss.[5] The lovely orchis in dark red, lilac, and some paler, almost white. The dusky bugle.[6] The geranium, the meadow crane's bill.[7] The great mullein.[8] The pansy, blue and yellow.[9] The fleabane.[10] The scarlet pimpernel, the poor man's weatherglass.[11] The yellow toad-flax,[12] sprung from Trojan Helen's tears, and in damp spots

[1] Rosa spinosissima.   [2] Mentha arvensis.
[3] Eryngium maritimum.
[4] Iris pseudacorus (yellow) and Iris fœtidissima (purple).
[5] Echium vulgare.   [6] Ajuga reptans.
[7] Geranium pratense.   [8] Verbascum thapsus.
[9] Viola tricolor.   [10] Pulicaria dysenterica.
[11] Anagallis arvensis.   [12] Linaria vulgaris.

the lovely turquoise blue forget-me-not,[1] and what is often called forget-me-not—and it is not unlike, if not regarded closely, the colour being almost the same—the Germander speedwell.[2]

All these and many more are there; they love the wild expanse, and strive to brighten a scene which would, without them, be more dreary still. The flowers I have seen on other days, when thoughts of Kenfig town were not those uppermost.

Life is here in plenty. The " wanton " plover wheels and swoops about, and seeks in plaintive cry to coax one from too great a nearness to its nest. The tawny owl finds happy hunting-grounds here, and the rabbit burrows ready-made places for its nesting. The kestrel, or windhover, hovers over its prey among the sand dunes; a hillock close by is called Twyn-y-barcud, the kite's mound. The cuckoo comes from sunny Africa to tell that spring is due; until it comes the spring seems still far off, for winter now holds fast so much of spring.

If one tarries till the glint of sun is somewhat worn, and rays come level from the west with cool shade cast from sandy mound, rabbits swarm, and, growing bold by dint of thoughts of waiting clover, gaze and wonder why you linger in their domain.

Yes, the sough of the summer wind here is sad, for it seems to bear the faint, far-off echoes of the busy town which once stood around this spot, eager and throbbing with life; here, where quiet reigns, was heard the hum of busy throng, the noise of work, the clang of men-at-arms, and sound of strident

[1] Myosotis palustris.   [2] Veronica chamaedrys.

trumpet from the castle-walls. Children babbled and played, and idlers basked and gossiped in the sunny streets.

Kenfig town once stood here, nestling close up to the castle-moat for feeling of security.

But the town has vanished, no vestige remains. The cruel sand, in league with storm, claimed it as its prey, and won it. Man was beaten ; the sand remained victorious. A little bit is left, it is true, but it is an outlying part, Mawdlam and the few scattered houses on the ridge, called Ton Kenfig. These look, in the drowsy summer heat, as if they had slept like Rip Van Winkle and had awakened surprised to find so little left of what had been before, and had gone to sleep again.

Refusing to be hidden by the sand, two gaunt arms rise from a grassy mound as if to bear witness of the great castle they had so long kept watch over—the only ruins of a lordly stronghold. These are the sole visible relics, with the moat in part, of Kenfig Castle.

At the foot of the mound, out of which project the two clumps of masonry, flows the Kenfig river. Beyond, to the northward, lies the great plain of Morfa,[1] and in the distance rise in bluish haze the bracken-clad hills of Margam, the scene of fierce struggles between Silures and Romans, and later, between Cymry and Normans. Bodvoc sighed his last breath on these hills long, long before this ancient castle rose in its pride.[2]

[1] Morfa, a moor which the sea overflows.

[2] The Sepulchural Stone on the Margam Mountain has this inscription :—

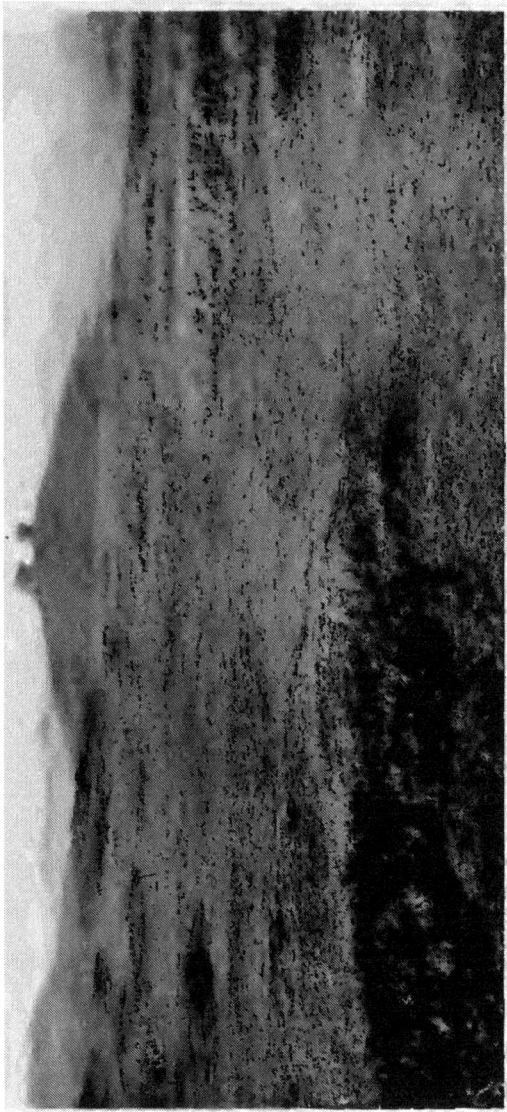

Just a little east of Kenfig Castle is the Roman highway through these parts, the Via Julia Maritima. In the stillness of the night fifteen hundred years ago, and more, one standing here—before Kenfig was

> " Bodvoci hic iacit,
> Filius Catotigirni
> Pronepus Eternali Vedomavi."

" Here lies (the body of) Bodvoc, son of Catotigirn, great grandson of Eternalis Vedomavus."

I believe Catotigirn to be Catigirn, son of Vortigern. Vortigern became King of Britain about forty years after the Roman power ceased in this country, *circa* A.D. 449. Catigirn fell in a battle against the Saxons under Hengist and Horsa, his brother Vortimer being the general. Nennius does not mention Bodvoc, but I believe he was a son of Catigirn. Westwood says " coins of gold and silver have been found with the name Bodvoc upon them ("Ruding's Coinage," British Series, App. pl. 29). The name Bodvognatus is mentioned by Cæsar, "De Bello Gallico," iii. 23. Pascent, the third son of Vortigern, reigned after the death of his father in Builth and Guorthegirnaim, a district of Radnorshire.

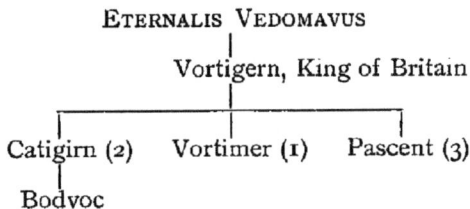

Eternalis Vedomavus
|
Vortigern, King of Britain
|
Catigirn (2)   Vortimer (1)   Pascent (3)
|
Bodvoc

Westwood, in his work " Lapidarium Walliæ," says the formula and orthography are debased Roman, so the date of the stone is probably of the fifth or early part of the sixth century.

Reference to the Margam and Penrice MSS. is made thus : T. 289 (Dr. Birch's Catalogue) ; and to the MSS. in Mr. G. T. Clark's " Cartæ et Alia Munimenta de Glamorgan " thus. (C. DCXIII).

2

thought of—could hear the tramp of the Roman soldiers of the Second Legion, the troops having the guardianship of the Western lands, and the rumble of the wagons conveying the *denarii*, or tax collected in the west, to the Imperial treasury at Isca Silurum or Caerleon.   Long since as this was, the road still recalls, by its name, the Roman occupation—Heol-y-troedwyr, the road of the foot-soldiers.

As I drove home along the Roman road, there lay basking in the sun, by the road-side, two modern "Latins" who little recked their proud ancestors had passed that way, they with sword, these with hurdy-gurdy, tax-collectors both.

Such is the site of Kenfig to-day ; silence and desolation reign supreme.

When did this desolation come about?   Did it come quickly, as a thief in the night, or was it a gradual overwhelming?   We cannot say.   Tradition has it that the besanding was caused by a great storm in the reign of Elizabeth ; but here tradition is at fault.   I believe the sand-fiend approached its prey with slow but sure strides, like a line of skirmishers sent out in front of the main body, and then with intervals of fierce rushes, always gaining ground, and retaining it.

We can, to some extent, judge of what took place from what is recorded as having occurred at Margam, near by.   A few of the Margam Charters mention the Hermitage of Theodoric[1] as a landmark in the description of the boundaries of the abbey lands.

[1] "The Hermitage of Theodoric and the Site of Pendar," Thomas Gray, *Arch. Cambrensis*, April, 1903.

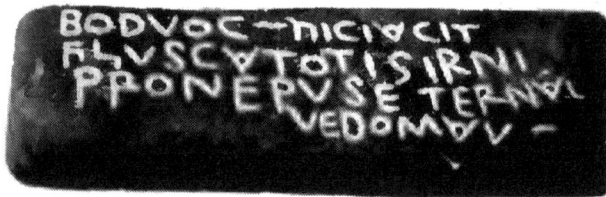

BODVOC STONE.

The original charter founding the Abbey of Margam is not extant, but its text is preserved to us in an Inspeximus by Edward le Despenser, Lord of Glamorgan and Morganwg, dated 13 July, A.D. 1358 (C. MCLXXXIII), of an Inspeximus by Hugh le Despenser, dated A.D. 1338, Oct. 9, T. 212 B (C. MCLI). The words here preserved of the original charter of Robert, Earl of Gloucester, bring to our knowledge that a Hermitage stood near the mouth of the Afan river on the east side at the date of the foundation of the abbey, A.D. 1147. The latest mention of the Hermitage in the Margam MSS. is found in a charter by Richard, Earl of Gloucester, between A.D. 1246 and A.D. 1249. After this date no mention is made of it in any of the MSS. The reason of this disappearance is probably given us by another abbey document dated 2 April, A.D. 1336, T. 211 (C. MCXLIII). In this it is related that the Abbot of Margam,[1] in obedience to the mandate of the Apostolic See and the Abbot of Clairvaux, the mother house, drew up a detailed account of the abbey's possessions, and following the list of the granges in the document, the abbot adds a complaint of the losses by mortality, wars, nearness of the abbey to the high-road, and the expense caused thereby through the entertainment of rich and poor who sought shelter and hospitality in the abbey, and that no small part of the land adjacent to the shore was subject to the inundation of the sea—doubtless meaning the sand-invasion and abnormal tides.

[1] Margam was called Margan, or Morgan, until the reign of Henry VIII.

In response Pope Urban VI. issued a Bull[1] T. 236 (C. MCCII) addressed to the Bishop of Llandaff sanctioning the appropriation of the patronage of the Church of Afan, Aberavon, by the abbey because, among other things, the Bull states the abbey lands adjacent to the shore had become unfruitful owing to the inroads of the sea. Dated 17 July, A.D. 1383. For the same reason, and by Papal authority, Penllyn Church was also appropriated.

In the Rev. J. D. Davies' "West Gower" a tradition is mentioned which would show that a great sand-invasion took place about A.D. 1317. A grant dated June, A.D. 1317, is in existence ; by it Sir William de Breos, Lord of the Seignory of Gower, gives liberty to his huntsman William and Joan his wife to take hares, rabbits, and foxes in the sand-burrows of Pennard. Mr. Davies remarks on this : " Here then, we have indisputable evidence that in A.D. 1317, Pennard burrows existed as a fact. The tradition is that it was formed by a terrible storm, all in one night, and . . . the conclusion is almost irresistible that both these burrows, Pennard and Penmaen, were formed at the same time, and the Church and village of Stedworlango were overwhelmed when the sand-storm occurred, and consequently the besanding of these two Churches (Pennard and Penmaen) must have taken place previous to A.D. 1317."

Here we have evidence of what took place not far from Kenfig about this time, and doubtless great progress was made by the sand-invasion at Kenfig

[1] So called from the leaden seal, or " bulla," attached.

about the year A.D. 1300. It is also to be inferred, from the absence of any mention of the Hermitage of Theodoric in all documents after the dates I mentioned before—A.D. 1246–1249—that it fell a prey to the devouring sand between these dates and A.D. 1317.

I quote from my paper on the Hermitage of Theodoric: "It is interesting to discuss the question of the overwhelming of the buildings (the Hermitage) by the the sand-storms. Were they covered up slowly, or at once? When I discovered the ruins, I was puzzled to know what part we were in, and later found we were in the upper storey. Dividing two of the rooms, I found a clay partition three inches thick, plastered with mortar on each side, still standing, supported by the sand, although the floor had disappeared. This seems to me to prove that the sand enveloped the building quickly; otherwise, if the sand took a considerable time to reach the upper storey, this fragile partition would have crumbled and fallen by the action of the wind and rain, to which it would soon be exposed after the buildings were abandoned."

Looking through the Ministers' Accounts in the Record Office recently, I noticed in one document mention of a field being destroyed by the sea about this period at Kenfig.

This is a return by John Giffard de Brymmesfeld, "custodis terrarum et tenementorum que fuerunt Gilberti de Clare Comitis Gloucestrie et Hertfordie defuncti in manu domini Regis existentium in Glamorgan et Morgannoc de exitibus eorundem a xx° die Aprilis anno Regis Edwardi nono usque xxix^m diem Septembris proxime sequentem." This is the account rendered in the ninth year of Edward II., not, as the heading would lead one to suppose, in the ninth year of Edward I. The endorsement, too, shows it to be Edward II., as he is there, as usually, styled "Regis Edwardi filii Regis Edwardi." I very nearly followed one writer who places the date of the document April 20, 1281. John Giffard de Brymmesfeld, called "Le Rych," had charge of the castles and lands of the lordship of Glamorgan and Morganwg on the death of Gilbert de Clare, eighth Earl of Gloucester and tenth and last Earl of Clare, on the 23 June, A.D. 1314, at the battle of Bannockburn ; the lordship of Glamorgan falling into the hands of the King. This account of Brymmesfeld is from 20 April to the 29 September, 1316. That this date is right is also proved by a reference to the account of Bartholomew de Badlesmere, who had charge in A.D. 1314.

Under the head of Villa de Kenefeg cum Castro is the entry in the " compotus " :—

(*a*) "Exitus Manerii. Idem respondet de ijs. vjd. receptis de quadam pastura que vocatur 'Conynger' vendita per idem tempus et ideo minus quia submersa per mare in magna parte."

(*b*) " Issues of the Manor. The same answers for 2 shillings and 6 pence received from a certain pasture which is called 'Conynger' sold for the same time, and there is less because the great part is drowned by the sea."

In the return made by Bartholomew de Badlesmere in the year A.D. 1314, when he was in charge of the castles and lands of the late Earl of Gloucester, he received 12 pence for pastura cuniculorum, or "the Conies' Pasture." This is the pasture called "Conynger" in the return made by John Giffard de Brymmesfeld two years after, namely, A.D. 1316.

The account is for one quarter of the year, so the rent for the year would be 4 shillings. But the account goes on, and for 2/6 received for pasture sold in the same place (namely, in the Conynger, or Conies' Pasture).

In 1314, therefore, the pasture yielded 12 pence and 2/6 in the quarter of the year, or 14/- for the year. In the year 1316, owing to the inroad of the sand, the yield for the half-year was only 2/6 or 5/- for the year.

Conyger is meant by Conynger. In Wright's "English Dialect Dictionary" is given Conyger, also spelt conieger, conigar, conigre—a rabbit-warren, coney-garth. Old French conniniere—a rabbit-warren.

The accounts of the two officials in charge of the late earl's property are important, in that they show that between September of 1314 and April, 1316, a great storm had covered the pasture called Conyger to the extent of one-half.

I can well imagine what the Conyger was like: a large, wind-swept, open grass-plain with rabbit-burrows here and there, close upon the marge of the Severn sea, similar to the fields along the sea-shore at Sker; probably the resort of the inhabitants of Kenfig for recreation and sweet sea-breezes from off the Atlantic.

Invasions of sand are often referred to in the ancient MSS. as inundations of, or drownings by, the sea.

Here, then, we have one of the earliest actual records of the besanding of land at Kenfig.

It is interesting to note, although it may not prove much, that Hugh le Despenser, Lord of Glamorgan and Morganwg, granted, T. 220 (C. MCLXVII) to Margam Abbey a free warren in his rabbit-warren or cuniculary in the Berwes, or burrows, between the Rivers Avene and Kenfig, on the west as far as the sea, and as the highway extends from the town of Avene to the town of Kenfig on the east. Feb. 16, A.D. 1344. It shows that the sands had by that time become so extensive as to become an important breeding-place for rabbits. This besanding took place apparently at about the same time in other parts. The learned historian, Abbot Gasquet, writing to me, says, "Your discovery of the ancient hermitage buried in the sand is most interesting. It reminds me of the discovery of the complete church of Soulac, near Bordeaux, which had been likewise buried for centuries."

I had at that time, A.D. 1898, discovered the ruins of the Hermitage of Theodoric [1] on the spot indicated in

---

[1] I thought the Hermitage (see " Hermitage of Theodoric and Site of Pendar," *Arch. Camb*., 1903) might have been founded by Theodoric, nephew of Sir Richard de Granavilla. I had but slender grounds for this idea, and I now have changed my mind. Looking through a "History of Heroes in Welsh Pedigrees" in the British Museum, I read that "Teithvach ap Kynan King of Glamorgan had a son Theodor who became King of Glamorgan and a Saint. The Register of the Church of Llandaff saith that St. Theodoric ap Teithvach King of Glamorgan lived about the time that Voitiper or Gwrthefir was King of Britain (A.D. 460–470). That having war with the Saxons was always Victorious in Battle till at length tired with

the charters of Margam Abbey; the foundation charter of Robert Earl of Gloucester mentions it, so that the Hermitage existed before the Abbey.

In the same Minister's Account we find damage was done to lands at Neath. Under the head Manor of Neath, we find the entry :—

"Issues of the Manor :—

"Meadows there, nothing for the same time, because they were drowned by the sea, except fifteen acres that were mown to get hay for the constables'

war he exchanged his crown for a Hermitage and Resigned his Royall Dignity to his son Meuric, upon which the Saxons miserably destroying his Country his People compelled him to quit his Desart to be their Generall whereupon Incouraged by an Angel with the promise of a Crown of Martyr Dom, being full of Divine zeale, he encountered the Infidell Enimies at Tintern by the River Wye in Monmouthshire totally overthrew them, but having received a dangerous wound in the Battle and perceiving it to be Mortall ordered his returne home and charged his son Meuric that in what place so ever he died he should there build a Church to God and Bury him and having not past aboue five miles, yielded his Blessed Soule to God at the meeting of the Rivers Wye and Severne where his son accordingly built a church and buried him, therefore called by his name Merthyr Tudoric, now by corruption Merthyrn or the Church of St. Theodor Martir." The church is now called Matherne or St. Theodoric.

I believe the Hermitage of Theodoric was where St. Theodoric, King of Glamorgan, retired upon resigning his royal dignity, and it was certainly situated at that time in a "Desart," a desert here meaning a lonely place such as hermits sought. Of course this must remain a conjecture, but there are good grounds for the idea. Here we have the Hermitage of Theodoric situated in a most weird and lonely spot, and we have the fact of St. Theodoric retiring to a hermitage; it is surely not necessary to look elsewhere for the place he retired to and erected his cell.

horses for the same time, and for the sheriff's horses against his coming for holding the Court . . . nil."

In the same document are mentioned the names of two granges, under the head of Kenefeg with the Castle; I am unable to locate them. The entry is :—

"The same answers for £9 6sh. 8d. from the farm of the granges of Pennth moyl and Portreveshavok, given to the Abbot of Morgan in fee-farm by the ancestors of the Earl (of Clare) and of the farm of two mills there for the same time. The mills may be Llanmihangel and the Pandy."

Mr. Clark writes these granges Pennch moil and Portreveshanok, but I came to the conclusion, after careful examination of the original document, they are Pennth Moyl and Portreveshavok; and although they are given under the heading of Kenefeg, I was inclined to think Pennth Moyl referred to Penhydd and Portreveshavok to Hafod-y-porth.[1]

The mists of ages are almost as impenetrable as the sands hiding the town of Kenfig, and I can only hope to enable you to peer into the past by intervals. First, then, we have this stormy period of about

[1] Since I wrote the above I have seen the account rendered by Bartholomew de Badlesmere. In Badlesmere's account the granges are given as Penuth Moyl and Portreueshauok.

Although they are returned for in the same account as in Kenfig, I have no doubt these granges are Penhŷdd, Moel Gallt-y-Cwm, and Hafod-y-Porth. Therefore they have no connection with Kenfig.

The two mills are the Dyffryn Mill and the fulling mill at Farteg, near Bryn, the latter long since disused. The former, a grist-mill for a very long period, is now a woollen factory.

A.D. 1300. After a long interval the immortal antiquary, John Leland, comes by, and in his quaint
language and odd spelling gives us a glimpse behind
the curtain of time of Kenfig as he saw it three
hundred and sixty-eight years ago, for he was there in
A.D. 1538 or 1539. His account proves the tradition
that Kenfig was besanded in Elizabeth's time to be
wrong. Leland writes thus in his " Itinerary " :—

"From *Newton* to *Kenfike* Ryver a VI. miles. of
these VI. miles 3. be higgh Cliffes on the shore : the
other low shore and sandy Grounde. For the Rages
of *Severn* Se castith ther up much Sand.

" I hard one say that this *Kenfik* water is caullid
Colebroke.[1] There is a Manor Place caullid *Sker* a
2 miles[2] from the shore wher dwellith one *Richard
Loughor* a Gentilman.

" There is good Corne and Gresse but little Wod
by 3. or 4. Miles from *Newton* towards *Kenfik* on the
shore. Kenfike is a smaull Broke and cummith by
estimation not past a 3. Miles of out of the Mores
there about."[3]

Here follows the important part :—

" There is a village on the Est side of *Kenfik*, and
a Castel, booth in Ruines and almost shokid and
devourid with the Sandes that the *Severn* Se ther
castith up.

"*Kenfik* was in the *Clares* time a Borow Toun.

---

[1] A small stream which flows from Hirwaun in Margam and
falls into the Kenfig river a quarter of a mile north of Kenfig
Church. Leland was wrongly informed.

[2] This may mean two miles further on the shore.

[3] Kenfig river is eight miles from source to sea.

It standith a litle within the mouth of *Kenfik* water.

"*Morgan* Abbey and Village standith a 2. Miles of by North Este.

"From *Kenfik* to *Aber Avon* a 2. Miles by low Shore, parte Morisch and sandy with the Rages of *Severn.*"

Leland seems to have been much impressed by the angry Severn Sea. Here, then, we see what Kenfig was like three hundred and sixty-eight years ago, ruin had already overtaken the town and castle, and both were almost choked and devoured with sand.

I use the modern spelling Kenfig for obvious reasons. Kenfig to-day is not known to us as Cenffig; further on I will give the derivation of the word Cenffig.

In the Kenfig Ordinance, which I will give later, we find a clause which was added in A.D. 1572, by which the burgesses agreed to inclosing, parking, and ditching part of the free common of Kefncribor, Cefn Cribwr, "because," the clause runs, "wee have and yett doe yearly fall in arrearages and losses the which is to the portreeves great charges by reason of the overthrow blowing and choaking up of sand in drowning of our *Town* and *Church* [italics are mine] with a number of acres of free land besides the burgages of ground within the said libertys except three for the which burgesses so lost by the overthrow Yett nevertheless the rent thereof, is and hath allways been paid to the lords receivers, to the portreeves great loss and hindrance yearly in making of auditt."

This was not long after Leland had seen Kenfig.

But we have evidence of the state of things 122 years later. In the Survey and Presentment of A.D. 1660, which will be given further on, the jury of burgesses, in describing "the Lordship, Manor, Town and Burrough of Kenffig," state : " They also present and say that severall of the free tenants have lost their freehold (time out of mind) by reason of the choaking blowing and over-blowing up of the sands what number of years they know not."

In another clause they state :—

" To the 13th article they say that they are not certain what messuages or dwelling houses were and are within the said burrough or corporation by reason that the sands had overcomed (time out of mind) a great number of dwelling houses within the said burrough and town."

The late Mr. J. Rowland Phillips, in his " History of Glamorgan," writes, " that at Kenfig, for instance, a great tract of land had been swept away and rendered waste by repeated sand-storms of unusual magnitude. The first of which there is any account was a great storm in the time of Richard II., when an unprecedented high tide, swollen and infuriated by a great wind, devastated the shore, carrying away lands and houses and leaving in their places nothing but sand-hills."

This storm was preceded by others as disastrous, such as the inundations of the sea referred to by the Abbot of Margam, with the result, as we have seen, that the advowson of Aberavon, and later of other churches, was given to the Abbey.

We find in the Margam Abbey documents indirect

evidence of the progress of the sand-fiend. For some
time I could not understand no mention being made,
in the Margam MSS., of the present main-road which
passes through Pyle. The grant of Thomas Gramus,
referred to later, for instance. He grants to Margam
Abbey three acres of land in the culture of Deumay[1]
from Goylake stream[2] (Afon Fach now) to the road
leading from Kenefeg to Catteputte, Pwll-y-gâth ;
this road crosses the present main-road at Pyle ; had
the main-road been in existence at the time of this
deed, *circa* A.D. 1258, it would have been mentioned.

And so it is in several instances. Thomas
Gramus' land is described as being between Goylake
on the south and Longland on the north, but the
main-road which now passes through this land is
not mentioned. The only road mentioned in the
MSS., as leading to Margam is that from Pwll-y-
gâth, which crosses the Kenfig river at Rhŷd Yorath
Goch, Yorath Goch's Ford, near Longland. Yorath
Goch[3] was the owner of the land between Pwll-y-gâth
and the Gramus land on the west.

The main highway at that time was, it is clear, the
Heol-y-troedwyr and the Heol-y-sheet, the ancient
Roman road, and the present turnpike road passing
through Pyle was not constructed. In the Margam
MSS., the Roman road is termed the Via Regalis,
the high way or royal way.

---

[1] Culture of Deumay, that is, the arable land of Deumay.
This is the land which lies between the Goylake and the road
leading from Kenfig to Pyle.

[2] Goylake—lake means a river or stream. If the monk could
have written in Welsh he would have written Gwyll-lake, or dark
stream   [3] Yorath Goch, Red Yorath.

It is interesting to note that there was a bridge over the Kenfig river on this highway as early as A.D. 1245. The bridge is known as Pont Felin Newydd, or New Mill bridge. Thomas Gramus, by a deed T 289.45 (C. DCCCCXXIV) gives to God and to Blessed Mary of Margam—the Abbey is dedicated to St. Mary—with the advice and consent of his father, Roger Gramus, and his wife and heirs one acre of his land near the high-way, the Via Regalis, which road leads from the *bridge of the river of Kenefeg* to the Goylake river. The monks gave him twenty shillings for charity.

This bridge over the Kenfig river was probably Roman. The whole has now been replaced by an iron structure.

We must bear in mind, as I remarked before, that this road was the highway between Cardiff and Swansea, but owing to the invasion of the sand, it had, at one time, to be abandoned, or at any rate, the traffic was perhaps maintained with difficulty. A new piece of road was therefore decided on further inland, and was constructed between Stormy Down and Cwrt-y-defaid at Margam, a length of about four miles.

The old road, we have seen by the grant of Hugh le Despenser, was in use as late as A.D. 1344 (see page 24); the grant of the rabbit-warren, west of the king's way, Via Regalis, from Aberavon to Kenfig town.

We have no knowledge of the date of the deviation of the main highway, but it can be fixed approximately by the date of the building of Pyle Church, which is

stated in a Margam Abbey deed to have been
"newly erected" in A.D. 1485. The church would
not be built before the new road was made; if
the church was built, say, in A.D. 1480, probably
the road was constructed some time before this date.
This deed will be referred to in the part dealing with
the churches.

The drift-sand, when it eventually reached the main
road, Heol-y-sheet, the Roman road, must have caused
considerable difficulty in keeping it free for passage.
At each storm the sand would be driven on to and
over it, and I have seen a similar case when three
or four feet of sand would be piled on a railway in
a single night. Although the open road lying between
Pont Felin Newydd, past the Groes-y-dadl and the
point where the lane begins near the bend of the Afon
Fach, is close upon two miles from the sea, the sand
passed over it and beyond it at one point, six hundred
yards, completing the two miles from high-water
mark.

It is extraordinary that this piece of road, of a little
over half a mile in length, should have had to fight for
its existence so far from the sea.

Any one who has seen and felt, as I have, the drift-
sand carried by a furious gale, stinging the face and
compelling the traveller to blunder on with almost
closed eyes, can imagine the difficulty experienced
in traversing this road in a time of strong winds.

Planting the *Ammophila arundinacea* is always a cure
for the moving of drift-sand, and it is probable this
method was attempted in those days; but the great inroad of the sand at this point seems to have been driven

with such fury as to defy planting and to render it of no avail, successful as it is with slower movements of the sand-drift.

The great devastation caused by these sand-storms aroused the attention of the authorities, and I am able, by the kindness of Mr. Ivor Bowen, barrister-at-law, to refer to an Act of Parliament passed touching the matter. The Act was passed in A.D. 1554, sixteen years after Leland found Kenfig town and castle almost "shokid" with sand. The Act mentions "The great nuisance and losses that cometh and chanceth to the Queen's Highness and her Subjects by reason of Sand rising out of the Sea and driven to Land by Storms and Winds, whereby much good Ground lying on the Sea coasts in Sundry Places of this Realm and especially in the County of Glamorgan, be covered with such Sand rising out of the Sea that there cometh no Profit of the same, to the great loss of the Queen's Highness and her loving Subjects, and more is like to ensue if speedy Remedy be not therein provided." The Commissioners of Sewers were given additional powers and authority to deal with the matter.[1]

Mawdlam, so called from the Church of St. Mary Magdalene, and the few scattered houses of Ton Kenfig lie to the south and east of the site of the ancient town; the Prince of Wales Inn, which had in recent years become the town-hall of the borough, being half a mile away.

These houses lie along the ridge above Kenfig

[1] "The Statutes of Wales," Ivor Bowen, barrister-at-law (T. Fisher Unwin). Also in "West Gower," Rev. J. D. Davies.

Pool, originally a marsh, drained to some extent by a stream which flowed, according to an ancient deed, northward into the Kenfig river, and no doubt have contributed to the idea that Kenfig is derived from Cefn-y-figgen, the ridge above the swamp.   It is not so, for the ancient town stood on the flat ground at the head of the swamp near the castle and river, and so the true name is Cen-y-ffig,[1] the head of the swamp.

The waters of the marsh in course of time became ponded up by the drift-sand, and resulted in the considerable lake it now is.   I believe the surplus water still finds its way under the sand, and its outfall into the Kenfig river may be the Ffynnon Llygad, near the western part of the castle-moat.

There is no doubt about the site of the town of Kenfig ; for Leland, who actually saw it, clearly indicates the position.   He says :—

"It standith a little within the mouth of *Kenfik* water."

The following extract from a manuscript of about A.D. 1678, "The Manors of the Earl of Penbrock in Glamorgan," shows how the present village came to bear the status and name of Kenfig :—

"The borough of Kynfigge Sir Robert Fitz Hamon kept in his own hands, and builded a castle there, and used the same as one of his dwelling-houses.   How-

---

[1] "Cen" and "pen" are, I believe, synonymous.   The spelling of name in the Abbey deeds is almost invariably Kenefeg, phonetically rendered by the Norman scribe, therefore the name formerly was Cen-y-ffig, shortened to Cenffig. *Ff.* in Welsh = English *f.*

KENFIG CASTLE RUINS.

From a sketch in Donovan's "South Wales," in 1804.

[To face page 35.

beit, in a short time, both the town and castle were
drowned by the sand of the Sea, and there remaineth
but out cottages bearing the name of the borough of
Kynfigge, which hath the whole liberties yet remaining as the town formerly had : saving that the weekly
markets and annual faires are lost. The King's
Majesty is patron of the Church there. Kynfigge
river springeth in Ceven Cribwr, and runneth to
Pile, and so under Kynfigge Castle to the sea of
Severn."

As I have said, the town and the church of St. James
have disappeared, and Morgan Gam, or Morgan the
crooked, lord of Afan, son of Morgan ap Caradoc,
would rub his eyes could he come to life again, and
wonder what had become of the town he did his
best to destroy seven hundred years ago.

CHAPTER II

IESTYN AP GWRGAN AND SIR ROBERT FITZHAMON

TWO figures loom large in the dim mist of ages which cover the past of Kenfig, and much of the glamour which attaches to the place would be missing without them. They are Iestyn ap Gwrgan and Sir Robert Fitzhamon, the former the Prince of Glamorgan, the latter the Norman knight and conqueror of Gwrgan's lordship of Glamorgan.

Prince Iestyn was the hereditary and rightful ruler of these parts, the descendant of a long and princely line. But, unlike his noble father, he was a wicked and cruel prince, and he incurred the hatred of his countrymen. His advent to power is thus related in the "Brut y Tywysogion," the Chronicle of the Princes :—

"The same year (A.D. 1043) Hywel, Lord of Glamorgan, died at the age of 130 years. He was the wisest prince in Wales, and the most beloved by every one of his tribe ; and he loved peace and equity. And Iestin, son of Gwrgan, was placed in his room ; and he was the worst prince ever seen in Wales, and loved neither peace nor equity ; and he did nothing but what caused molestation and spoliation to his country and nation ; on which account no wise or orderly person assisted him when he was opposed."

Of course, a man of this character would be open to attack from others desiring to reign in his stead, and this actually came to pass. It is stated by Welsh chroniclers that Kenfig Castle was one of Iestyn's residences. By others Kenfig Castle is said to have been built by Sir Robert Fitzhamon. I believe the castle, and probably the town, owes its origin to Iestyn. Caradoc (*Myv. Arch. II.*) goes further still, and says that Iestyn, notwithstanding his incessant wars, *rebuilt* the castles of Kenfig and Boverton.

Still, with all his faults, Iestyn ap Gwrgan is a pathetic figure. Glamorgan comprised the country between the Rivers Usk and Neath and between the sea on the south and the Black Mountains on the north, so Iestyn ruled over a large and important territory, but he lost all and died a monk in Keynsham Monastery, near Bath. Sir Edward Mansell, writing in A.D. 1591, says that "Iestyn turned monk in Kensam Priory where he lived not giving out who he was till the time of his death when he discovered all, now being 129 years old."

The story of the conquest of Glamorgan has long been accepted, but it is probable, as Mr. Clark says, that the invasion by the Normans was part of a settled policy for completing the English conquest. This policy was undertaken by Fitzhamon, while other adventurers at the same time were taking possession of Monmouth, Brecknock, and South-West Wales.

At the risk of wearying some of my readers, who have read the story from my previous papers and from other works, I must briefly give an account of Fitzhamon's coming to our county.   It is probably fabulous, but it is interesting and there may be in it some substratum of truth.

In A.D. 1088 Cadivor, the son of Colwyn, Lord of Dyvet,[1] died, and his sons Llewelyn and Einon moved Gruffyd, son of Meredydd, to make war against Prince Rhys ap Tewdwr.   But Rhys put them to flight, killing Gruffydd.   Einon fled to Iestyn, Lord of Glamorgan, who likewise was in rebellion against Tewdwr, and promised he would on certain conditions marry Iestyn's daughter.   Einon having been in England, and knowing the English nobility, proposed to Iestyn that the aid of the Normans should be sought against Rhys.   So Einon went to England and was the means of bringing into Glamorgan Sir Robert Fitzhamon and twelve Norman knights with a large army [A.D. 1090].   The Norman army, and Iestyn's, burned and spoiled Rhys's land, and destroyed his people.   Rhys fought them at Bryn-y-beddau, near Hirwain,[2] and in the terrible battle he was slain.[3]

Mathew Paris,[4] in his quaint language, shall give you the sequel :—

"These Normanes, after they had received their promised Salarie and great rewardes of Jestyn, returned

----

[1] Dyved, the land between the Rivers Teivy and the Towy, or the present county of Pembroke and part of Caermarthenshire ; the south-western part of Wales.

[2] Hirwuen Wrgan, Gwrgan's Long Meadow.

[3] "Historie of Cambria, translated into English by H. Lloyd, gentleman, A D. 1584."

[4] Mathew Paris was a monk of the Monastery of St. Albans, *circa* 1217–1250.   His great work is the "Chronica Majora."

to their ships. When Eneon burthened Jestyn with the promise of his daughter in marriage, Jestyn laughed him to scorn and told him he would bestow his daughter otherwise; whereupon Eneon, full of anger and despite, followed the Normanes. And when he came to the shoare, they were all a shipboard : then he shouted to them, and made a signe with his cloake to call them back, and they turned again to know his meaning. Then he went to the chiefest of them, and shewed of his abuse at Jestyn's hands : declaring withall, how easie it was for them to winne that faire and pleasant countrie from Jestyn, whome for his treason to Rees none other than Prince of Wales would succour; whereupon they were easilie persuaded, and so ungratefullie turned all their power against him, in whose defense they had come thither, and at whose hands they had been well entertained, and recompensed with rich gifts and great rewards. And first they spoiled him of his countrie, who mistrusted them not, and tooke all the fertile and valey ground to themselves, and left the barren and rough mountains to Eneon for his part."

Prince Rhys, as we have seen, was killed ; Goronwy, his son, was also killed, and Cynan, another son, was drowned in the marshy bog called Pwll Cynan, on Crymlyn[1] Burrows, between Briton Ferry and Swansea.

The Normans are said to have been paid for their services at y Filldir-aur, the "Golden-mile," near Bridgend ; but, as is related, Einon brought them back. To Einon was given the lordship of Seinghen-

[1] Crymlyn, perhaps the curved lake.

nydd, but he ever after retained the name of Einon-y-bradwr, Einon the traitor.

Iestyn, in one account,[1] is accused of rebellion against Rhys ap Tewdwr, Prince of Deheubarth, but the charge of rebellion is untrue; for Morganwg was never included in the dominion of Deheubarth.[2] On the contrary, Caradoc and other writers mention it as an independent state throughout the whole of its history. Morgannwg has also been identified as the Essyllwg of remote antiquity, which, on some occasions of imminent danger, gave war-kings, Catteyrn, to the whole British confederation.

Rees Meyrick, in his " Morgania Archaiographia," written in A.D. 1578, says the war "sprang of the unsatiable desire of Rice ap Tewdwr to Justin's wife, and not for any title of subjection, as some lately of misreport affirmed."

The descendants of Iestyn were well treated, and were the only Welsh nobles who possessed lands in the lowlands of Glamorgan. To Caradoc, son of Iestyn, was granted the lordship of Margam, or Morgan, which comprised the lands from Crymlyn to Ogmore. It has been erroneously stated that Caradoc's lordship was confined to the district between the Rivers Afan and Neath. But we find from the Margam MSS., that the lords of Afan owned lands between the Afan and the Ogmore; lands at Newcastle, Bridgend, and Laleston being frequently mentioned. Sir Edward Mansel

---

[1] Iolo M. 3, in substance

[2] Deheubarth, "the south part," comprised the district of the Towy; part of the present counties of Caermarthen and Brecknock.

SEAL OF LEISAN AP MORGAN AP CARADOC AP IESTYN, APPENDED TO A DEED CONFIRMING THE LAND OF PULTHMOK, NEAR COWBRIDGE, TO MARGAM ABBEY. CIRCA 1213.

SIGILLVM. LEISAVN. FILII. MORGAN.

wrote, *circa* A.D. 1591 : "Some say that it was the lordship of Morgan or Margam which then consisted of the Country from Cremlyn to Ogwye and was the largest of all the lordships which Caradoc had with a deed securing to him the Principality of Glamorgan after his, Iestyn's, death."

Although the history of Kenfig begins with the Norman Conquest it is far older.

Mr. Clark, in his " The Kenfig Charters," says :—

" Kenfig is reputed by the Welsh to have been a private possession of Jestyn ap Gwrgan, which is exceedingly probable, seeing that in the general settlement it was reserved by the Earls of Gloucester, Lords of Glamorgan, as their private demesne ; and was by them, at a very early period, erected into a borough together with Cardiff, Cowbridge, Neath, Avan, and Llantrisant. A Castle was, in those days, a necessary adjunct to a borough town, and at Kenfig a castle was accordingly built. The Register of Neath Abbey cited by Sir E. Stradling attributes the Castle to William, son of Robert the Consul, who died in 1183. Rees Meyrick says he also built here 'a town for merchandize upon the sea bank.' "

William the Earl only re-built the town, for Meyrick says re-built.

The earliest mention of Kenfig which I have found is in the " Brut y Tywysogion," the Chronicle of the Princes :—

" Oed Crist 893, y daeth y Paganiad duon i Gymru dros for Hafren ac a losgasant Llanelltyd fawr, a Chynffig, a Llangarvan, ac a wnaethant ddrygau mawrion yn Morganwg, a Gwent, a Brecheiniawc, a

Buellt, ac ar eu gwaith yn dychwelyd yng Ngwaunllwg,
a nhwy yn anrheithiaw Caerllion ar Wysg y daeth
Morgan tywysawg Morganwg a chad yn eu herbyn,
au gyrru tros for i wlad yr Haf lle y lladdwyd
llawer o honynt gan y Saeson a Bryttaniaid y wlad
honno."

("The black Pagans came to Wales over the Severn
Sea, and burnt Llanelltyd the great and Chynffig and
Llangarvan ; and did great damage in Glamorgan and
Gwent and Brecknock and Buellt ; and during their
return through Gwentllwg, while ravaging Caerleon
upon Usk, Morgan prince of Glamorgan, fought a
battle with them, and drove them over sea to the
Summer Country (Somersetshire) where many of
them were killed by the Saxons and Britons of that
country.")

The black Pagans were apparently the Danes. I
may mention that a small camp made by a Danish
army exists in Cwm Philip behind Margam Park.

Here, therefore, we find Kenfig mentioned 254
years before William, Earl of Gloucester, succeeded
his father.

Interesting events followed the coming of Fitzhamon
into these parts, as we shall see. Some account, therefore, of this prominent man who became the possessor
of Kenfig is necessary.

Really not much is available as to his history, and
Mr. Clark, in his " Land of Morgan," writes : " It is
singular that of so notable a man as Fitzhamon so little
should be known."

Sir Robert Fitzhamon was the son of Hamo
Dentatus, a great lord and kinsman of William the

Conqueror, and descended from Rollo, first Scandinavian conqueror of Normandy.[1]

Sir Robert came to England in the train of William the Conqueror, and took part in the great conquest of this land, soon after himself to conquer our own county of Glamorgan.

In the " Annals of Tewkesbury " we find it stated " Anno D. 1066 William, duke of the Normans gained England ; Robert, a young man, son of Haymon lord of Astreville in Normandy came to England with William the Conqueror." [2]

Sir Robert was count of Corbeil and baron of Thorigny and Granville. He was, like his father, a great soldier ; but what is of interest for us is the fact that after the winning of Glamorgan he retained for

---

[1] The curious genealogy as given in the Register of Tewkesbury is as follows. Fitzhamon is stated in it to be the grandson of Hamo Dentatus, which is not correct.

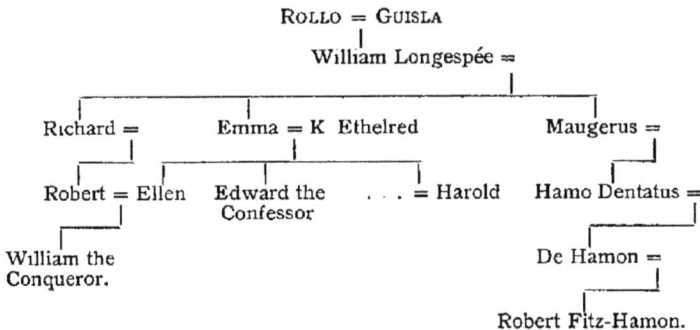

[2] " An° D. 1066 Gulielmus *dux* Normann. *acquisivit* Angliam. Robertus, *juvenis, filius* Haymonis *domini* de Astrevilla in *Normannia, venit* in Angliam *cum* Gul. Conquestore" (Leland's " Itinerary ").

himself Kenfig Castle and territory, and Cardiff. It is clear that the Castle of Kenfig was in existence at this period, otherwise it could not be said that he retained it for himself. He also retained the lands called Tir Iarll, "the earl's land." It includes to-day two parishes, Llangynwyd, which adjoins Margam, and Bettws; formerly Tir Iarll embraced a much larger district.

Sir Robert Fitzhamon, after the conquest of Glamorgan, styled himself, "by the grace of God, Prince of Glamorgan, Earl of Corbeil, Baron of Thorigny and Granville, Lord of Gloucester Bristow Tewkesbury and Cardiff, Conqueror of Wales, near kinsman to the King and Generall of his army in France." [1]

We now find Kenfig in the possession of Fitzhamon the Norman, and the former owner, the Welshman Iestyn ap Gwrgan, leading the contemplative life in Keynsham Priory, near Bath.

Sir Robert had four daughters by his wife Sybil, daughter of Roger de Montgomery. The daughters were Cicely, who became Abbess of Shaftesbury; Hawise, Abbess of Wilton; Amice, who married the Earl of Bretagne; and Mabel, the heiress.

Fitzhamon, like many of the great landowners of his time, devoted large sums in benefactions to the Church. Thus, at the persuasion of his wife, he endowed Tewkesbury Abbey, which was founded by the Dukes of Mercia in A.D. 715, and he came to be regarded as its founder, this was in A.D. 1102. He built much of the existing Church of Tewkesbury, dedicating it to St. Mary. His descendants, lords of

[1] Rees Meyrick.

Glamorgan, were patrons of the Abbey and had a right of veto on the election of the abbots.

One consequence of Fitzhamon's possession of Kenfig was that Tewkesbury Abbey came on the scene, and by gift of Sir Robert became possessed of lands at Kenfig, and so thereafter closely identified with the history of the town. We find in the Margam MSS. early references to the Abbey of Tewkesbury in connection with Kenfig. In a charter of King Edward I. he recites and confirms the several charters of King William II. and King Henry I. to the Abbey of Tewkesbury. That of William grants to the Monastery of St. Mary of Tewkesbury " these particulars following which Robert Fitz-Hamon and his tenants did give, to wit, . . . and the churches of Walis, with the lands, tithes, rents, and other things." Also Henry I., in another charter, grants churches and tithes in Cardiff and the " tithes of all the demesnes which Robert, son of Fitz-Hamon, held in Wales, and the tithes of all the barons' holding of Sir Robert Fitz-Hamon throughout all Wales."

Sir Robert Fitzhamon met a soldier's death. He was wounded in the temple at the battle of Tinchebrai in France, and of this wound he died in the year A.D. 1107, and was buried at Tewkesbury Abbey.

Mabel, his heiress, now became the owner of Kenfig, among other possessions. She inherited the Honour of Gloucester, the Lordship of Glamorgan, her father's lands in that county and elsewhere, and, in addition, her uncle's lands in England and Normandy.

As can be well imagined, she was much sought after in marriage. King Henry I., thinking she would be a suitable wife for his natural son Robert,[1] conducted negotiations for the marriage himself, so Mr. Clark says.

Womanlike, seeing no less a personage than the King sueing for her hand for his son, she became a little suspicious. Mabel told the King she was sought more for what she possessed than for herself, and that with such a heritage as hers she ought not to marry a lover unless he had two names—that is, a Christian name and a surname.

The King admitted that and said his son should be named Robert le Fitz le Roy. Then, with an eye to the future, Mabel asked what their son is to be called. The King answered, " Robert Erle of Gloucestre hys name ssal be."

Malmesbury says of the Countess Mabel, " She was a noble and excellent woman, a lady devoted to her husband and blest with a numerous progeny."

The title of Earl of Gloucester was conferred on Robert after the marriage by the King, and by right of his wife Mabel he became lord of Glamorgan, and the lords of Glamorgan were little less than kings. The marriage is thought to have taken place in A.D. 1117.

Robert Earl of Gloucester was a great soldier, and took part with his father, King Henry I., in the battle of Brenneville in A.D. 1119, and was present at the taking of Byton Castle in A.D. 1122. Geoffrey of Monmouth dedicated to the Earl his translation from the British tongue into Latin of the " Ystoria Bren-

[1] Earl Robert's mother is believed to have been Nest, daughter of Rhys ap Tewdwr, Lord of Deheubarth.

hined y Brytanyeit"—the "Historia Regum Britanniæ."
He writes : "To you, therefore, Robert, Earl of
Gloucester, this work humbly sues for the favour
of being corrected by your advice, that it may not
be thought to be the poor offspring of Geoffrey
of Monmouth, but when polished by your refined
wit, and judgment, the production of him who had
Henry the glorious King of England for his
father, and in whom we see an accomplished scholar
and philosopher, as well as a brave soldier, and
expert commander ; so that Britain with joy
acknowledge that in you she possesses another
Henry."

Such, then, was the husband of Mabel, Sir Robert
Fitzhamon's heiress.

One can understand that the Welsh could have
no liking for Fitzhamon, the conqueror of their
country ; but his son-in-law, not being associated
with the conquest, stood on a different footing,
and by his royal connection, great power, and con-
ciliatory character, brought the Welsh to think well
of him and to submit to his rule.

I often wondered what, in the first place, induced
Robert Earl of Gloucester and Mabel his wife to
give Margam to the monks of Clairvaux. I am now
able to show how it came to pass.

"*To Henry, King of England,* A.D. 1132.

"To the illustrious Henry, King of England,
Bernard, Abbot of Clairvaux, that he may faithfully
serve and humbly obey the King of Heaven in hi
earthly kingdom.

"There is in your land a property belonging to your

Lord and mine, for which He preferred to die rather than it should be lost. This I have formed a plan for recovering, and am sending a party of my brave followers to seek, recover, and hold it with strong hand, if this does not displease you. And these scouts whom you see before you I have sent beforehand on this business to investigate wisely the state of things, and bring me faithful word again. Be so gracious as to assist them as messengers of your Lord, and in their persons fulfil your feudal duty to Him. I pray Him to render you, in return, happy and illustrious, to His honour, and to the salvation of your soul, to the safety and peace of your country, and to continue to you happiness and contentment to the end of your days." [1]

The object of Bernard, the Abbot of Clairvaux, was to gain the sympathy and help of the King towards founding houses of the Cistercian Order in England. The monks sent by Bernard were received with honour by the King and the realm ; the Abbey of Rievaulx, in the province of York, was one result and the Abbey of Margam, fifteen years later, another.

Henry I., to whom this charmingly metaphorical letter was written, was, as you will remember, the father of Robert Earl of Gloucester, and when the King received the monks Robert and his wife were probably present, and this gave them a preference for the Cistercians and created in them the desire to emulate the example of Mabel's father, who had

[1] "Some letters of Saint Bernard, Abbot of Clairvaux," selected by Francis Aidan Gasquet, Abbot President of the English Benedictines.

largely endowed Tewkesbury Abbey, and of Sir Richard de Granville, her uncle, also, who founded Neath Abbey.

And so the Earl and his wife gave Margam, part of her dower-land, to the monks of Clairvaux, and the Abbey was founded and the white-robed Cistercian monks came and settled here, and their successors held the lands for nearly four hundred years.

Earl Robert also gave Ponte,[1] Briton Ferry, and Sker to Neath Abbey.

The charter conveying Margam to the monks is not extant, but the text is preserved to us in various other documents. On the back of a charter of King Henry III., notifying to his bailiffs and lieges that he has taken under his protection all men, lands, rents, and possessions of the monks on sea and land, is written the following :—

"The Foundation Charter of Margam Abbey—a charter of Robert (of Caen) natural son of King Henry I. Consul or Earl of Gloucester, addressed to Robert Norreis his sheriff, and all his men, French, English, and Welsh, whereby he grants to the monks of Clairvaux *i.e.* the Cistercians, all the land between the Kenefeg and Aven streams, his fisheries of Aven, etc., for founding an Abbey, etc., by consent of Mabilia (daughter of Robert Fitz-Hamon Lord of Glamorgan) his Countess of whose inheritance the land forms part."

This took place before A.D. 1147, for in that year

---

[1] Perhaps so called from the Latin *ponto*, a flat-bottomed boat such as would be used at the ferry.

we find the entry in the "Annales de Margan" of
the founding of the Abbey :—

"MCLXLVII. Fundata est abbatia nostra quae
dicitur Margan et eodem anno comes Gloucestriae
Robertus, qui eam fundavit, apud Bristollum obiit,
pridie kal. Novembris."

("1147. Our abbey which is called Margan was
founded, and in the same year Robert Earl of
Gloucester who founded it died at Bristol 31
October.") And so the pious founder died before
the Abbey buildings rose and displayed their mag-
nificence.

Margam Abbey, thus endowed by Sir Robert
Fitzhamon's daughter and her husband, and owning
the lands adjoining the Kenfig river on the west,
naturally soon became, with Tewkesbury Abbey,
largely interested in Kenfig and acquired lands and
tenements, in and about the town, the gifts of
pious persons.

Some brief account of the Cistercian monks who
thus came to Margam, and in course of time
became the owners of lands and tenements in
Kenfig, may be of interest.

The land, you will notice, was given to the monks
of Clairvaux in France, and doubtless the first
monks in Margam came from that Abbey. Clairvaux
is 120 miles east-south-east of Paris on the river
Aube.

False statements as to the lives of the monks were
so industriously taught at the period of the Reformation that these ideas have been handed down almost
to the present day. Thanks, however, to men like

Abbot Gasquet, Mr. Thorold Rogers, and others, we in our day have opportunities for learning the truth regarding the monks. There were some monks who led dissolute lives, but it is now known they were comparatively few.

Abbot Gasquet, although he writes with a Roman bias as regards the events which occurred in connection with Henry VIII.'s quarrel with the Pope, on account of the latter refusing to allow him, the King, to divorce his wife Catherine of Aragon, because he had awakened to the fact that she had been his brother's wife, is so fair and so accurate that I gladly quote from him.

He says: "Two great and fruitful ideas were kept constantly before the mind of the nation by the existence of these monastic houses — the life of perpetual praise and the life of associated labour. *Laborare et orare* [1] was the familiar principle which animated the course of every well-conducted monastic house, and which was, so to speak, the conservation of the spiritual forces, whereby the energy of faithful work became interchangeable with the energy of unremitting prayer. . . . To carry out this principle of perpetual praise with the utmost solemnity attainable was the first end of the monastic life.

"But though the service of God was beyond all question, the prime object of monastic life, yet the more closely that life is examined the more clearly does it exhibit the element of associated labour. In the popular estimate current at the present day . . .

[1] "To work and to pray."

it is not unusual to imagine that a monk, although possibly a pious, was at all events a very indolent personage, and that the utmost he accomplished was to mumble—he was always supposed to mumble —a good many more prayers than other people, and to live on the fat of the land. . . .[1]

A deeply read writer of modern times may here be quoted : " The monks were men of letters in the Middle Ages, the historians, the jurists, the philosophers, the physicians, the students of nature, the founders of schools, authors of chronicles, teachers of agriculture, fairly indulgent landlords and advocates of genuine dealing towards the peasantry."[2]

The monks of Clairvaux were of the Cistercian order, who had left the Benedictines to found a more. austere rule than that of the Black Monks, as the Benedictines were called. Both orders were great landowners, the Cistercians being also farmers and farming their own lands ; this they did by the institution of *fratres conversi*, or lay brethren. The various farms belonging to Margam Abbey were worked by these lay brethren.

In course of time this system died out and the farms were let out to secular persons, at Margam from towards the end of the fifteenth century.

The Cistercians were the only monks who had lay brethren attached to the monasteries ; all other orders had paid servants and officers.

It was the possessions of the monastic houses in

[1] " Henry VIII. and the English Monasteries," Abbot Gasquet.
[2] Mr. Thorold Rogers.

particular that to use the words of an old writer [1] were popularly regarded as "Oblations to the Lord" and "the patrimony of the poor to be bestowed accordingly" : The monks whereof "taught and preached the faith and good works and practised the same both in word and deed ; not only within the monasteries, but without."

"They made such provision daily for the people that stood in need thereof, as sick, sore, lame, or otherwise impotent, that none or very few lacked relief in one place or another. Yea, many of them, whose revenues were sufficient thereto made hospitals and lodgings within their own houses [*i.e.*, the monastic houses,] wherein they kept a number of impotent persons with all necessaries for them, with persons to attend upon them, besides the great alms they gave daily at their gates to every one that came for it. Yea, no wayfaring person could depart without a night's lodging, meat, drink, and money ; it not being demanded, from whence he or she came, and whither he would go.

"They taught the unlearned that was put to them to be taught ; yea the poor as well as the rich, without demanding anything for their labour, other than what the rich parents were willing to give them of mere devotion.

"There was no person that came to them heavy or sad for any cause that went away comfortless. They never revenged them of any injury, but were contented to forgive it freely on submission. And if

[1] B.Mus Cole MS. XII. Written 1591 by one who remembered the ancient days.

the price of corn had begun to start up in the markets they made thereunto with wainloads of corn and sold it under the market price to poor people to the end to bring down the price thereof. If the highways, bridges, or causeways were tedious to the passengers that sought their living by their travel, their great help lacked not towards the repair and amending thereof : yea, often times they amended them on their own proper charges.

"If any poor householder had lacked seed to sow his land or bread or corn, or malt, before the harvest and came to the monastery, he should have had it until harvest, that he might easily have paid it again. Yea, if he made his moan for an ox, horse, or cow, he might have had it upon his credit." "All sorts of people were helped and succoured by abbeys. Yea, happy was that person that was tenant to an Abbey, for it was a rare thing to hear that any tenant was removed by taking his farm over his head."

Such, then, were the White Monks who played an important part in the history of Kenfig for close on four hundred years.

Countess Mabel died in A.D. 1157, ten years after her husband, Earl Robert. Her eldest son William became second Earl of Gloucester and lord of Glamorgan, holding Kenfig as part of his possessions. He it was who when at war with Ivor Bach, lord of Seinghenydd, was surprised in Cardiff Castle, and, with his wife and son, were carried off to the hills, Ivor dictating his own terms.

Earl William added much to the town of Kenfig;

he enlarged Keynsham Priory in Somerset at the request of his dying son, and it then became an Abbey. He also contributed largely to various religious foundations.

In a charter of William, the second Earl, to Nicholas Bishop of Llandaff and others in favour of the Cistercian monks, is a gift of a burgage [1] in Kenefeg, and a grant of the fishery of Kenefeg water, *i.e.*, river, provided his mill at Kenefeg is not affected by it. The charter, similar to that of his father Earl Robert, constitutes the grant to the monks of all the land between Kenfig and Afan. It is not extant, but we have the text in an *inspeximus* by Edward le Despenser, lord of Glamorgan and Morganwg, dated 13 July, 1358 (C.MCLXXXIII) ; also in an *inspeximus* by Hugh le Despenser dated 9 Oct., 1338, T. 212 B (C.MCL).

Here, then, we find at a very early date—for Nicholas, Bishop of Llandaff, held the see from A.D. 1149 to A.D. 1183—the Abbey of Margam commenced to have possessions in Kenfig, and we shall see as we go through the numerous documents which belonged to the Abbey how, year by year, lands and houses were given to the monks by various persons, so that just before the dissolution of the monasteries

---

[1] Burgage. " Bur " meant a bower, cottage or dwelling, and is said to be from a root signifying to cover, to protect, hence our word to " bury " and burrow (of a rabbit). The word also appears to be used in the same sense in the ancient Norman laws, when there were lands called *borgage* or *bourgage* (which were freeholds, partible among co-heirs), not only in boroughs, properly now so called, but in hamlets and rural parishes.—" The Ancient Laws of Wales," by Hubert Lewis.

—Margam in 1537—a great part of Kenfig manor lands had become theirs.

One of the first gifts to Margam Abbey in the manor of Kenfig is a grant—T. 18 and 289 (12); (C. DCCXVII)—by Ririth, or Richeret, son of Breavel, of land in Clammorgan de supra Corneli for the souls of himself, his ancestors, and his wife, who is buried in the cemetery outside the gate of Margam Abbey. Subject to royal dues of 12d. yearly. The witnesses are : W. de Lichesfeld, Jordan de Hereford, W. de Valle, monks of Margam ; Ernald the Constable of Kenefec, and others.

As we have no description of the metes and bounds of Kenfig borough at this early date, although they are well known to us to-day, I leave a description of them to a later period, when we will find them given in the charter of Thomas Lord le Despenser, which is dated 16 Feb., A.D. 1397.

CHAPTER III

KENFIG CASTLE

KENFIG CASTLE was probably erected before the town came into existence, so it may be well to refer to it at this early period.

One of the chief approaches to the castle from the northward would be the Roman highway as far as Pont Felin Newydd or the bridge of the new mill. From this point the way would lie west-south-west 600 yards at the time of its occupation. Judging from the name, a mill apparently at one time existed near the bridge, but no record of it remains in writing or tradition. The Rev. Thomas Howell informs me that one of the millstones is in use as a step to a cottage near the bridge. When the old bridge was taken down a barrel-arch of 3 feet diameter was found under the south wall of the bridge above. The barrel-arch pointed a little south of east, obliquely to the bridge, and probably served to convey the water from the tail-race of the mill, which would thus seem to have been on the south-east of the bridge.

The other roads converging on the Castle from east and south are the highway from Cefn Cribwr past Marlas, the Roman road from Cardiff from the south-east, Heol-las and the road through Ton Kenfig from the south.

Probably an army advancing to attack Kenfig would debouch on to the open ground by all these roads. Any roads which in those days led to the west side of the town are now lost in the waste of the sand-dunes; as the sea lay on the west of the town and castle the chief approach was necessarily from the landward side.

As I have said, very little remains to be seen of this once important stronghold. Probably if the mound above which appear the two clumps of masonry were excavated, some parts of the walls might be discovered, and it is desirable this should be done.

The site of the castle had evidently been selected with a view to the utilisation of the Kenfig river with which to form part of the moat. This it does on the north-west side, the other sides being protected by the artificial moat, of which a considerable part can still be traced. The artificial part was supplied with water by damming up the river at the point where moat and river united on the eastern side. Practically, therefore, the castle was encircled by the River Kenfig.

At first sight one is struck by the large area comprised within the moat, about eleven acres, so that the castle-bailey,[1] or outer court of the castle, was an extensive one. But it must be remembered in the Middle Ages the garrison were usually disposed in

[1] Viollet-le-Duc, the eminent French architect, in technical terms in his "Annals of a Fortress," gives Bailey, forecourt; court of the outer works or yard.

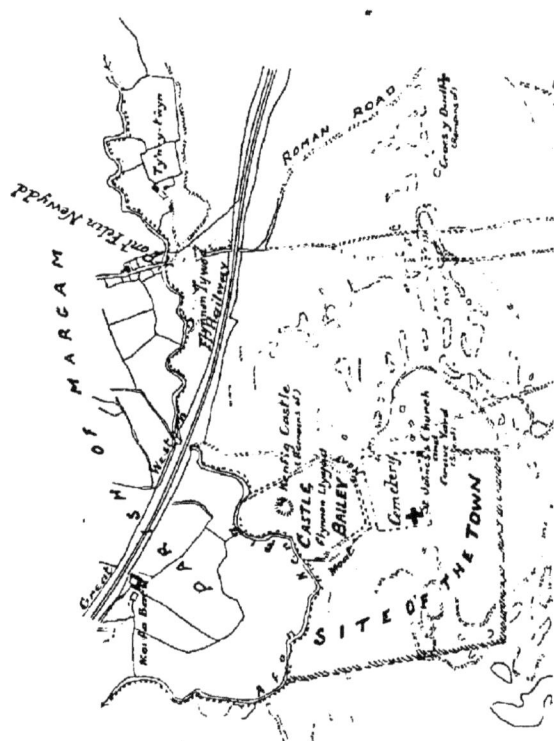

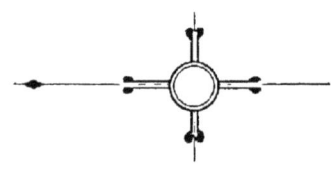

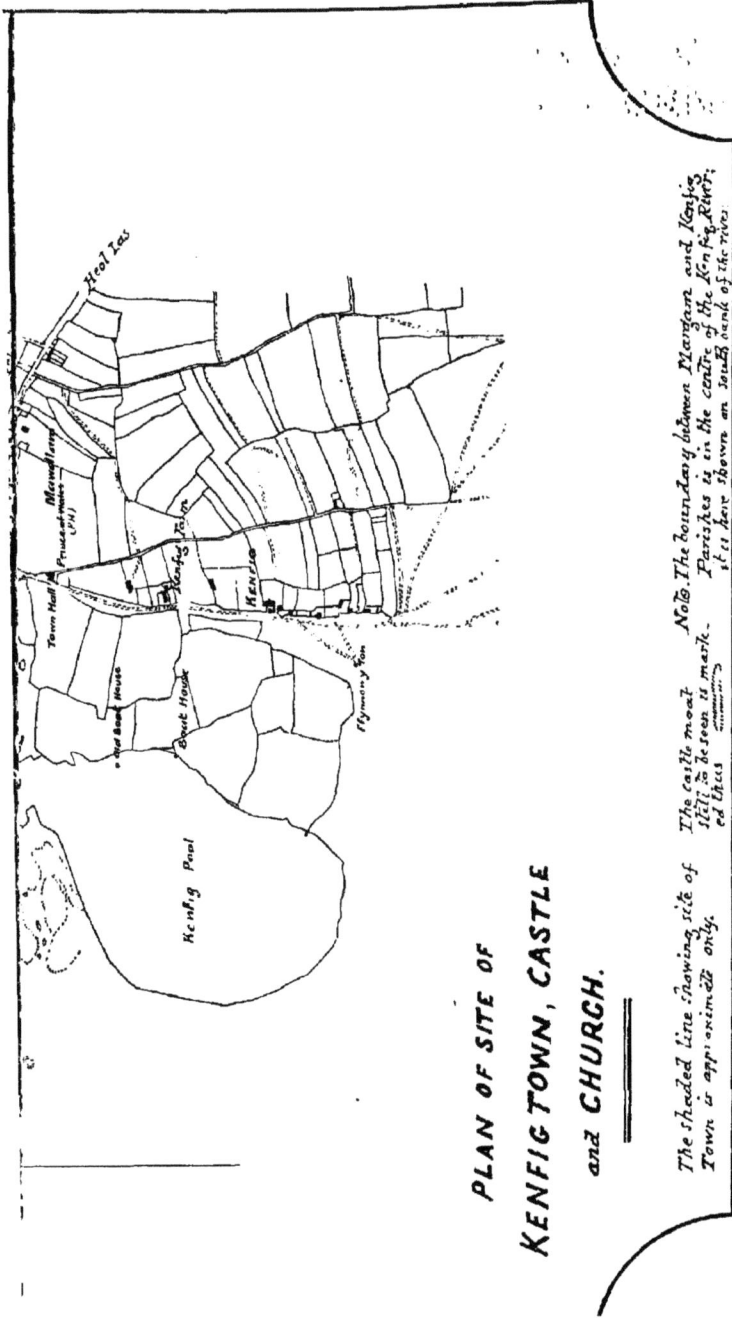

PLAN OF SITE OF

KENFIG TOWN, CASTLE

and CHURCH.

The shaded line showing site of Town is approximate only.

The castle moat still to be seen is marked thus.

Note. The boundary between Margam and Kenfig Parishes is in the centre of the Kenfig River; it is here shown on south bank of the river.

Kenfig Pool

Heol Las

Mawdlam (PH)

Town Hall

Prince of Wales House

and Back House

Break House

Kenfig Town

Kenfig

Flymin-y-Ton

[To face page 58.]

the bailey of the strong castles. And so it must have been in this case, for we find in the Margam MSS. mention made of houses occupying part of the space within the bailey. One such house we find had been occupied by the parson (*clericus*), who was probably the castle-chaplain. It is an interesting document, as it gives us not only an instance of a dwelling in the castle-bailey, but it also gives us the position of the cemetery of St. James's Church.

The deed T. 202 (C. MCLXXXVI) is a grant by Thomas, son of William de Sancto Donato (St. Donat's) to Robert Cavan de Sancto Fagano (St. Ffagan's) of a messuage *within* the bailey (the castle bailey), on the east near the wall of the cemetery of Kenefeg, which Richard the parson formerly lived in, and one acre of arable land which he held in the field of the Church-land.

In the Magnus Rotulus Pipæ, or the Great Roll of the Pipe,[1] we have a glimpse of the castle in active occupation.

A return of the expenses of the lordship of Glamorgan is made, and an entry is there of the castle costs.

"And in corrody for the servants dwelling in the castles of Neth and Kenefeg and of New Castle, £22. 19sh. 4d. by the King's Writ : And in bread for the servants of Kenefeg seven marks, by the King's writ."

In the same document Mauricius de Berkelay renders account of the following :—

---

[1] The Great Roll of the Pipe contains the Sheriffs' returns of the revenues of the Crown.

"And from Reginald son of Simon ten marks for the custody of the castle of Kenefeg by writ of the King. And from Walter Luvel [the Knight of Corneli, who will often appear in these pages as a witness to numerous deeds] 40sh. for the custody of the New Castle for half a year. And in repair of the castle of Kenefeg and mending the gates and palisades, £16. 11sh. 6½d. by writ of the King."

In the Compotus of Johannis Giffard de Brymmesfeld, referred to before, is the cost of various works done to Kenfig Castle and also to repairs done to houses in the castle.

John Giffard of Brymmesfeld, the warden for the King Edward II., in A.D. 1316, in his account preserved in the Record Office, under the head of "Villa de Kenefeg cum Castro," gives: 20 April A.D. 1316. "*Expenses of the Castle.* 2,000 shingles [1] for the mending and repairing the houses in the Castle [in the castle-bailey is meant no doubt] 8 shillings. Wages of one carpenter making and placing the said shingles by the job (*ad tascham*) and repairing other defective houses in the castle, half a mark. For nails for the same, two shillings."

The total cost is xvjs. viijd., 16s. 8d. ; taking out the 10/- for shingles and nails, 6/8 remain as the value of the half-mark.

This would show there were several houses in the castle-bailey.

A curious item in the account of expenses is the

[1] The shingles (*scindulæ*) were made of wood ; in Neath Castle accounts are " 1,500 shingles made and prepared out of the Lord's timber by the job."

following : " Out-of-pocket expenses for hanging two
robbers 8d. Two ropes for the same 2d. A new
' calefurciis,' or gallows, for hanging the robbers,
made by the job 6d. The total cost xvjd., 16d."

The town and castle were often attacked, and the
town was on several occasions burned, as we know
from various chroniclers. So frequently did this
occur that one chronicler writes, evidently in surprise,
" Kenfig had not been burned for a year or more."
We must bear in mind that at that time the houses
were built of wood, and so the town was easily set
on fire.[1]

As far back as A.D. 1167, Kenfig is reported to have
been burned. In Leland's "Itinerary" it is stated
"Anno Dom. 1167 *villa* de Kenfik *prope* Nethe in
Wallia *combusta* est in *nocte* S. Hilarii." The
" Annales de Margan " states that this was done by the
Welsh on the night of St. Hilary the Bishop, 13 Jan.[2]
From this it would appear that the town was chiefly
occupied by Normans, as the castle certainly was
garrisoned by them.

In A.D. 1185 the Welshmen—an eclipse which presented the sun the colour of blood, having been
construed in their favour—began to lay waste the
district of Glamorgan with fire and rapine ; they
burned Cardiff, and Kenfig town for a second time

---

[1] Probably timber with brickwork or stone in sections, known
as " half-timber," such as Leland probably meant when he wrote
" The Towne of *Gloucester* is antient, well builded of Tymbre."
This was about A.D. 1537 (Leland's "Itinerary," vol. iv., part 2,
fol. 171).

[2] " Annales de Margan," p. 16.

fell a prey to the flames; it had not been burned for a year or more. The Castle of Neath was again besieged and stoutly defended until the arrival of *French soldiers*, who put the Welshmen to flight and burned their engines of war.

This must have been in the eyes of the people a remarkable year, for besides the eclipse causing the sun to be the colour of blood we read in the " Annales de Margan " that at Llanrhidian in Gower, at this time, St. Iltyd's spring flowed with milk, and that of so excellent a quality that the butter rose upon its surface.

And now we come to an important event in the history of Kenfig Castle and town. In one chronicle we find stated in brief terms: " MCCXXXII. Combusta est villa de Kenefeg per Morganum Cham "[1] (" 1232 the town of Kenfig was burned by Morgan Cham ").

But we find from another chronicle that if Morgan Gam succeeded in burning the town he failed to take the castle. Morgan Gam, "the hunchback," was the third son of Morgan ap Caradoc ap Jestyn; he inherited the lands of his brothers Leisan and Owein, lords of Afan. He was a turbulent man, and delighted in quarrels and battle.

At Eastertide of the year 1232 there must have been great alarm at Kenfig, for it was known there was to be war and bloodshed. At the command of Lewelin a large number of the nobler princes of the Welsh were marching, with a large army, on Kenfig, with the object of plundering the inhabitants and

[1] " Exchequer Chron." in *Arch. Camb.*, 1862, p. 278.

destroying the town. The chronicler says the people having had timely warning of the coming of the foe, were enabled to send away their cattle to other places for safe keeping. The inhabitants also burned part of the town inside the gates so as to render an entry more difficult. The Welsh, under the leadership of Morgan Gam, lord of Afan, afterwards coming up to the assault, first burned the part of the town outside the gates and then rushed with great clamour and seized the tower,[1] or keep, which was at that time only encircled and fortified by a fosse and palisade.[2]

But the men who were inside defended themselves so bravely that many of the enemy were seriously wounded and others killed, whereupon all the others after the first assault quickly withdrew and went up into the mountains.

The annalist adds he was much astonished at one thing, that although the besiegers were in great want of food they spared the church and the cemetery and all who were therein.[3] I wonder if he expected they would have eaten some of the inhabitants.

Thus Morgan Gam succeeded in burning the town, but he failed to capture the castle, and had to retire ignominiously to the mountains. William de Rievalle

---

[1] Note Viollet-le-Duc, in "Annals of a Fortress," gives: Donjon or Keep, chief retreat of the defenders of a strong castle. The donjon was always separated from the defences of the castle, and put in direct communication with the exterior.

[2] Fosse and palisade. The ditch or moat which is dug outside the walls, parapet, or rampart, filled with water or with palisades or stakes in the bottom.

[3] "Annales de Margan," p. 39.

was constable of the castle, and seems to have been a brave and capable officer.

In the year 1243 Kenfig town was burned in the struggle between Howell ap Meredydd and Richard Earl of Clare, who was the eighth Earl of Gloucester and lord of Glamorgan.[1]

Kenfig suffered much in the year A.D. 1295. There was a general rising; one Madoc destroyed towns in North Wales, and another Madoc overran Pembroke and Carmarthen, and Morgan, lord of Afan, gained complete mastery over Glamorgan. Clare, lord of Glamorgan, at this time was, says Mr. Clark, probably disabled by disease. But the King, Edward I., acted with vigour. He began in North Wales and passed through the whole of Wales with immense rapidity, "amazement in his van, with flight combined." The terror of his name seems to have reduced the rebels to order. In the Eulogium Historiarum the King's movement is noticed thus :—

"Rex de Snowdoun per Walliam progrediens occidentalem intravit Glamorgan."

At the end of the year the Earl de Clare died in the Castle of Monmouth, 7 Dec., 1295.

In 1315 things had changed, and we find the son of Morgan Gam defending the castle. An entry in the Close Roll of 12 March A.D. 1315, addressed to Bartholomew de Badlesmere as warden of Glamorgan, mentions the petition of Sir Leisan de Avene, stating that during a recent Welsh insurrection he defended Kenfig Castle at a cost of above forty marks, and

---

[1] MCCXLIIJ. "Combusta est villa de Kenefeg, et Howell ap Maredut contra Ricardum de Clara " (" Welsh Annals")

NEAR VIEW OF KENFIG CASTLE RUINS.

asking compensation. As Sir Leisan was in truth
defending his own lands, the King allowed him
twenty marks only, which Badlesmere was to pay
him.[1] Kenfig was not in Sir Leisan's lands, but it
must have been used in a general scheme for defence,
Sir Leisan's castle at Aberavon being included.

We find the echo of this disastrous insurrection in
the account sent in in 1316 by John Giffard de
Brymmesfeld, the warden of the Earl's lands and
castles in Glamorgan :—

"*Villa de Kenefeg cum castro.*

"Rents of Assize. The same answers for 71s.
received of rent of assize of 100 burgages of the
town of Kenefeg at the terms of St. John Baptist
and St. Michael. And not more because 42 burgages which formerly yielded for the same period
21 shillings, were burned in the war and the tenants
left and the burgages remained empty.

"And 4 shillings and 6d. from the small cottagers of
the term of St. Michael.

"And 16 shillings, 6d. from the prise (tax) of beer of
the town of Kenefeg for the same time. And not
more because the greater part of the town was burnt
in the war."

Less beer was consumed, and the prise of beer was
reduced.

In the reign of Henry IV. the castle made resistance to the victorious arms of Owen Glyndwr.
But it fell to him, and he dismantled it and reduced
it to ruin.

The castle had been provisioned before Owen came,

[1] "Kenfig Charters," G. T. Clark.

for we find in the Calendar of Patent Rolls the entry :—

"1403, Sep. 12th.   4 Henry IV. m. 23.   (Rotulus Viagii.)

"Commission to Richard, Bishop of Worcester, Henry Bruyn, Sheriff of Worcester, and John Ryall to take . . . 8 quarters of wheat, one tun of wine, 3 tuns of ale, 200 fish and 60 quarters of oats to the castle of Kenflyc (*sic*)."

I presume this event must have taken place after 1405, for in the same Calendar, under date April 6, 1405, 6 Henry IV., Part 2, m. 30, is the entry :—

"Grant to the king's consort, Joan, queen of England, of the custody of . . . the castle and town of Kenfeg, with the lordship of Tyriarth . . . which Constance late the Wife of Thomas le Despenser lately had . . . during the minority of Richard, his son and heir."

Had the castle been destroyed by Glyndwr before, the grant of the custody would have been a farce.

Hugh le Despenser presented a petition to Edward the Second in which he complains that the Castle of Kenfig had been plundered and burnt by Roger Mortimer, the Earl of Hereford, and his nephew, who were confederated against him.

East of the castle about 650 yards, near the river, are some wonderful springs, one of which is called Ffynnon Tywod (the sand-spring).   The water rushes out with unconquered vigour and sweetness, leading the sand an everlasting dance ; quite a sight.   I wonder how its throat does not get choked.

CHAPTER IV

THE CHURCH OF KENFIG AND THE CHAPELS

UNLIKE the practice of our times, the church was usually erected first, or with the beginning of a town ; in these times a church is thought of when the population has become numerous or too numerous for the makeshift. I think it probable that the chapel of St. Thomas, which will be referred to later, was the first religious edifice in the town.

The ancient church of Kenfig, dedicated to St. James, lay 300 yards to the south of the castle: the walls of its cemetery adjoin the castle-bailey, as we have seen in Chapter III.; the grant of a messuage within the bailey of the castle, on the east near the wall of the cemetery [1] of Kenefeg assists in locating it.

The Church of St. James was erected about the same time, or soon after Margam Abbey, for the records of Tewkesbury Abbey show that Henry Thusard, clerk in Holy Orders, had a licence from William Earl of Gloucester to found and build at Kenefeg the Church of St. James, and in the British

[1] Cemetery is derived from *Cœmeterium*, "a dormitory," it being in the Christian sense the sleeping-place of the dead (Gasquet).

Museum MS. Cott., Cleop., A. VII., we have the foundation charter :—

Earl William's Charter de Prima Fundatione
Ecclesiae S. Jacobi de Kenefeg.

"Carta Willelmi Comitis testificantis, quod ipse requisivit abbatem et conventum Theokesberiae ut permitterent Henrico Thusard clerico ejusdem comitis erigere ecclesiam in Kenefeg tenendam dum vixerit ab ipsis, solvendo pensionem ii. solidorum ad festum omnium Sanctorum, sine minoratione aliqua decimarum suarum quas antiquitus habebant ; ita ut post decessum ipsius Henrici, edificia et virgulta et cetere emendationes in terra ecclesiae facte, et ornamenta ecclesie in ipsa ecclesia, sicut sua propria perpetuo remanerent. Ita etiam quod si ministri dicti comitis de aliqua parochia ipsius abbatis in parochiam de Kenefeg causa guerre, vel majoris pasture oves suas vel vaccas removerent et ibi non sint remanentes residue, decimam habebit illarum."

The charter bears no date ; the following is the translation :—

(MS. Cott., Cleop., A.VII., A.D. 1147–1183.)

"Charter of William the Earl testifying that he has required the abbot and convent of Tewkesbury that they shall permit Henry Thusard, clerk of the same earl, to erect a church in Kenefeg, to hold from them while he shall live, paying a pension, or payment, of two shillings, at the feast of All Saints, without any diminution of their tithes, which they have had in former times, so that after the death of the same Henry, the building and shrubberies and other improvements or repairs made in the land of the church and the church ornaments in the same church shall remain as their own for ever. So also that if the ministers of the said earl shall by reason of war or larger pasture remove either his sheep or cows from any parish of the said abbot into the parish of Kenefeg and there be no residue there remaining, he shall have a tithe of them."

It would seem from this charter that the church land was planted with shrubs.

As Earl William succeeded his father, Earl Robert, in A.D. 1147, the year of the foundation of Margam Abbey, St. James's Church was probably built soon after; in fact, we find the church was in existence before A.D. 1154, for in T. 378 (C. DCIX)we have a record of an arbitration in that year by Theobald, Archbishop of Canterbury, Primate and Legate of the Apostolic See, directed to Nicholas ap Gwrgan, Bishop of Llandaff, settling the dispute between Job the priest, parson of St. Leonard, Newcastle, Bridgend, and Master Henry Tusard, parson of St. James, Chenefeg, so that the said Henry relinquishes to the church of Newcastle the tithe of Geoffrey Esturmi (from whom comes the name Stormy—Stormy Farm and Stormy Down), and thirty acres of land belonging to the church of Chenefeg, dated at Canterbury A.D. 1154. St. James's Church was therefore built between A.D. 1147 and A.D. 1154.

Among the Cottonian MS. in the British Museum

is a long charter, Cleop., A VII. 68, by Nicholas, Bishop of Llandaff, confirming to Tewkesbury Abbey all churches and benefices which the Abbey holds in the diocese of Llandaff.

The document discloses the large number of churches held by the Abbey in these parts, presented to it by Fitzhamon, his son-in-law, Robert Earl of Gloucester, and the latter's son, William Earl of Gloucester. Thus did these lords gain the powerful support of the Church.

In this charter we find there were two churches in the town of Kenfig, betokening a large and important place. There was also a chapel in each Corneli. The Bishop confirms to Tewkesbury the church of St. James of Kenefeg, with the chapel of St. Thomas in the same town; the chapel of Corneli which is the town of Thomas; the chapel of St. Wenduin in the town of Walter Lupellus, or Luvel. The date of the charter would be between A.D. 1149 and 1183, the period in which Bishop Nicholas held the see.

The name Corneli is derived from the dedication of its chapel to St. Cornelius. In Brittany he is called St. Cornély, so by a kindred race he is given the same name in Wales. The use of the title of saint before a name is seldom met with in mediæval Welsh, hence the place is called simply Corneli.

Above the western door of the parish church of Carnac in Brittany is the figure of the patron, St. Cornelius, having on either side of him an ox, for he is the patron saint of horned cattle. The Pardon of St. Cornély takes place on September 13th; the " pardon " is the feast of the patron saint of a church, and it is to the Bretons what the Mabsant of early days was to the Welsh. I say early days, for in later times the Mabsant had lost all connection with religious feeling. In Brittany the "pardon" retains its mediæval aspect almost unchanged ; it is the feast or revel of the parish with strong religious adjuncts.

All the farmers for miles around make a point of bringing their cattle in pilgrimage to the saint. They drive them round the church; then the owners kneel before the figure over the west door, say a prayer, after which they drive their beasts to the holy well, where they sprinkle their heads with the water. It is customary for such farmers as can afford it to give a beast to St. Cornély. After High Mass these cattle are ranged about the principal porch ; the clergy come forth in procession and bless the oblations, which are then led away to be sold by auction for the good of the Church.[1]

In Leland's "Collectanea" is an article on Superstitious Practices prevailing in Wales in the year 1589. The article describes the offering of part of a bullock to St. Beuno. It appears to have been the custom in North Wales of offering cattle to St. Beuno.

"And as the Bullocke dyd enter throughe a little Porche into the churchyarde, the young man spake aloude. Thy halfe to God and Beyno. Then did I aske, "says the writer," his Hoste [with whom the young man stayed], Why he said Halfe and not the Whole ? His Hoste answered in the yonge Man's hereing, He oweth me thother Halfe, therefor he offereth but the One Halfe. This was in the Parish

[1] "A Book on Brittany," by the Rev. S. Baring-Gould.

of *Clynnog* in the Bishopricke of *Bangor*, about Fifteen Myle from *Bangor* in the Yere of our Lord 1589."

The town of Sir Walter Luvel, the knight, was North Corneli; his lands lay around it, therefore the chapel of St. Wenduin must have been in North Corneli. It follows that the chapel of Corneli, or St. Corneli, was in South Corneli, "the town of Thomas"; so called probably after Thomas de Corneli. At the time of Bishop Nicholas's charter, Thomas de Corneli and Walter Luvel were persons of high position in North and South Corneli.

In the copy of the charter of Nicholas, Bishop of Llandaff, referred to (C. XXX), Wendun is given as the name of the saint to whom the chapel of the town of Walter Luvel was dedicated. I have had the charter examined recently, with the result that the name is found to be Wenduin.

Saint Wenduin, or Wendelin as he is named in German Calendars, is the patron saint of sheep.

The Rev. H. H. Knight, in his book on Newton, refers to a sculptured figure of a lamb fixed in the wall of a cottage at Newton Nottage called Ty John Morris, and he considers it may have reference to St. Wenduin. It is possible the sculptured stone may have been removed from the chapel of St. Wenduin at North Corneli.

Passing along Heol-las[1] recently, I noticed a

[1] Heol-las, called "Blue Street" by the inhabitants, from a spirit of contrariness, I suppose, glâs standing for green as well as blue. Heol-lâs means green street, from the wide grass sides which the road has.

DOORWAY IN THE PINE END OF A COTTAGE AT NORTH CORNELL.

pointed doorway in the south side of the east pine-end of a cottage standing in a cluster of others between Mawdlam and Corneli. The doorway cannot have belonged to a cottage; it is an ecclesiastical doorway of Early English date. The jambs and arch have a plain chamfer, or chamfer plane, as Mr. Paley terms it. The cottage stands about five hundred yards east-north-east from North Corneli.

I am inclined to think the cottage or part of it stands on the site of and embodies part of the chapel of St. Wenduin.

At this date the church of St. Mary Magdalene was not built, and we shall see further on the first reference to it in the Margam MSS. It was built between the years 1245–1266.

A deed by Ketherech, son of John Du, proves that the town of Walter Luvel was North Corneli. He grants to Margam Abbey five acres of his land in Peitheuin, near the highway which leads from Kenefec towards Cardiff along the " vill" of Walter Lupellus, or Luvel; he made a further grant of fifteen acres adjoining the five in the same terms. Now the road from Kenfig to Cardiff does not lead to South Corneli, so that the " vill" must be North Corneli.

One of the charters of Hugh de Hereford, referred to elsewhere, mentions land on the west part of Corneli, from the old cemetery to the boundary of the land of Walter Lupellus, or Luvel, then to the land of Joaf, then as far as the highway coming from the chapel of Corneli belonging to Walter Lupellus, and so forth. Here we find that a cemetery, that is, churchyard, existed at Corneli.

Another deed puzzled me, for it would almost show that the "vill" of Walter Luvel might be South Corneli. It is the deed of Philip, son of William de Cornely, by which he grants to Margam Abbey the minerals of iron and lead on the east side of the high-road which leads from the "new town," or Newton Nottage, to the town of Walter Luvel, which is called Cornely. Which Corneli? The road from Newton first reaches South Corneli, and it is near that place the lodes of minerals exist; there are none, so far as I know, at North Corneli.

Walter Luvel granted to Margam Abbey all manner of iron and lead in his whole land. As the minerals lie at South Corneli it is probable he had land there as well as at North Corneli.

Luvel was a considerable landowner and a bene-factor of the Abbey; in a deed dated A.D. 1202 he granted, T. 80 (C. DCCII), all his land in the fee of Llangewydd [1] viz., one hundred acres, which he had with his wife in marriage of David Scurlag, his wife's father, whereby he became a "homo," or dependant, of the said David, free of rent except five shillings paid by the monks for the land of Penvei. [2] Seven years' rent paid beforehand.

In another deed he notifies to William, Bishop of Llandaff, and all the faithful of Holy Church, that he has granted to Margam Abbey seven acres of his free tenement, one acre being in exchange for the same quantity which the monks had near to his land, the

[1] The church of St. Cewydd; there are slender remains of the Hen Eglwys at Llangewydd.

[2] Pen-y-fai, near Aberkenfig; head or top of the field.

rest in frank almoign.[1] Five of these are adjacent to
the grange of St. Michael, on the mountain near the
River Kenfig to the west of the grange, the land of
Rodbert Corvesarius being to the south, and Alex-
ander's on the north ; the two acres remaining near
Alexander's on the north, between the land of Walter
Ulf and Richard the priest. For this the monks give
him in charity twelve shillings.

Witnesses : Walter Lupellus, his son ; David and
William, his sons ; Athelewa, his wife ; Einulf de
Kenefec, and others. T. 43 (C. DCCCXLVI).

The question as to which Corneli was Sir Walter
Luvel's[2] is, I think, decided by a quit-claim by Sir
Walter's son, Walter, nephew of David Scurlag. In
it he is styled lord of Upper Corneli, which is North
Corneli. A witness to the deed is Maurice, lord of
Lower Corneli.

I think we may safely conclude that St. Wenduin's
Chapel was in North Corneli.

Perched high up on the side of the hill in the
village of South Corneli, sheltering under an escarp-
ment of the limestone rock, and quite near its perpendicular face, stands a small thatched cottage which is
known as Ty Capel, or the Chapel house.

The approach to it is by a street which leads up the
hillside at a right angle to the main road, and then
up a grassy slope on to a plateau on which the cottage
stands. The aspect of the quiet little old-world
village nestling under the west end of White Cross

[1] Frank almoign, free alms.
[2] He is styled Sir Walter Luvel in a deed dated 26 May,
A.D. 1219.

Down is picturesque.   The hill above is in part
wooded, and here and there the ivy-clad limestone
shows white, and makes pleasing contrast with the
green of grass and trees.   From the cottage itself
a fine view is obtained of the country around and of
the Channel beyond.

The important house in South Corneli is, of course,
Ty Maen, but this poor little cottage was once an
important building in the place, and one can imagine
in far-off days the inhabitants wending their way up
the steep to wedding or baptism or funeral, and at
night the beacon light from its window beckoning
the faithful to evensong.

For Ty Capel represents the ancient chapel
dedicated to St. Corneli.

The building, the highest in South Corneli, stands
about 180 feet above sea-level.   Its east pine-end
is only about 12 feet from the face of the rock and
in it, as if hiding from inquisitive eyes, is a small
Perpendicular window 15 inches high to the springing
of the arch, which itself rises 5 inches to the apex, in
width 12½ inches.   Over it is a label, but the return
on each side has been broken off.   Holes in the jambs
indicate the position of the stanchions and saddle-bar.
A small window on the south side has holes for the
same purpose.   The doorway had at some time been
shifted to its present position at the south side of
the west pine-end ; the doorway arch is slightly pointed
and has a chamfer plane.   Inside is a huge fireplace
with flat arch, opening to a width of 7 feet 4 inches.
The east window is in a cupboard-like recess 2 feet
wide and 2 feet in depth, the light itself being in the

EAST WINDOW OF THE CHAPEL OF ST. CORNELI AT SOUTH CORNELI.

[To face page 76.

upper part of the recess. I omitted to add that the window chamfer (on the outside) is hollowed and the cill is level with the ground.

The site of the chapel is verified by a cyrograph or indenture between Philip de Corneli[1] and the Abbot and Convent of Margam concerning an exchange of land. The Abbot and Convent by a deed, T. 163 (C. DCCCCLXX), grant to Philip de Corneli and his heirs all their land at the Sanctuary[2] of the Chapel of Corneli; which land lies on the south near the land of Walter, son of Anselm, and extends in length to the place which is called "Twelve acres," in perpetual exchange for the land of the said Philip which adjoins the land of the said Abbot and Convent of Margam, and begins at the land called Tangestellond[3] and reaches in length along the highway as far as the place called Orchardescroft on the south; Philip's heir to make provision elsewhere for the dowry of his wife, Amabilia, if she outlives him.

The seal of Philip is 1 inch in diameter, dark green wax; an ornamental fleur-de-lis or lily. SIGILL . . . LIPPI D' . . . ELI.

Witnesses: David Siward, William le Flemeng, Philip de Nerbert, and others. Dated St. Benedict's Day, A.D. 1257.

The "Twelve acres" field is on the east of the main road, a hundred yards south of Ty Maen, and is now divided in two by the railway, and its south end is along the Heol-y-Splot.

[1] Occurs A D. 1254–1262.
[2] In the Middle Ages the churchyard was often called the "sanctuary."   [3] Ty Tanglwys.

The field lies to the south of the chapel of St. Corneli 137 yards, and in between the chapel and field lies the land which belonged to the abbot, with probably Walter's land on its north.

The abbot evidently coveted Philip's land and wished to complete a compact area for Ty Tanglwys and to obtain access to the main road on the south, in addition to the access to the Roman road, or Heol-y-Sheet, on the north.

An old man, so old-looking that I thought at first sight that he might have been living at the time of the old chapel, told me human remains had been found in the ground about the Ty Capel. He also told me Orchard's Croft is the field adjoining South Corneli on the north and east of the main road.

At South Corneli stands a residence, mentioned already, Ty Maen, or the "Stone House"; the name evidently points to a remote date when all the others were built of wood, or what is termed "half-timbered" houses. The present house is, I have no doubt, a reconstruction of a much older building. This is shown to be the case by the jambs and pointed arch of an ancient doorway in the wall of an outbuilding belonging to Ty Maen on the opposite side of the road; it is now walled up. It is similar to the doorway at Heol-las.

The entrance doorway in the wall of the grounds is a good piece of Perpendicular work with flattened arch, spandrils, and square label. On each side in the spandril is a small shield bearing the date, apparently at first sight 16 and 50. But I cannot think such work was carried out at so late a period as 1650;

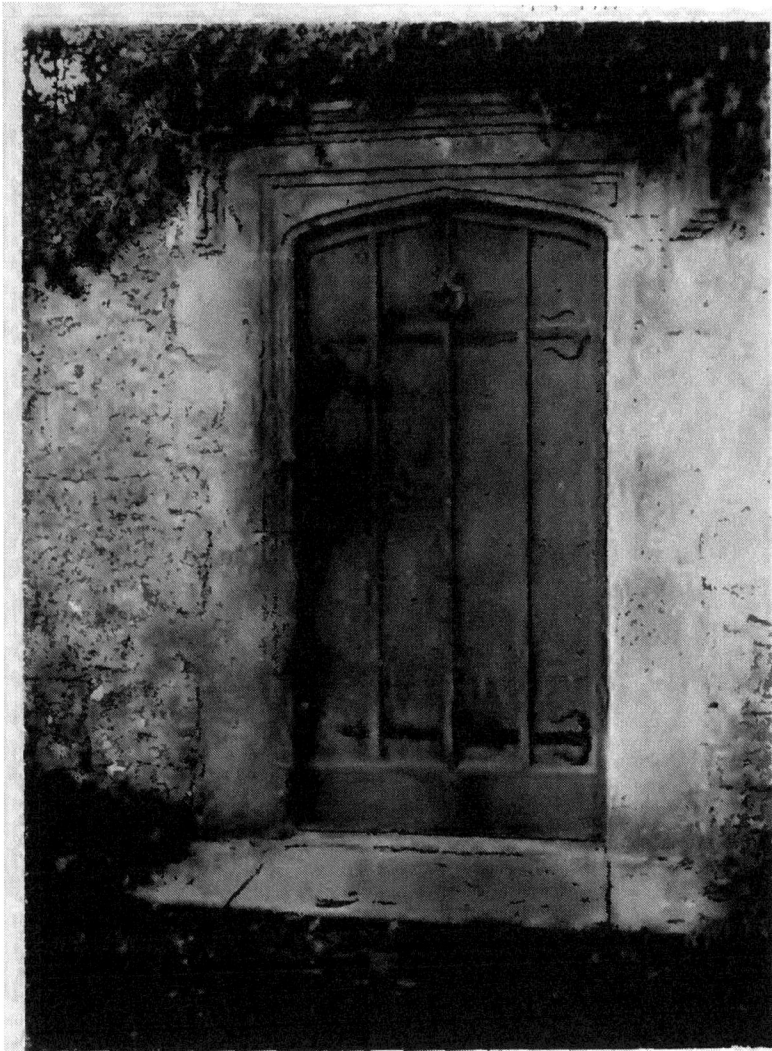

DOORWAY AT TY MAEN, SOUTH CORNELL.

on examining the figures closely I came to the conclusion that what looks like a 6 is really a 5, and
that the date is 1550. The 5 of the 50 has a much
better shape than the 5 of the 15; probably the
architect came by and found fault with the first 5
and the workman made the second 5 in a better
shape.

Over the entrance-door of the house are the words
from the 115th Psalm, "Non nobis, Domine, non
nobis." In the older part of the building is a wide
fireplace, now walled up, the flattened arch of the
Perpendicular period, with square label.

In panels around the dining-room were painted the
names of the leading families of Glamorganshire.
These have been painted over, but Mr. Lipscomb,
Miss Talbot's Margam agent, has kindly given me
the names.

Window.

1. Co. Glamorgan	Kemys of Cefnmably	1
2. Reginald De Sully	Lisle	2
3. Peter Le Sourd De Petersen	Hoby	3
4. John Le Flammand De St. George	Mansel of Margam	4
5. Richard Syward De Tala-van	Worcester	5
6. Gilbert d'Omfreville De Penmark	Lewis of the Van	6
7. Wm. Lesterling De St. Donats	Stradling of St. Donats	7

Fireplace.

8. Roger Berkerol De E. Orchard	Turberville	8
9. Robert St. Quintin De Llanblethian	Carne of Ewenny	9

10. Oliver St. John De Fonmon	Herbert of Cardiff	10
11. Payne Turbeville De Coity	Beaufort	11
12. Richard Granville De Neth	Butler of Dunraven	12
13. Wm. De Londres De Ogmore	Lougher of Tythegstone	13
14. Robert Fitzhamon *Library door.*	Cantelupe of Cantleston and Cornelly	14
	St. John of Fonmon	15
	Talbot of Margam	16
	Gamage of Coity	17
	Sydney	18
		19
		20

Entrance to the room.

Mr. Lipscomb writes me : " It looks as if the painted names in the panels may have replaced some decayed and faded record of old times—the painting was quite plain, and would otherwise be rather meaningless; but probably you will concoct a plausible theory "—a generally accepted idea of an antiquary's capability of invention !

Most of the above knightly names appear in the monastic deeds of Margam, generally as witnesses to deeds and charters. The greater number are of Norman descent. And now for the concoction. Over each name in the panel was probably painted the armorial bearings belonging to the person named. I believe it is a fact that the armorial bearings were painted as I suggest.

South Corneli, with Peiteuin, was given to Margam Abbey in the early days of the monastery by members of the Du family. Ketherech Du and his wife Tanguistel gave Peiteuin land and Ty Tanglwys. Caradoc Du, brother of Ketherech, gave

Corneli and part of the Peiteuin lands. These gifts would date from A.D. 1190 onwards.

In A.D. 1208 an important arbitration took place concerning a dispute between the two great Abbeys of Margam and Neath. The deed of arbitration, T. 101 [C.DCCI], is by J., Abbot of Fountains, L., Abbot of Wardon, and R., Abbot of Boxley,[1] arbitrators, and was entered upon in accordance with a recited mandate by the Abbot and General Chapter of Citeaux.[2]

The assessors were the Abbot of Rievaulx, Tintern, Caerleon, Cumbermere, Cwmhyr. The Abbots of Margam and Neath were present to present their case.

The arbitration deed is dated at the Margam Abbey Grange of Orchard, Wednesday after St. Julian's Day, 28 May, A.D. 1208.

What an array of abbots—ten lord-abbots!

Orchard Grange must have been a manor-house and of a superior kind to have accommodated ten such great personages, for doubtless they were entertained there.

I believe Orchard Grange is now represented by Ty Maen, part of the old grange being incorporated in the reconstructed building. Tradition, too, points to its monastic origin, for it is said to have been a

---

[1] Fountains, co Yorkshire; Warden, co. Bedford; Boxley, co. Kent

[2] Citeaux, in the department of Côte d'Or, France, is 73 miles south-south-east of Clairvaux, and lies in the centre, about, of a triangle formed by the towns of Dijon, Dôle, and Beaune. Doubtless the cellars of the Abbey were fully stocked with the generous burgundy of that famous Golden Slope.

nunnery. The idea of the nunnery may have come from the word convent, so generally believed to mean a nunnery, whereas it means the body of monks. "The Abbot and Convent of the Monastery of Blessed Mary of Margam" was the full description.

South Corneli, long treated as a separate manor, seems, from some fragments of an early document, to have been included in Newton. However this may have been, the Herbert Manor, coming through the Hortons of Cantleston to Sir Mathew Cradock, was transmitted with Corneli Lower, South Corneli, to the Herberts of Swansea.[1] By his first wife, Alice Mansel, Sir Mathew Cradock had an only daughter, who married Richard Herbert, Esq., of Ewias, father of Sir William Herbert, created Earl of Pembroke A.D. 1551.

Newton Nottage Manor was divided between the Earl of Pembroke, Richard Loughor, Esq., and the heir of Sir William Herbert, Knt.[2] It is probable that the present Ty Maen was reconstructed by one of the Herbert family on the site of the older building.

After the digression, which came in incidentally, on Ty Maen, we must return to the subject of this chapter—the churches. We have but little knowledge of the ancient church of St. James. Mr. G. T. Clark, in the "Kenfig Charters," says the church was swallowed up by the sand, and taken down. I presume he means that the sand encroached so much

[1] "Newton," by the Rev. H. H. Knight.
[2] Extract from "Glamorganshire Pedigrees," *circa* 1678.

that the building was taken down and the material used elsewhere.

The site of the church, as marked on the Ordnance Survey, is three hundred and six yards from the centre of the castle mound; no trace of it remains. Mr. Robert W. Llewellyn some years ago found a worked stone on the site, and he told me that in certain dry seasons the outlines of graves were plainly seen. Mr. C. F. Cliffe, in the "Book of South Wales," A.D. 1848, says of the church: "An arch of the ancient Castle, and part of this ancient church and churchyard . . . in which human bones are often exposed, may be traced amongst the sand hills." Personally, I have not been able to find the slightest trace of church or churchyard.

At Kenfig Farm, a building of the Tudor period, is part of the jamb of a window in Sutton stone, and this may have come from St. James's, but I am inclined to think rather that it was brought from the Capel Papistiad near Margam Abbey. At the back of the house, too, a small window has been interpolated; the jambs evidently belonged to an ecclesiastical building. The only relic, besides two altar-slabs referred to later on, of which we can be tolerably certain is a finely ornamented tomb-slab, which, I am told by Mr. Lipscomb, was discovered on the site of St. James's Church several years ago and removed to Margam Church for safe keeping. It was the tomb-slab of an important personage, probably an ecclesiastic. It is somewhat defaced, and I regret I have been unable to make out the inscription, along the right side as one looks at it, but from the characters one can place the date as the fourteenth century. It seems to me to have a crook on either side of a floriated staff which ends in a circle which probably inclosed a cross. Donovan, writing in A.D. 1804, mentions this slab as a large coffin-like stone embellished with an *elegant flowery* cross.

Margam Abbey continued to increase its holding in Kenfig, and disputes arose between it and Tewkesbury Abbey. Among the Margam deeds is one by Henry, Bishop of Llandaff,[1] T. 49 (C. DCL.), granting to Margam Abbey all its proper tithes in the parish of Kenefeg, the tithes of the sheaves of the church of Kenefeg and its chapels, and all the lands of the church and its chapels, paying 10 marks yearly to Tewkesbury Abbey, which latter Abbey retains the cure of souls, the altarage, and the right of presenting a vicar to the said church, and is answerable to the Bishop for the episcopal dues, the lands and tithes alone going to Margam. This deed was inspected and ratified by Bishop Elias, T. 137 (C. DCCCCXCV).

By another deed Bishop Henry, T. 102 (C. DCCXXII), notifies between A.D. 1203–1213 that at the petition of Dom Walter, abbot, and the Convent of Tewkesbury, he has granted to Margam Abbey the church of Kenefeg, at an annual farm rent of 10 marks to the said Convent, saving the episcopal dues.

In Harley Charter, 75, A. 51 (C. CCXIV and DCLXXV), the Abbot and Convent of Tewkesbury agree with the Abbot and Convent of Margam that after the death of Jurdan de Hamelduna, the latter

[1] Henry of Abergavenny, A.D. 1196–1218.

THE CENTRE SLAB IS THE TOMBSTONE FROM THE DESTROYED CHURCH OF
ST. JAMES'S, KENFIG.

[*To face page* 84.

Abbey shall be quit of the annual payment of 22 shillings made on his behalf to Tewkesbury, and have back the charter which binds the Abbey to the payment.

I cannot find the reason for this payment.

Another document, T. 103 (C. DCCXXI), is an important one, for it definitely settles the matter of the church and fixes a regular payment. This is an agreement between Tewkesbury and Margam Abbeys concerning the church of Kenefeg. By it, A.D. 1203–1213, the Abbot and Convent of Tewkesbury grant the church to Margam Abbey for a perpetual payment of 10 marks yearly ; the Abbot of Tewkesbury to be honourably provided for at Kenefeg or Margam when he visits these parts. Margam to maintain a chaplain and perform the services.

Apparently this agreement did not secure peace between Tewkesbury and Margam Abbeys, for the following deed points to quarrels and litigation. In deed T. 136 (C. DCCCCXII) Bishop Elias, on the 18th, May, A.D. 1239, notifies to all faithful Christians that in his presence Dom Robert of Fortingdon, Abbot of Tewkesbury, has for ever renounced all litigation with the Abbot and Convent of Margam. Moved before S——, Prior of Strigull [Chepstow], by authority of Otto, the Papal Legate of England, respecting tithes and other property in Kenefeg.

Tewkesbury Abbey received yearly from the Abbot of Margam a rent of £11 10s. for the farm of the churches of Kenefec and Newcastle. One of the acquittances is T. 226 (C. MCLXXX). Dated at

Tewkesbury 20 March, A.D. 1353–1355. There are several extant of later dates.

In Harley Charter, 75, A. 27 (C. MCXXXIX), Bishop John of Llandaff, in the visitation of his diocese, notifies that the Abbot and Convent of Margam have exhibited by Brother Thomas Benet, monk, their proctor, sundry muniments and deeds of a grant in perpetual fee farm, by the Abbot and Convent of Tewkesbury, to them of tithes of their labours in the parish of Kenefeg, tithes of sheaves appertaining to the church of Kenefeg and all its chapels, and so forth, Dated 23 July, A.D. 1332.

In A.D. 1397 a dispute arose between the Abbey of Tewkesbury and Margam as to the repairs of Kenfig Church. John Burghill, Bishop of Llandaff, adjudicated by a deed, T. 242 (C. MCCXVII), during his visitation in an inquiry into the responsibility of Tewkesbury Abbey, John Tuder, Vicar of Kenefek, and Margam Abbey to repair the chancel of Kenfek Church ; whereby it was agreed and ordered that the Abbot and Convent of Tewkesbury must repair the chancel before the Feast of SS. Philip and James next, and afterwards the Vicar of Kenfek shall be answerable for the maintenance and repairs of the same. Llandaff Palace, 10 July, A.D. 1397.

The latest acquittance by the Abbot of Tewkesbury to the Abbot of Margam for this annual payment which I can discover is the Harley Charter, 75, B.1, in the British Museum, dated 4 Nov., 1522. No doubt it was paid up to the end which came and swept away both monasteries in 1537.

The church of St. James was in existence as late

as A.D. 1397, according to the above adjudication, by John Burghill, Bishop of Llandaff, We find from another document, which I will refer to later, that Pyle Church was built about A.D. 1485, so that probably St. James's Church was finally overwhelmed between the above date A.D. 1397 and A.D. 1485.

A document among the Margam MSS. reveals an interesting fact in the life of ancient Kenfig and in connection with the church of St. James.

From the deed T. 777 (C. MLXVIII) we find that some time between A.D. 1254 and 1267 a lonely recluse or anchoress dwelt at Kenfig in a narrow cell built, as was the custom, against the wall of the chancel of St. James's Church. This is a grant by John, son of Hosebert of Kenefeg, to Alice, the *famula*, or servant, formerly the *inclusa*, or recluse, of St. James's Church of Kenefeg, of a messuage in Kenefeg town, on the south part of St. James's cemetery, at a yearly rent of two peppercorns at Michaelmas, and eleven shillings in *gersumma*,[1] or consideration money.

Witnesses : W. Franklein, who occurs A.D. 1254–1267 ; Philip the cook ; Thomas de Corneli ; John

---

[1] The low rent, with the fee on the death of a tenant, quite accords with the Welsh Breyr-tenure. This fee was called a *grassum*, which is said to have been the same as *gersum*. And in an ancient deed cited by Somner (Somner, "Gavelkind," p. 177), there was a grant to Jordan de Serres and his heirs *ad gavelkindam* xi acres to be held of the church of Canterbury in hereditary right in perpetuity at an annual rent of 6s. 6d. ; for that *concessione*, i e., grant, the said Jordan gave to the church one hundred shillings de *Gersume*.—" The Ancient Laws of Wales," Herbert Lewis.

Albus; W. Ruddoc; Maurice Gramus, who occurs
A.D. 1258–1267; and Thomas Walensis.

Alice had evidently in the course of time recovered
from her grief; maybe she had been disappointed in
love, which had induced her to take upon her the
austere life of a recluse immured in a narrow cell
and never leaving it. Time softens all things, and
Alice became the servant attending to the cleaning
of the church, and so, as to be always at hand, had
her dwelling near the churchyard.

"Besides monks and friars, rectors and vicars,
cantarists and chaplains of various kinds, there was
still another kind of religious persons to be found in
many towns, viz., Recluses. The first recluses were
inclosed in the Egyptian deserts in a narrow cell, but
in process of time a churchyard was taken to be a
sufficiently solitary place, and the cell sometimes consisted of two or more fairly comfortable rooms built
against the chancel wall of the church. There lived
an old hermit or priest, or a religious woman, supported partly by an endowment, partly by the offerings
and bequests of the people. Their picturesque
asceticism attracted the interest and veneration of
impressible people, who would consult them in the
affairs of their soul. Richard the Second, before
proceeding to Smithfield to quell Wat Tyler's rebellion, consulted the recluse who lived in a cell in
Westminster Abbey. And Henry V. consulted the
same recluse before one of his French expeditions.

"Thomas Bolle, Rector of Aldrington, Sussex,
having resigned his living in 1402, applied to the
Bishop, Robert Rede, for leave to build a cel

CHURCH OF ST MARY MAGDALENE.

against the wall of the church, in which he might be shut up, as a recluse, for the rest of his life. The licence was granted, and the Reclusorium remains to this day in the shape of a room 29 feet by 25 feet with ingress to the chapel of the Blessed Virgin on the north side of the church."[1]

The first reference to St. Mary's which I can find is in a deed, T. 289, 60 (C. MXXV), by which Margery, daughter of Roger, and concubine of Richard, the clerk of Kenefeg, grants to Margam Abbey three acres of land in the fee of Kenefegh of her free patrimony, one acre and a quarter of which adjoins the road from the Old Castle[2] to Corneli on the west, between the land which William Alexander holds of the monks, formerly the land of Thomas Hosman, and of Hugh Walensis. They begin at the said road and lie to the west; as far as an acre held by the said William, formerly by John Wittard. One acre and a quarter lies between William's land, formerly W. Coh's, and that of W. Fronkelen; these begin at the said road and lie along to the west as far as the highway leading from St. Mary Magdalene's Chapel to Corneli; half an acre lies on the east of the road leading from the Old Castle to Corneli, between the lands of William, son of Alex-

[1] "Parish Priests and their People in the Middle Ages in England," Rev. E. L. Cutts, D.D.

[2] Old Castle. This refers to the British Camp on the western end of Cefn Cribwr, near which is Pen Castell Farm. In an early deed by which Gunnilda wife of Roger Sturmi, gives her dower land of eighty acres to Margam Abbey, it is referred to as Vetus Castellum super montem—the Old Castle on the mountain.

ander (formerly W. Coh's), and the land of Thomas Cole. This begins at the said road and lies east towards the land of Thos. Gramus.

Witnesses : Philip de Corneli ; Thomas Gramus ; W. Fronkelen ; Philip the clerk ; Thomas Walensis ; Brother W Ailward, monk of Neath ; Nicholas de Kenefegh, monk of Margam.

(Round seal, green wax ; a star.)

✠ S. MARGERIE·FIL'E:ROG'I.

The witnesses supply us with the date approximately. Philip de Corneli occurs A.D. 1254–1262, Thomas Gramus A.D. 1245–1267, Philip the clerk A.D. 1254–1282. The deed exhibits great care in fixing the locality of the land.

The chapel of St. Mary Magdalene has recently been restored by Miss Talbot, and there remains of the original building the tower only. Inside is a Norman font with fish-scale ornament.

Sir Stephen R. Glynne describes the church as it was before restoration, after a visit on Sept. 26, 1848.[1]

" A rude church of the South Wales stamp, comprising a nave and chancel, with a large coarse western tower, to the west of which is attached a very large porch It is probable that the whole is Third Pointed, though there is little distinction of an architectural character. The tower is much ruder than that of Pyle ; it has a battlement, below which on the north and south sides is the usual plain corbel-table ; but

[1] *Arch. Cambrensis.*

none on the east or west. In the centre of the
western battlement is a kind of pediment, a common
feature in this country. The belfry is lighted only
by a narrow slit on each side; on the south is a
large stair-turret lighted by slits, but not reaching
up very high; some of these slits are barred. The
tower arch is low and plain, rude, and misshapen,
of very obtuse form upon coarse imposts. The
chancel is also very low; there are a square recess
on the north-east side and brackets in the east wall.
The font is Norman and curious; the bowl-cup
shaped with a cable-moulding round the rim and
courses of scaly mouldings. The whole church is
whitewashed externally, even the roof. The site
is elevated, and commands a sea-view over flat, sandy
burrows."

A few years ago I noticed two altar-slabs on which
the consecration crosses were still plainly visible,
lying on the edge of the path leading from the
entrance gate to the church porch. I mentioned this
to Mr. Lipscomb, but before he could have them
removed I found, to my astonishment, they had
actually been utilised to form part of the pavement
in front of the porch. I brought this to Mr. Lipscomb's notice, and he had the slabs taken up, by
permission of the vicar, and placed for safe keeping
inside the church.

Here we have two pre-Reformation altar-slabs
with some of the consecration-crosses still to be
seen. In a very short time these would have been
entirely obliterated and the slabs lost sight of. Tradition has it that these ancient relics were actually

it supplies us with the date of the building of Pyle Church.

This document, T. 2812, is a Royal *Inspeximus* of a record in the Court of Augmentation of Crown Revenues, showing that in Easter Term, April, A.D. 1539, the townsmen (*villani*) of Pyle came into court with a deed dated at Cowbridge 23 May, A.D. 1536, under seal of John Vaughan, LL.D., Visitor in Wales for Thomas Crumewell, the King's Vicar-General in Spirituals, reciting testimonial letters of William Morgan, LL.D., Vicar in Spirituals and Official of the Bishop of Llandaff, which declare that at a Consistory held at Margam, 12 Aug., A.D. 1485, in the cause of the townsmen of Pyle against the burgesses of Kenfig, a sentence definitive was pronounced that all the burgesses of Kenfig should attend the church of Pyle, newly erected, as their parish church ; and the court allows the sentence.

Witness : Sir Richard Ryche, Knt., at Westminster.

Dated : 27 April, 31 Henry VIII., A.D. 1539.

When the dissolution of the monasteries was taken in hand, provision had to be made for carrying out the transfer of the property of the religious corporations to the Crown, and so a measure was passed in Parliament creating a Court of Augmentations. This court consisted of a chancellor, a treasurer, two legal officers, ten auditors, seventeen particular receivers, a clerk of the court, with an usher and messenger. The court had a busy time, dealing with the monastic assets coming into the King's possession through the sup-.pression of the religious houses. The church of Pyle

CHURCH OF ST. JAMES, PYLE.

(St. James) was probably just completed at the above date, A.D. 1485. It is a little over a mile and a half as the crow flies from the old church of Kenfig town (St. James) then destroyed by sand. It was, no doubt, intended to replace the latter, and, seeing that the cost was partly incurred for the burgesses of Kenfig, the latter were made to understand that the new church was their parish church, and they must attend it, and contribute to its service and maintenance. For some reason or other apparently the burgesses did not so wish to regard the new church or to attend it.

One of the Margam deeds, T. 2075, is a deed of sale by Lodowicus,[1] or Lewis, Abbot of Margam, of the Cistercian Order, and the Convent thereof, in the diocese of Llandaff, to Master Maurice Byrchynsha,[2] LL.B., Hugh Salisbury, Thomas Troutbeck, and Richard Jonys, laymen, of the advowson, disposition, and donation of the parish church of St. James of Kenfick, same diocese, etc. This is, of course, St. James's Church, Pyle. Dated in the Chapter House, 4 March, A.D. 1528 (for 1529). Seal of the Abbey, with two small counterseals of T. S., green wax.

The little church is interesting, and still more so as we know, very nearly, the date of its erection. At the Consistory Court at Margam, mentioned before, 22 August, A.D. 1485, the church was stated to have been newly erected, so I think the date may be safely put at A.D. 1480 to A.D. 1485.

The architecture is Perpendicular. The plan com-

[1] Lewis Thomas, last Abbot of Margam.
[2] A John Byrchynshaw was created Abbot of Chester, A.D. 1493.

prises a chancel and nave, western tower, and south porch. The east window is of three lights; the window and the east wall appear to be original, the north and south walls having been restored. In the east wall, about 5 feet up on each side of the altar, is a bracket on which formerly stood a statue. The drip-stone over the east window has square, somewhat rudely worked terminations of the period. On the south side of the chancel are two square-headed lights and a priest's door, now blocked up.

Sir Stephen R. Glynne, Bart., writing of Pyle Church, September 26, A.D. 1848, states : "In the nave are square-headed windows on the south side with labels and of two and three lights," so that the large pointed Perpendicular window near the porch must have been inserted since then.

The corbels for carrying the rood-loft remain.

The chancel arch is pointed, and the arch mouldings spring directly from the jambs, and are not continued below the curve. The tower arch is similar; the arch mouldings spring directly from the jambs.

The roof is of barrel form ; on the wall-plate are alternately a shield and a human face.

The tower is strongly built, embattled, with corbel-table below the battlement; from the top are to be seen fine views of the country, the sea, and Mumbles Head.

The base of the churchyard cross, having still part of the shaft of the cross, remains in the usual position —in front of the south porch. It is to be hoped that the cross may be repaired, seeing that all over the

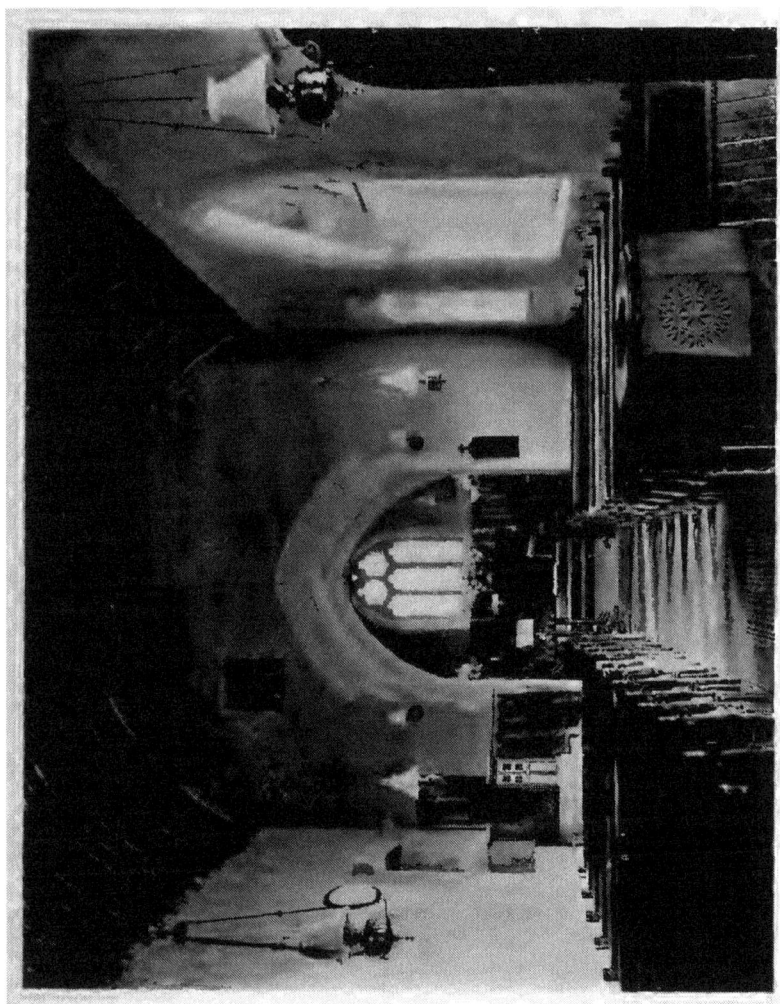

country the churchyard and village crosses are being restored.

It is extraordinary how things that have been used in past ages in the Divine Service have so little reverence paid to them in this land. I found part of the *mensa* of the pre-Reformation altar forming the step to the belfry ; two of the consecration crosses remain as clear as when they were first cut, over four hundred years ago. The altar-slab had been cut to form the step, and is now only 18 inches wide, the central cross being near the edge ; the other three crosses were in the parts cut away. The *mensa* is very similar to the larger one at Mawdlam, which is 5 feet 6½ inches long by 2 feet 6 inches wide, so that about 6½ inches have been taken off the end and 12 inches off the side, which originally was against the east wall. The slab is of the usual section, as at Mawdlam, but is much newer and the edges are still sharp.

And so the altar *mensa* on which the Holy Mystery was celebrated, and from which the Bread of Heaven was distributed for nearly a hundred years, had become a foot-step.

Mr. Lipscomb, so soon as I told him of the desecration, took steps and had the altar-slab removed from its position as a foot-step. A past age was responsible.

Now I think I have told all that can be told of Kenfig old church and its chapels.

7

CHAPTER V

CHARTERS OF KENFIG

MR. CLARK, in the "Kenfig Charters," says the documents preserved in the municipal chest in the Town Hall, at Kenfig are nine in number. 1. The Charter of Thomas Lord le Despenser, dated 16 February, A.D. 1397. 2. The Charter of Richard Beauchamp, Earl of Worcester, dated 1 May, 1421. 3. The Charter of Isabella, Countess of Worcester, dated 1 May, 1423. 4. The Ordinance of Kenfig, 4 Edward III. This is a translation of the original which is lost. 5. A copy of No. 4. 6. A Presentment or Survey of the Lordship, Manor, Town, and Borough of Kenfig, taken in A.D. 1660. 7. A copy of No. 6. 8. A translation of the Charter of Lord Thomas, on paper. 9. An abstract of the Charter of Countess Isabella in English.

Thomas, sixth Lord le Despenser, was the youngest son of Edward, son of Hugh le Despenser, who married Eleanor, sister and co-heir of Gilbert de Clare, the last Earl of Gloucester, by whom the Despensers became lords of Glamorgan. Lord Thomas married Constance, daughter of Edmond of Langley, Duke of York, and among the estates allotted to her in dower occur the castle and town of Kenfig. His son

Richard was the last male of the house of Despenser, and a second daughter was Isabella, whose charter follows. The recited Charter of Edward le Despenser, fifth baron, and father of Thomas, is dated 14 May, 34 Edward III. (1360). Among the witnesses to the latter is Thomas, Abbot of Neath.[1]

I give here the Charter of Thomas le Despenser, lord of Glamorgan, 16 February, 20 Richard II. (1397), in Latin, followed by a translation in English. The Latin text is taken from "Cartae et Alia Munimenta quæ ad Dominium de Glamorgan pertinent," vol. ii. p. 45. Curante G. T. Clark :—

CHARTER OF THOMAS LE DESPENSER, LORD OF GLAMORGAN, 16 FEBY., 20 RICH. II. [1397].

Thomas le Despenser filius et heres domini Edwardi le Despenser et domine Elizabeth consortis sue dominus Glamorgancie et Morgancie. Omnibus sancte matris ecclesie filiis ad quos hoc presens scriptum pervenerit salutem. Noveritis nos inspexisse confirmacionem bone memorie domini Edwardi patris nostri nuper domini Glamorgancie et Morgancie quam fecit burgensibus nostris de Kenfeg de libertatibus eorum in hec verba.

Edwardus le Despenser dominus Glamorgancie et Morgancie omnibus ballivis et ministris nostris ac aliis fidelibus presentem cartam inspecturis salutem in Domino sempiternam

Sciatis quod de gracia nostra speciali dedimus et concessimus burgensibus nostris ville nostre de Kenfeg omnes libertates subscriptas imperpetuum videlicet

[1] " The Kenfig Charters," G. T. Clark.

Quod ipsi et heredes sui quieti et liberi sint de thelonio muragio pontagio pavagio et terragio kayagio et picagio et aliis diversis custumis et consuetudinibus per totum dominium nostrum tam in Anglia quam in Wallia

Et quod ipsi eligere debeant annuatim ballivos nostros de burgensibus nostris eiusdem ville videlicet tres prepositos de quibus Vicecomes Glamorgancie seu Constabularius castri nostri de Kenfeg unum recipiet ad voluntatem suam duos ballivos ex quibus prepositus recipiet unum et duos tastatores cervisie qui debent recipi et iurari in castello nostro de Kenfeg coram vicecomite seu constabulario eiusdem castri ad bene et fideliter faciendum quecumque ad officia sua pertinent

Et quod idem prepositus onerari debeat in compoto suo de exitibus ballivie eorum.

Et eciam predictus prepositus et ballivus qui pro tempore fuerint pro serviciis suis de redditu unius burgagii sint quilibet eorum quietus per annum.

Concessimus eciam predictis burgensibus nostris quod de omnibus merchandisis tam per terram quam per aquam ad predictam villam venientibus seu transeuntibus demonstracio primo fiet constabulario nostro predicto seu preposito ville priusquam aliquid inde sit venditum seu remotum sub pena qua decet

Et quod nullus de burgensibus nostris capi nec imprisonari debeat in castro nostro predicto pro aliquibus eos tangentibus dum manucapcionem seu plegiagium extra pontem castri predicti seu portam possent invenire nisi in casu felonie cum manu opere tantum capti fuerint seu pro aliquibus nos aut familias nostras specialiter tangentibus.

Et de omnibus rebus infra libertatem ville nostre predicte factis prefatos burgenses tenementa et catalla eorum tangentes unde inquisicio capi debeat quod illa inquisicio sit terminata per intrinsecos eiusdem ville et non per alios.

Concessimus insuper eisdem burgensibus nostris quod ipsi nec heredes sui esse non debeant receptores denariorum nostrorum nisi tantum de denariis exeuntibus de ballivia prepositatus ville nostre predicte nec distringi debeant ad blada carnes vina seu alia victualia nostra contra eorum voluntatem emendum sed quod liberi sint per libertates eorum vendere omnia que habent vendenda cuicunque et quibuscunque et quo tempore voluerint absque aliquo impedimento

Preterea concessimus prefatis burgensibus nostris quod ipsi et heredes sui libere legare possent omnia burgagia sua per ipsos adquisita tam de tenementis quam de redditibus cuicunque et quibuscunque voluerint ad voluntatem ipsorum

Et quod iidem burgenses nostri distringi non debeant exire antiquas bundas libertatis ville predicte contra eorum voluntatem ad aliquid faciendum   Et tales sunt bunde libertatis eorum videlicet inter locum vocatum Newdich et Taddulcrosse et quandam divisam ducentem de Newdich usque Taddulcrosse inter terram Abbathie de Margan et terram Abbathie de Teokesburie in parte orientali et quendam rivulum vocatum Blaklaak qui solebat currere 'de aqua australi usque aquam borialem de Kenfeg in parte occidentali et medietate cursus aque de Kenfeg in parte boriali a Howlotesford currentis ad mare et Regiam viam ducentem de Taddulcrosse ad crucem et sic de dicta cruce usque Blaklaak in parte australi

Et quod nullus extraneus extra nundinas vel forum
infra bundas predictas aliquas merchandisas de aliquo
extraneo emat nisi tantum de burgensibus nostris
eiusdem ville preter gentiles homines de Glamorgancie
et Morgancie pro victualibus eorum et non racione
merchandise Nec aliquis teneat seldam apertam de
aliquibus merchandisis nec tabernam nec Corf faciet
in villa nostra predicta nisi fuerit cum predictis burgensibus nostris lotatus et escotatus et infra guldam
mercatorium ipsorum receptus

Necnon concessimus eisdem burgensibus nostris
quod ipsi et heredes sui guldam inter eos facere
possint quo tempore et quandocunque voluerint ad
proficuum ipsorum.

Et quod distringi non debeant pro debito alicuius
nisi debitores aut plegii pro eodem fuerint Et quod
nullus ballivus seu minister noster colore ballivie sue
summoniciones sue attachiamenta faciet nec infra
bundas predictas districciones capiet nisi tantum constabularius predictus et ballivi ejusdem ville qui per
ipsos burgenses electi fuerint.

Insuper concessimus prefatis burgensibus nostris
quod omnes mercatores tam Pannarii Cerdones
Pelliparii et Cirotecarii quam alii diversi qui ex
empcione et vendicione vivant infra dominium nostrum
Glamorgancie et Morgancie residere debeant in villis
de burgh et non upland.

Et quod omnimodas⁴ merchandisas faciant in nundinis foris et villis de burg et non alibi Et eciam
omnes mercatores cum eorum merchandisis alibi non
transeant quam per regales vicos et per villas de
burgh. Ita quod nos nec heredes nostri tolnetum

nostrum nec aliquas custumas nobis debitas aliquo tempore amittamus

Et quod predicti burgenses nostri nec eorum heredes aliquam vigilacionem faciant nec aliquem fugitivum in aliqua ecclesia custodiant extra muros ville nostre predicte

Concessimus vero predictis burgensibus nostris quod per ordinacionem constabularii predicti ordinaciones et clamaciones libere facere possint de assisa panis et cervisie et aliis diversis rebus ad voluntatem eorum eandem villam tangentibus quandocunque necesse fuerit ad emendacionem illius ville et proficuum populi nolentes quod iidem burgenses nostri sint ligati per ordinaciones et clamaciones in comitatu nostro Glamorgancie aliquo tempore factas.

Preterea concessimus prefatis burgensibus nostris quod due nundine sint in eadem villa nostra quolibet anno sicut esse solebant tempore antecessorum nostrorum videlicet nundine que incipiunt in vigilia Sti. Jacobi apostoli durante per octo dies sequentes In quibus vero nundinis predictus constabularius seu prepositus capiet tolnetum nostrum et alias custumas nobis debitas et quod de cetero in eisdem nundinis predictus constabularius seu prepositus teneat omnia placita corone de omnibus feloniis infra bundas libertatis eiusdem ville durantibus illis nundinis factis ac alia placita de transgressionibus debitis et convencionibus et aliis diversis contractis ubicunque fuerint facta. Et concessimus predictis burgensibus quod durantibus predictis nundinis nullus mercator aliquas merchandisas emat vel vendet extra illas nundinas inter Rempny et Polthcanan sub forisfactura

earum merchandisarum et gravi amerciamento. Et
alie nundine sint die Martis in septimana Penticostes
que nundine quiete sint de tolneto tantum in vigilia
et in die sequenti

Concessimus insuper prefatis burgensibus nostris
quod constabularius seu prepositus ville nostre predicte
teneat placita vocata Pepoudres de die in diem quandocunque necesse fuerit

Et omnia alia placita terminentur de mense in
mensem coram Vicecomite Glamorgancie in curia
ville nostre predicte

Concessimus eciam quod constabularius noster de
Kenfeg qui pro tempore fuerit de cetero faciet officium
Coronatoris de omnibus infortuniis infra libertatem
predictam contingentibus

Preterea concessimus prefatis burgensibus nostris
quod ipsi et heredes sui habeant communem pasturam
in communibus pasturis quibus usi fuerint ex antiquo
pro averiis suis pasturandis et aliis aisiamentis in
eisdem habendum prout habere solebant tempore
antecessorum nostrorum.

Nos autem donaciones et concessiones predictas
ratas habentes et gratas eas pro nobis et heredibus
nostris predictis burgensibus nostris concedimus et
confirmamus easque tenore presencium innovamus.
Volentes et concedentes pro nobis et heredibus nostris
quod carta predicta in omnibus et singulis articulis
suis imperpetuum firmiter et immobiliter observetur
eciam si aliqui articuli in eadem carta contenti huc—
usque forsitan non fuerint observati.

In cuius rei testimonium huic presenti carte sigillum
Cancellarie nostre de Kaerdyf duximus apponendum.

Hiis testibus venerabilibus patribus Henrico abbate de Margan Thoma abbate de Neth domino Johanne de Coventre archidiacono Landavensi et custode dominii Glamorgancie et Morgancie dominis Ricardo de Thurberville Johanne le Norreis Johanne de la Seer Elya Basset militibus et aliis.

Data apud Kaerdyf quartodecimo die mensis Maii anno regni Regis Edwardi tertii post conquestum tricesimo quarto

Nos vero prefatus Thomas le Despenser de gracia nostra speciali concessimus predictis burgensibus nostris et eorum successoribus quod habeant unum messorem super [idem pasturam] eorum vocatam le Rugge que se extendit in longitudine de Catput usque ad Rugge de Coitiff et in latitudine de Kevencribor usque aquam decurrentem de Lowerkesmore usque Kenfeg qui quidam messor si aliquos alios preterquam burgenses ville nostre predicte inveniat super dictam pasturam manuoperantes cum eorum averiis ipsos attachiari faciat et attachiamenta presentet ad hundredam ville nostre predicte et sint ibi amerciati secundum quantitatem delicti.

Concessimus insuper predictis burgensibus nostris et eorum successoribus unam pasturam communem vocatam le Doune de Kenfeg que se extendit in longitudine a prato comitis usque ad Goutesfurlong abbatis de Neth et se extendit in latitudine a Wadeslond quam Willielmus Stiward tenet usque le Burghes de Kenfeg super quam communam predictus messor pro commodo nostro attachiamenta faciat. Et si aliquos de burgensibus ville nostre predicte ad comitatum nostrum Glamorgancie aliquo tempore attachiari

contigerit volumus et concedimus quod medietas inqui-
sicionis que supercapi debeat sit de de burgensibus
ville nostre predicte et altera medietas viceneto

Concessimus insuper prefatis burgensibus nostris
centum perticas terre in augmentum ffranchesie eorum
videlicet de capella Sancte Marie Magdalene versus
partem orientalem et citra circumquaque antiquas
bundas et limites dicti Burgi de Kenfeg ratificantes et
confirmantes imperpetuum per presentes pro nobis et
heredibus nostris omnes predictas libertates tam de
novo per nos [concessas] quam per predictas ante-
cessores nostros predictis burgensibus nostris de Kenfeg et eorum successoribus prius datas.

In cuius rei testimonium huic presenti carte sigillum
cancellarie nostre de Kaerdyf duximus apponendum.

Hiis testibus Domino Johanni de Sancto Johanne
tunc vicecomite nostro Glamorgancie Domino Wi-
lelmo Stradelyng milite Johanne Basset Roberto
Walssche et Johanne le Eyr et aliis.

Datum apud Kaerdiff sexto decimo die Ffebruarii
anno regni Regis Ricardi secundi post conquestum
vicesimo

" This, the oldest extant Kenfig charter, is engrossed
upon a skin of stout parchment, sixteen inches broad
by twenty inches long, with a fold of three inches to
carry the label for the seal. The character is small
but clear, and the ink good. The document is perfectly legible throughout, save where small holes have
been worn by constant folding. Where this occurs,
the words are supplied, in this print, in brackets.
The seal is of red wax of excellent quality, shown by

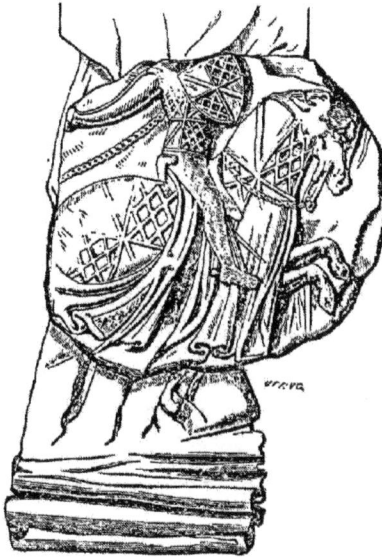

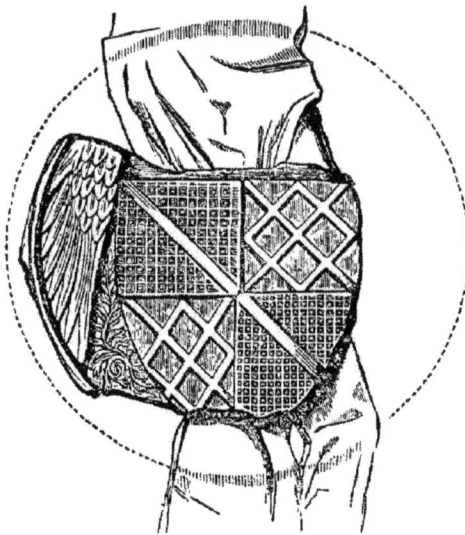

SEAL TO THOMAS LE DESPENSER'S CHARTER.

the sharpness of the impression retained by what remains of it."

Charter of Thomas le Despenser, Lord of Glamorgan, 16 Feb., 20 Ric. II. [1397].

Thomas le Despenser, son and heir of Lord Edward le Despenser and of the Lady Elizabeth, his consort, lord of Glamorgan and Morgan, to all the sons of Holy Mother Church to whom this present writing shall have come, greeting. Know that we have inspected the confirmation of Lord Edward of worthy memory, our father, late lord of Glamorgan and Morgan, which he made to our burgesses of Kenefeg concerning their liberties in these words.

Edward le Despenser, lord of Glamorgan and Morgan, to all our bailiffs and ministers and other faithful people who shall inspect the present charter, greeting everlasting in the Lord.

Know that of our special grace we have given and granted to our burgesses of our vill of Kenfeg all the underwritten liberties for ever, namely, that they and their heirs be quit and free of toll for repairing walls, bridges, paving, and earthworks, quayage,[1] picage,[2] and divers other the tolls and customs throughout all our lordship as well in England as in Wales.

And that they may yearly elect our bailiffs from our burgesses of the same vill, namely, three provosts (or reeves, "*prepositus*" [3]), of whom the sheriff of Glamorgan or the constable of our castle of Kenfeg

---

[1] Quayage, toll for using a quay.

[2] Picage, payment for breaking the ground to set up a booth.

[3] Prepositus, chief municipal officer.

shall receive one, at his will, two bailiffs, out of whom the provost shall receive one, and two tasters of beer, who ought to be received and sworn in our castle of Kenfeg before the sheriff or the constable of the same castle, well and faithfully to perform whatsoever things belong to their offices.

And that the same provost ought to be charged in his account with the issues of their bailiwick.

And also the aforesaid provost and the bailiff for the time being shall for their services each be quit of the rent of one burgage by the year.

We have granted also to our aforesaid burgesses, that of all merchandise coming to or passing through the aforesaid vill as well by land as by water an inspection shall first be made by our aforesaid constable or the provost of the vill before any thereof be sold, under a suitable penalty.

And that none of our burgesses ought to be taken or imprisoned in our castle aforesaid for anything touching them so long as they can find surety or pledge without the bridge or gate of the aforesaid castle, except that in the case of felony only they shall be taken with stolen goods in hand, or for anything specially touching us or our household.

And that concerning all things done within the liberty of our aforesaid vill touching the burgesses aforesaid, their tenements and goods, whereof an inquisition ought to be made, that inquiry be determined by inhabitants of the same vill and not by others.

Furthermore we have granted to our said burgesses that neither they nor their heirs be receivers of our moneys except only of the moneys issuing from the bailiwick of the provost of our aforesaid vill, nor ought they to be distrained to buy our corn, flesh, wine or other our victuals against their will, but that they be free by their liberties to sell all things which they have to sell to whomsoever and at what time they shall wish without any impediment.

Furthermore, we have granted to our aforesaid burgesses that they and their heirs may freely bequeath all their burgages by them acquired, as well of tenements as of rents, at their will to whomsoever they shall wish.

And that our same burgesses ought not to be distrained to go beyond the ancient bounds of the liberty of the aforesaid vill against their will to do anything. And these are the bounds of their liberty, namely, between the place called Newditch and Taddulcrosse and a certain boundary leading from Newditch to Taddulcrosse between the land of the Abbey of Margam and the land of the Abbey of Teokesburie on the east and a certain stream called Blaklaak which used to run from the southern water to the northern water of Kenfeg on the west and the middle of the water-course of Kenfeg on the north running from Howlotesford to the sea and the highway leading from Taddulcrosse to the cross and so from the said cross to Blaklaak on the south. And that no stranger outside the fair or market within the aforesaid bounds shall buy any merchandise of any stranger but only of our burgesses of the same, except the denizens of Glamorgan and Morgan for their victuals and not by way of trade. Nor shall any one keep an open shop of any merchandise nor tavern nor make "corf"[1] in our aforesaid vill unless he shall be of lot and scot with our aforesaid burgesses and received into the guild of their merchants.

Also we have granted to our same burgesses that they and their heirs can make a guild among themselves for their profit at what time and whensoever they shall wish. And that they ought not to be distrained for the debt of any except they be debtors or pledges for the same. And that no bailiff or minister of ours by colour of his bailiwick shall make summonses or attachments or take distraints within the aforesaid bounds excepting only the aforesaid constable and the bailiffs of the same vill who shall be elected by the burgesses themselves.

We have further granted to our aforesaid burgesses that all merchants as well clothiers, cobblers, pelterers,[2] and glovers, as divers others who live by buying and selling within our lordship of Glamorgan and Morgan, ought to dwell in the vills of the borough and not "upland." And that they shall do all manner of trading in the fairs markets and vills of the borough and not elsewhere. And also all merchants with their merchandise shall not travel otherwise than along the highways and through the vills of the borough, so that neither we nor our heirs lose our toll or other the customs due to us at any time.

And that neither our aforesaid burgesses nor their

---

[1] "Corf" is probably a mistake for "cervisiam," the word being contracted in the original, and "e" is easily confused with "o." Cervisia (beer) seems to be the only word that would make sense.

[2] A dealer in raw hides.

heirs shall keep any watch or guard any fugitive in any church outside the walls of our aforesaid vill.

We have also granted to our aforesaid burgesses, not willing that our same burgesses be bound by ordinances and proclamations (*clamationes*) made in our county of Glamorgan at any time, that by ordinance of the constable aforesaid they can freely make ordinances and proclamations of the assize of bread and beer [1] and divers other things touching the same vill, at their will, whenever it shall be necessary to the improvement of the same vill and the profit of the people.

Furthermore, we have granted to our aforesaid burgesses that there shall be two fairs in our same vill in each year as there used to be in the time of our ancestors, that is to say, a fair which begins on the eve of St. James the Apostle, lasting for eight days following. In which fair moreover the aforesaid constable or provost shall take our toll and other customs due to us, and that further in the same fair the aforesaid constable or provost shall hold all pleas of the Crown of all felonies done within the bounds of the liberty of the same vill during that fair, and other the pleas of trespass, debts and agreements and divers other the contracts wherever they be made. And we have granted to the aforesaid burgesses that during the aforesaid fair, no merchant shall buy or sell any

---

[1] "Assize of Bread and Beer. A franchise conferred on lords of manors from a very early period, the frauds in these trades being severely punished ; by a statute of Henry III. a baker breaking an assize was liable to be condemned to the pillory, and knavish brewers to the tumbril, or dung-cart."—Gasquet, "The Manors."

merchandise outside that fair between Rempny[1] and
Polthcanan[2] under forfeiture of the same merchandise
and heavy amercement. And the other fair is on the
Tuesday in Whitsun week, which fair shall be free of
toll on the eve and the day following.

We have furthermore granted to our aforesaid
burgesses that the constable or provost of our vill
aforesaid shall hold the pleas called pie poudre from
day to day whenever it shall be necessary. And all
other the pleas shall be determined from month to
month before the Sheriff of Glamorgan in the court
of our aforesaid vill.

We have granted also that our constable of Kenfeg
for the time being shall perform the office of coroner
on all fatalities happening within the aforesaid liberty.

Furthermore, we have granted to our aforesaid
burgesses that they and their heirs shall have common
pasture in the common pastures which they have used
from ancient times for pasturing their cattle and for
other easements in the same, as they were accustomed
to have in the time of our ancestors.

We moreover, holding the aforesaid gifts and grants
ratified and gratified, grant the same for us and our
heirs to our aforesaid burgesses and confirm the same
which by the tenor of the presents we renew. Willing
and granting for us and our heirs that the aforesaid
charter in all and singular its articles be for ever
firmly and unchangeably observed, even if any articles
contained in the same charter may not hitherto per-

[1] Rumney River.
[2] Pwll Cynan in Crymlyn Bog, between Briton Ferry and
Swansea.

chance have been observed. In witness whereof we have ordered to be affixed to this present charter the seal of our chancery of Kaerdiyf. These being the witnesses, the reverend fathers, Henry, Abbot of Margam, Thomas, Abbot of Neth, Dom John de Coventry, Archdeacon of Landaff and warden of the lordship of Glamorgan and Morgan, Sirs Richard de Thurberville, John le Norreis, John de la Seer, Elyas Basset, knights, and others.

Given at Kaerdyf, the fourteenth day of May in the year of the reign of King Edward the third after the conquest the thirty-fourth [A.D. 1360].

We moreover the aforesaid Thomas le Despenser of our special grace have granted to our aforesaid burgesses and their successors that they shall have one hayward upon the same their (pasture) called le Rugge which extends in length from Catput to the Rugge of Coitiff (Coity) and in breadth from Kevencribor to the water running from Lowerkesmore [1] to Kenfeg, which hayward, if he shall find others except burgesses of our aforesaid vill occupying the said pasture with their cattle shall cause them to be attached and shall present the attachment at the hundred court of our aforesaid vill, and they shall there be amerced according to the extent of their offence.

We have further granted to our aforesaid burgesses and their successors one common pasture called le Doune of Kenfeg which extends in length from the Earl's meadow to Goutesfurlong of the Abbot of Neth, and in breadth from Wadeslond which William

[1] Llywarch's moor, so named from Llywarch, son of Meredydd, now called Hirwaun Margam.

Stiward holds to the Burrows of Kenfeg, upon which
pasture the said hayward shall make attachments for
our advantage. And if any of the burgesses of our
aforesaid vill shall happen at any time to be attached
to our county of Glamorgan, we will and grant that a
moiety of the panel, which ought to be taken concerning the matter, be of burgesses of our aforesaid
vill, and the other moiety of the neighbourhood.

We have further granted to our aforesaid burgesses
one hundred perticas of land in augmentation of their
franchise, namely from the chapel of St. Mary
Magdalene on the east, and round about the ancient
bounds and limits of the said borough of Kenfeg,
ratifying and confirming for ever by the presents for
us and for our heirs all the aforesaid liberties, as well
new ones by us instituted, as those formerly given by
our aforesaid ancestors to our aforesaid burgesses of
Kenfeg and their successors.

In witness of which thing to this present charter we
have ordered to be affixed the seal of our chancery of
Kaerdif. These being the witnesses, Sir John of St.
John, then our Sheriff of Glamorgan, Sir William
Stradelyng, Knight, John Basset, Robert Walssche
and John le Eyr and others.

Given at Kaerdyf, the sixteenth day of February in
the year of the reign of King Richard the Second
after the conquest, the twentieth.

The following charters are by Richard Beauchamp,
Earl of Worcester, and Isabel le Despenser, his
Countess. Isabel was the daughter of Thomas le
Despenser, the grantor of the preceding charter. She
married Richard Beauchamp who became lord of
Glamorgan.

CCCXXXII. Richard, Earl of Worcester, Confirmation of Charter to the Burgesses of Kenfig.

(Cartae . . . quae ad Glamorgan pertinent.)

Curante G. T. Clark, vol. ii. p. 96.

1 May. 9 Hen V. 1421.

Richard Beauchamp, Earl of Worcester, Lord le Despenser and of Bergavenny, to all faithful people to whom this present writing shall come, greeting.

We have inspected the confirmation of Thomas Le Despenser and Lady Elizabeth, his consort, which he made to our burgesses of Kenfig concerning their liberties in these words. (*Vide* C. CCCX.)

And we therefore the aforesaid Richard Beauchamp, Earl of Worcester, because by the charters of our progenitors it was granted to our aforesaid burgesses that if any of our burgesses of our vill aforesaid shall happen to be attached any time to our county of Glamorgan that a moiety of the panel which ought to be taken concerning them be of the borough of our aforesaid vill and the other moiety of the neighbourhood, and now at the supplication of the aforesaid burgesses of our aforesaid vill, have granted (that as often as it shall happen that any) of the said burgesses at any future time be attached to our county of Glamorgan that an inquisition thereof be made concerning them in the manner abovesaid at the first, second and third commote of Glamorgan, after which (it shall happen) that they or any of (them who there ought to be attached so he be not) a common or notorious thief. And further, holding the said gifts and grants ratified and gratified, we grant and confirm the same for us and our heirs to the said burgesses, and by the tenor of these presents renew the same. Willing and granting for ever for us and for our heirs that the aforesaid charter of our confirmation and of our gift aforesaid in all and singular its articles shall be firmly and unchangeably observed, any interruptions notwithstanding. In witness of which thing to this our present charter of confirmation and gift we have affixed the seal of our chancery of Kaerdiff. These being the witnesses, the reverend men, William, Abbot of Margam, Lleisant, the Abbot of Neth, John Stradelyng, then our Sheriff of Glamorgan and Morgan, John St. John, Oliver St. John, Gilbert Denys, and Edward Stradelyng, knights, John Laurence, Robert Walsshe and Walter Moreton, esquires, and many others. Witnessed by myself at Kaerdif, the first day of May in the year of the reign of King Henry the fifth after the Conquest, the ninth.

NOTE.—The words in brackets above are apparently incomplete. They are thus bracketed in the book.

C. CCCXXXVII. ISABEL, COUNTESS OF WORCESTER. CONFIRMATION CHARTER TO THE BURGESSES OF KENFIG.

(Cartae . . . quae ad Glamorgan penitent.)

Curante G. T. Clark, vol. ii. p. 101.
1 May, 1 Hen. VI. 1423.

Isabell, Countess of Worcester, Lady de Despenser of Glamorgan and Morgan, to all the faithful in Christ to whom this present writing shall come, greeting.

We have inspected the confirmation of Thomas le Despenser, lord of Glamorgan and Morgan, our father, in these words. (*Vide* C. CCCX.) Here follows the *Inspeximus* of Thomas le Despenser.

And we therefore, the aforesaid Isabel, Countess of Worcester, Lady le Despenser of Glamorgan and Morgan, because by the charter of our progenitor, etc. (*Vide* C. CCCXXXII.)

Here follows the charter of Richard Earl of Worcester.

With these witnesses : the reverend men, William, Abbot of Margam, Lleisant, the Abbot of Neth, John Stradelyng, then Sheriff of Glamorgan, John St. John, Oliver St. John, and Edward Stradelyng, knights, John Laurence, Robert Walsshe, Walter Moreton, esquires, and many others. Witnessed by myself at Kaerdiff, the first day of May in the year of the reign of King Henry the sixth after the conquest, the first.

Lord Thomas recites and confirms his father's charter, which granted to the burgesses of Kenfig certain liberties for ever.

For the first time we have a description of the boundary of the ancient borough, but it is not easy to follow.

I have no doubt " Newditch " is the new ditch, or leat, constructed for conveying the water necessary for working Llanfihangel Mill [1] from the Kenfig river ; and the point at which the ditch starts from

[1] St. Michael's Mill.

the river is the parish boundary on the east as it is to-day ; from this point the boundary follows an imaginary line along the middle of the Kenfig river to the sea and forms the northern boundary. From this same point the boundary passes south to a stone on the roadside named Groes Siencyn, thence to a stone in Cae Pwll-y-Cyffylau,[1] from that point to Groes-y-Gryn, or perhaps Groes-y-gryniau—the cross of muttering. No cross remains here : from its name it was probably a prayer- or weeping-cross. The cross stood near the present' blacksmith's shop at the intersection of Heol-las and Heol-y-sheet, then to a stone in Hoel-y-Broome, then to a stone in Y Cae Isaf and to a stone in the road at the point where it debouches on to Kenfig Down, and thence through Sker Farm building, called Ty-yr-Ychen,[2] to the sea at Gwter-y-cwn,[3] the low-water mark forming the boundary on the western side. From Gwter-y-cwn to the point called "Newditch" the boundary is the same for parish and borough. From "Newditch" the parliamentary boundary and that of the lordship take in part of the parish of Margam—upper Kenfig—and part of Trissent,[4] the line passing north from "Newditch" to a point near Cae-garw,[5] thence north-west to the Pumpeius Carantorius Stone near Eglwysnynydd, and from there to the sea.

---

[1] The field of the horses' pool.

[2] Oxen's house.   [3] Dogs' ditch.

[4] Trisaint, so called from the chapel near Hafodbeulog, dedicated to three saints, probably SS. Philip and James and St. Michael.

[5] Cae-garw, rough or coarse field.

The ancient boundary clearly refers only to the boundary as is represented by the bounds of the parish   From " Newditch " to Taddulcrosse, Groes-y-dadl, to which I will refer later, is easy.   But on the west " the stream called Blaklaak, which used to run, or formerly ran, from the southern water to the northern water of Kenfig," is a puzzle.

In a deed of confirmation by Robert Earl of Gloucester of the gifts of Maurice de Londres and Gilbert de Turberville to Ewenny Priory, he adds on his own account twenty-one acres of arable land adjoining 'the town of Kenefec, with a burgage in the west street as far as the black water without the gate of the town of Kenefeke.

This certainly points to a " Black River " on the west of the town.   The deed would be about 1139–1147.

The Latin text is : " Et addo ex parte mea viginti et unam acram terrae arabilis juxta villam de Kenefec, cum uno burgagio in vico occidentali usque ad aquam nigram extra portam villae de Kenefeke."

It appears clear from the charter and this deed of Robert Earl of Gloucester that a river ran at one time on the west of the town.   The conclusion seems to me irresistible that the stream, the Black River, was the overflow of the waters of the Pool into the Kenfig river.

From the west the description jumps to the north " and the middle of the water-course of Kenfig on the north running from Howlotesford to the sea " : this is as it is to-day.   Howlotesford is not known, but it is either the ford of the Owlet or Heolan-tes-ford—the ford of the sunny lane. I believe this is the lane passing Llanfihangel mill on the way to Llanfihangel Farm.

The reference in the charter to the burgesses not being liable to keep any watch or guard any fugitive in any church outside of our vill,[1] means the watching of any person who, flying from the law officers, had gained a church having the privilege of sanctuary, claimed safety from his pursuers. A Margam MS. gives us an instance of this privilege. John Smith, Bishop of Llandaff, issued a certificate, T. 267 (C. MCCLXXXI), declaring that the Llangynwyd tenants of Margam Abbey are exempt from ecclesiastical taxation, and are therefore not to be taxed for the escape of Jevan Glas, who had taken refuge at the step of the church of Llangonyth, Llangynwyd, the parishioners, in accordance with the custom and practice of the county, being bound to set a watch over him for forty days under penalty of a hundred shillings. In consequence of which, the said penalty had been laid upon the parishioners. Llandaff, 5 July, A.D. 1477.

The reference that all merchants and divers others who live by buying and selling within the lordship ought to live in the vills of the borough and not "upland" means that they are to live within the boroughs and not in the land beyond, *i.e.*, the waste or upland, in the latter case escaping contributions exacted by the town authorities.

Although certain churches had a special right of sanctuary, to some extent every church and

[1] Vill, the Normans' name for an urban district.

churchyard shared in the privileges of sanctuary; people in danger of life or liberty frequently took refuge in the churches. Property was often placed in the church for safety. The churchyard also gave protection. Ordericus Vitalis relates that the villagers in time of war sometimes removed themselves and all their goods there, and built themselves huts within the precincts, and were left unmolested.[1] We have seen how the inhabitants of Kenfig sought sanctuary in the church and cemetery that Easter-time in A.D. 1232, when the Welsh under Morgan Gam, lord of Afan, tried to capture the castle. They were not molested, to the surprise of the narrator, sanctuary being respected.

I always wondered what became of the person who had found sanctuary in a church, for he could not live in the church like the church-mouse—he would fall, sooner or later, into the hands of his pursuers; now I can give you this information.

"It was provided that when a thief, manslayer, or other malefactor, availed himself of the very ancient custom of privilege of sanctuary, that is, fled to obtain the protection afforded by the Church, the Coroner was to summon all the good and lawful men of his neighbourhood, and to cause the abjuration of the realm of the fugitive in the following manner. The felon was to be brought to the church door, a seaport was assigned for him by the Coroner, and then the felon abjured the realm. A time-allowance was given to him to reach the seaport, and he was to be set on his journey on the

[1] Cutts' "Parish Priests," etc., in part.

King's highway bearing in his hand a cross, being commanded to depart the realm as speedily as possible, turning neither to the right hand nor upon the left. This privilege entailed perpetual banishment into a foreign Christian country. His lands were escheated; his chattels were forfeited; and if he came back he was outlawed." [1]

This may have been a good way of getting rid of an undesirable, but bad for the Christian country on which he thrust himself.

In a deed among the Margam MSS., the sanctuary of the chapel of Corneli is mentioned. It does not mean, however, in this case that the chapel possessed the privilege of sanctuary. See footnote page 77.

The privilege of sanctuary must have been somewhat rare. Leland in his "Collectanea" only mentions Morgan abbat. Cistert. (Com. Glamorgan): Has the privilege of sanctuary, but it is very rarely, if ever, made use of by the Welsh.

Nethe abbat. Cistert. (Com. Glamorgan): Has the privilege of sanctuary; seldom used.

Edward de Despenser granted the burgesses the right to make their own ordinances and proclamations of the assize of bread and beer and divers other things, not wishing his burgesses to be bound by ordinances and proclamations made in his county of Glamorgan. This was giving the burgesses of Kenfig great liberty and independence. A copy of the ordinances for the government of the town of A.D. 1330,

[1] " Statutes of Wales," Ivor Bowen, barrister-at-law (T. Fisher Unwin).

altered and added to from time to time, will be given in its place.

A grant of two fairs is made in each year, "as there used to be in the time of our ancestors." One of the fairs began on the eve of St. James, and lasted eight days after. This was the Gŵyl Mabsant, the Patronal Festival, the church being dedicated to St. James.

Gŵyl is the Welsh for festival. Originally it meant the vigil or watch that was kept the evening preceding a Holy Day. It is the same as the Latin *vigilia*—"a watch." Salesbury, in his "Dictionary," 1547, gives "Gwyl, ne vysilia—vigyll."

In the course of time the term "gŵyl" came to be applied to the festival itself.

In the Myvyrian *Brut y Tywysogion* we are told that Joseph, Bishop of Llandaff, in A.D. 1030, "reformed the Festivals of Patron Saints, Gwyliau Mabsant, so that they were to be reserved entirely for prayer to God, showing good works, almsgiving, and a due remembrance of God and His Saints and of their prayer—worthy works."

Again, we are told that Uchtryd, Bishop of Llandaff, who died in A.D. 1146, "reformed the Sundays and the Holy Days, and Festivals of Patron Saints, y Suliau a'r Gwyliau, a Gwyliau Mabsant, and caused them to be observed with religious services (yn olychwydawl) where that had not been done willingly and customarily."

The Gŵyl Mabsant was an important event in the social life of the Welsh people ; the time was observed as a general holiday. In days gone by it would probably be the most important and joyous event connected with a parish, and it eclipsed every other festival. Old and young looked forward to it, and those who had left the parish to live elsewhere made a point of paying a visit to their old homes during its continuance. Great preparations were made for it, everybody kept open house, and there was a general welcome to those who came from a distance.

By the early part of the last century the Gŵyl Mabsant had lost its religious character entirely, and had become a festival for different kinds of rustic games and sport, trials of strength and agility, dancing (several old people have told me of the dancing at Margam and Kenfig, and it seems to have been the great attraction), feasting, drinking, and every kind of merrymaking.[1]

In Mr. I. C. Hughes's "Merch o'r Sker" is an amusing reference to a Mabsant at the "Black Lion" in Newton Nottage. While dancing and drinking were at their height a man of singular aspect was seen approaching the "Black Lion." In his hand he carried a long wand, holding it by the middle. There was something extraordinary and out of the common in his appearance. His eyes seemed to be burning in their sockets, and fire seemed to flash from them. The strange-looking man gave three loud taps on the door, and on being admitted profound silence reigned.

"Young men and young women,'" he thundered, "if you will not cease this very moment to carry on your carnal pleasure and ungodliness, every one of

[1] In substance from "The Welsh Calendar," the Rev. J. Fisher, D.D.

you will be flung head-foremost through the window on to the dunghill below, and will be dancing to the music of the damned in hell within five minutes."

No more was needed to be uttered by him, for the majority present recognised the old man as Siencyn Penhydd, who was believed to possess power to bring about things that no other mortal could, and quickly every one rushed to the door and left with all speed.

In the early part of the last century Siencyn Penhydd, called at Underhill, the house in which I live, to ask Mr. Philip Jones, the manager of the works of the Old English Copper Company, to use his influence in freeing a native of the village who had been carried off by a press-gang for the navy. Mr. Jones refused, upon which Siencyn warned him that he would be sorry for refusing and left. Siencyn had not gone far before he heard some one calling him back. One of Mr. Jones's daughters had fallen down the stairs and was injured. Siencyn got what he had asked for.

I have before me a copy of a memorandum that Mr. Jones was admitted a burgess of Kenfig on the 13th of June, 1808. This was kindly shown to me by Mr. G. Prichard, of Bryntirion, a relative.

In time its riotous character brought the Gŵyl Mabsant into disrepute, and eventually determined its discontinuance.

Mabsant is composed of *mab* in the sense of "man," and the adjective *sant*, "holy." He was the typical "holy man" connected with the parish.

The earliest use of the word *mabsant* is probably in an eulogy of the Welsh patron saints, *Canu y Dewi*, by Gwynfardd Brycheiniog, A.D. 1160–1220 (*Myv. Arch.*, 194). The friar-bard, y Brawd Fadawg ap Gwalter, A.D. 1250–1300 (ib., 275), addresses the Archangel Michael as Mihangel fy Mabsant.[1]

A court was held during the fair, presided over by the constable or provost. All merchants were prohibited from selling or buying outside the fair between Rhymney river and Pwll Cynan in Crymlyn Burrows, between Briton Ferry and Swansea. The prohibition doubtless brought together a great concourse of merchants, and the fair must have been an important event in the county.

The second fair was held on the Tuesday in Whitsun week.

The charter grants to the burgesses that the constable or provost shall hold the pleas called Pie Poudre from day to day (presumably during the fair). This was a court formerly held at a fair on St. Giles's hill, near Winchester. It was originally authorised by the Bishop of Winton from a grant of Edward IV. Similar courts were held elsewhere at wakes and fairs for the rough-and-ready treatment of dishonest pedlars and hawkers, to compel them and those with whom they dealt to fulfil their contracts. French, *pied poudreux*—dusty foot. A vagabond is called in French *pied poudreux*.

> " Have its proceedings disallowed or
> Allowed, at fancy of pie-powder."
>
> Butler, " Hudibras," pt. ii. 2.[2]

---

[1] " The Welsh Calendar," by the Rev. J. Fisher, D.D.

[2] " Dictionary of Phrase and Fable," by Rev. E. Cobham Brewer, LL.D.

The constable of Kenfig was to exercise the office of coroner. Extensive common rights were given the burgesses by the charter.

Among the witnesses to the charter are the reverend fathers, Henry, Abbot of Margam, and Thomas, Abbot of Neth (Neath).

Following this, Thomas, Lord le Despenser, gives the burgesses certain rights upon the Rugge, or Cefn Cribwr, extending from Catput, Pwll-y-gâth, to the Rugge of Coitiff (Coity). In breadth from Cefn Cribwr to the stream running from Lowerkesmore, Llwyarch's moor, to Kenfeg. Also the common of Kenfig Down —which extends in length from the Earl's meadow to Goutesfurlong of the Abbot of Neth, and in breadth from Wadeslond to the Burrows of Kenfeg. I am not able to identify these names, Goutesfurlong and Wadeslond.

He also grants to the burgesses 100 perticas of land in increase of their franchise. This is from the chapel of St. Mary Magdalene on the east and round about the ancient bounds and limits of the said borough of Kenfeg. A *pertica* is a rod or pole—a piece of land measured by a rod. I think pertica must have meant more than a perch, and one result of the increase probably was the extension of the boundary from Taddulcrosse, which is mentioned as being one point in the boundary eastward to the River Kenfig.

The other charters are simply confirmation charters, and call for no remarks.

CHAPTER VI

MARGAM ABBEY AND PROPERTY ACQUIRED IN KENFIG

I THINK it may be interesting at this point to show, by quoting from the monastic deeds of Margam Abbey, how that powerful corporation increased its possessions in Kenfig. Also I shall mention some of the sales and exchanges of lands and tenements among other persons besides the monks.

William Earl of Gloucester notifies, T., 544, 9 (C. MCCCXCVIII), that he gives to Helias the clerk five acres of land at Kenefeg, lying between the land which belonged to Robert Passelewe and that which the Earl gave to Gregory de Turri and to the said Helias. Helias to pay to the Earl's son, Robert, yearly three *decii* of ivory. Witness : The Countess Hawisia.[1]

The Earl also gave [1] T., 544, 8, to Gregory, son of Robert, three shillingsworth of land in Margam, viz., twenty acres of land and a burgage at Kenfig. This is interesting as showing that Kenfig was in, what is

[1] Hawisia died in A.D. 1197.

termed in another deed, the hundred of Margam.
Margam evidently embraced a far larger area than it
does to-day.   The value of twenty acres of land is put
at three shillings.

Gregory, by the Earl's consent, gave this land to
Helias his clerk, at a rent of one pound of cumin [1]
yearly.   Witness : The Countess Hawisia.

Helyas de Turre in a deed, T. 5 (C. DCXXXVII),
grants to Margam Abbey, for the soul of his lord
Gregory, the land which William Earl of Gloucester
gave to Lord Gregory and the grantor at Kenefeh,
within and without the vill.   This is an early deed, as
William Earl of Gloucester succeeded his father in
A.D. 1147 and died in A.D. 1187.

Conan,[2] the Abbot of Margam, re-granted, T. 6
(C. DCXXXVIII), to the nephews of Helyas, Gregory
and John, all the land which William Earl of
Gloucester gave to Gregory de Turri and Helias
his clerk, at Kenefeg, both within and without the
vill, and which the said Helias, with assent of the
Earl and of William, son of Gregory, gave to
the Abbey at a yearly rent of one pound of pepper [3]
at Michaelmas, saving to the mother of Helias her
dower which she holds for life, and to the father and
mother of John, their tenement for life.   On the death
of Helias's mother the land was to be divided between
Gregory and John.   The messuage in which she
dwelt to be included in Gregory's share.

[1] Cumin—caraway seed ; Latin, *cuminum*.
[2] *Circa* A.D. 1170–1188.
[3] The cumin of the former deed is replaced by pepper
in this.

Conan was Abbot of Margam at the time Baldwin, Archbishop of Canterbury, visited the Abbey when preaching the Crusade in Wales, in A.D. 1188. Giraldus Cambrensis, who accompanied the Archbishop, mentions that after the Archbishop had celebrated Mass at the high altar at Llandaff Cathedral "we immediately pursued our way by the little cell of Ewenith [Ewenny] to the noble Cistercian Monastery of Margam. This monastery, under the direction of Conan, a learned and prudent abbot, was at this time more celebrated for its charitable deeds than any other of that order in Wales. On this account it is an undoubted fact that, as a reward for that abundant charity which the monastery had always in time of need exercised towards strangers and poor persons, in a season of approaching famine, their corn and provision were perceptibly by Divine assistance increased, like the widow's cruse of oil by the means of the prophet Elijah."

The Earl later, on the death of his son Robert,[1] granted, T. 544,10 (C. MCCCXCIX), to the Lady Alienor, Queen of England, the three *decii* of ivory which Helias paid yearly for the five acres of land at Kenefeg. Helias de Turre, or Turri, was clerk or chaplain to Lady Alienora, Queen Consort of King Henry II.

William, son of Gregory, in a deed, T. 4 (C. DCXXXVI), granted the pound of cumin to Margam Abbey, which Helias de Turri used to pay for his land in the town of Chenefeh. Earl William

---

[1] Robert died 1166 A.D.

confirmed this gift to the Abbey at William de Turri's request.

An interesting document is a grant by William Earl of Gloucester to Richard de Kardiff, T. 289, 66 (C. DXCIII). This deed embraces a considerable part of Kenfig.

The Earl notifies to his dapifer, or steward, and sheriff of Glamorgan, and all his barons and men, French, English, and Welsh, that he has given to Richard de Kardiff, for his services, the New-Town in Margan, with all its appurtenances, beginning at the old dyke, which begins at the sea-shore, and running along Dewiscumbe as far as the dyke from S. Tudoc's,[1] then to Alweiscnappe and Bulluches-brue,[2] then as far as the Vale of Corneli, then to Dane's Vale, then to Catteshole,[3] then direct to the sea-shore along the valley to Baien which is in *Sabluno*.[4] The boundaries of the meadows which appertain to this New-Town, as well as the above, are from the ford of Baithan [5] to the high-road from Langewy [6] to Treikic.[7]

We shall see why Richard de Cardiff claimed to be the owner of Sker.

We have already, in pages 73, 80, and 81, met

---

[1] S. Tudoc, Tythegston.

[2] Alweiscnappe and Bulluchesbruhe.   I give the probable derivations further on

[3] Dane's Vale is between Marlas and the Hall.   Catteshole, Pwll-y-gâth.

[4] *Sabluno*, an error, doubtless, for *Sabulo*, on the sands.

[5] Baithan, Baiden . a lively little brook.

[6] Langewy, Llangewydd, church of St. Cewydd.

[7] Treikic, Tre-y-gedd near Baiden

with the name Peiteuin ; a grant by Espus, son of
Caradoc Du, also gives us this name ; which is no
longer in use.

Espus grants, T. 15, 289, 9 (C. DCLVII), to the
Abbey of Margam all his land on the fee of Peittevin
in the territory of Kenefek at a rent of half a mark
yearly, with three marks, the rent of six years, paid
beforehand. If he dies before he has an heir by his
wife, the daughter of Rees, son of Euhan, the Abbot
to hold all the land in frank almoign ; if he has an
heir, then twelve acres and his body for burial in the
Abbey, and two shillings abated from the rent. One
of the witnesses, Canethur or Canaithur Du, occurs
circa A.D. 1200, *temp.* Morgan ap Caradoc.

Peitheuin, Peiteuin, Peytevin, Petetevin, Petuien,
the land of Peyteuin, as it is variously spelled, is inter-
preted by the late Mr. Clark in his "Cartæ," as
meaning the land of the Poictevine. In his "Land of
Morgan," p. 70, Mr. Clark calls it the Manor of
Pettun. Peiteuin is the ancient name for Pyle.
This is clearly shown from some of the MSS. of
Margam. The name is probably derived from
pydewau (pits, wells, or quags), and so called from the
pits or quarries for limestone, of which there are
many ; some of them doubtless were worked many
centuries ago. Or it may be the land of the Poitêvin,
or native of Poitou in France, perhaps a soldier in
the service of the Norman knights.

Sir Edward Mansell, in reply to complaints of the
Earl of Pembroke, says, "And on the west lieth the
Manor of Pitteuin or Pile."

A son of John Du, Ketherech, gives, T. 16

(C. DCCLXXIII), in the same Manor, to Margam Abbey, five acres of land in his free tenement in the land of Peitheuin near the old highway which leads from Kenefec towards Cardiff along the vill of Walter Lupellus or Luvel, viz., North Corneli.

Walter Lupellus bore on one of his seals a wolf for Lupellus, and on another, an ornamental fleur-de-lis.

Katherech later demised and bequeathed to the Abbey, T. 17 (C. DCXXXIII), fifteen acres of land in the land of the Peiteuin adjacent to the five acres of the previous deed. Under seal of the Prior of Oweni (Ewenny), as the grantor has no seal.

Witnesses : William Killimichel ; Eniaw son of Richered ; Bruel ; Ketherech son of Caradoc Du ; Griffin son of Kneithur ab Herebert, his kinsmen and "nepotes," who have sworn to observe the conditions of the deed on the holy reliques at Margam Church ; together with Tanguistell, his wife. Conan, Abbot of Margam ; James, Prior ; Roger, cellarer ; William, porter ; Godefrey, monk ; Jordan, conversus ; Roger, hospital conversus ; Gregory ; John, master of the Grange, probably the Abbey Grange at Kenfig ; Aithan, the clerk ; Robinus, famulus (servant) of the hospice ; Ithel, son of Ruwel.

Gistelard, son of John, son of Belius, by a deed, T. 56, 289, 20 (C. DCCLXXVII), granted to Margam, Abbey his land near the water of Kenefec ; rent 4s. to the lord. Sworn on the reliques at Margam by Gistelard, his wife and sons and relations, namely, Espus son of Caradoc, Traharn son of Conan and Ketherec his brother.

Gistelard's son Joruard followed his father's example

and granted by a deed, T. 68 (C. DCCLXXVIII), to the Abbey his right to the land of Jeovaf his grandfather at Catteput, Pwll-y-gâth, twelve acres. This land is near that of Hugh de Hereford. Twelve acres and one acre of meadow and sixteen acres at Corneli near Walter Luvel's land.

Tatherech, daughter of Katherech Du, with consent of Joruard or Yoruard ab Gistelard her husband, quitclaimed her rights to the Abbey, T. 69 (C. DCLV), in the land of Peyteuin, sworn on the reliques at Margam.

The seal bears a fish hauriant ✠ SIGILLVM. TADERECH.

Thaderech, or Tatherech, also by a deed, T. 289, 6 (C. DCLII), granted to the Abbey all her lands in the fee of Peiteuin, at an annual rent of half a mark during her life, afterwards of four shillings, the remainder two shillings and sixpence being remitted for her soul. Six years' rent, three marks, paid in advance on the Feast of the Purification of the Virgin next after the capture of Griffin son of Res.

Mr. Clark gives the date as A.D. 1197. The record of the capture of Griffin ab Res was an event apparently of such importance as to be used for calculating the dates of deeds. The Glamorganshire *Annals* preserved in a MS. in the Record Office state that in A.D. 1242, "Pacem habuit Griffin ap Reys," and in A.D. 1266, "post festum Epiphanie die Sabati, *captus est Griffinus ap Reys* in castro Keredive, postea missus ad Kilkennie ad incarcerandum " (C. vol. iii. pp. 557, 558).

Dr. Birch says that the events related in the deed

appear to belong to an earlier period than A.D. 1266, but it may be that a previous capture of Griffin preceded the peace mentioned in the *Annals* for the year 1242.

And now the sons of Tatherech uphold their mother's gift. Tudur, Cradoc, Knaithur, Alaithur, and Gronu, sons of Joruard ab Gistelard and Tatherech, by a deed, T. 70 (C. DCCLXXIX), quit-claimed to the Abbey their right in the land of Peyteuin; and with abjuration, upon the reliques of the Church of Margam, of the land of their mother Tatherech.[1]

An early deed, T. 1945, is a notification by William Earl of Gloucester to his sheriffs and all his barons and Welshmen that he has granted to Hugh de Hereford 100 acres of land in the parish of Kenefech in

[1] King John on the 15 May A D. 1207, confirmed the Peyteuin land to Margam (but this may have been the land granted by Espus son of Caradoc, for the date of his grant is *circa* A.D. 1200) He also confirmed to the Abbey among other grants that of the burgesses and freemen of Kenfig, holdings within and without the vill

The Fine Roll for A.D. 1207 contains an entry (C. LXXIV) showing that the Abbot of Margam gives to the King 100 marks and two good horses for the land of the Welshmen in the territory of Kenefeg in free almoign, for which the Abbey used to pay 30s. yearly to the King's bailiffs of Glamorgan; and for getting a confirmation charter for their other lands and tenements in the bailiwick of Glamorgan according to reasonable tenour of their charters.

(C. LXXXIII) this is a copy of a royal acquittance to William, the Abbey cellarer, dated Sunday after St Matthew's Day, A D. 1207, with delay granted for the delivery of the two "palfreys." Bradenstok, co. Wilts, 24 Sep., A.D. 1207

At last the two horses were delivered at Lutegar, i e , Ludgershall, co Wilts (C. LXXXV), on Sunday after St Luke's Day, 18 Oct., A.D. 1207. An acquittance is given for them.

reward for his service in one of the Earl's castles for forty days. Hugh de Hereford seems to have been a soldier of fortune and apparently fought on alternate sides, if we can judge by the result.

Witnesses: Hamo, son of Geoffrey the Constable; William, son of Nicholas the Marshal; Gilbert de Turberville; Geoffrey Sturmi and others. Geoffrey Sturmi occurs as a witness to a charter of the Earl's of about A.D. 1166.

Hugh de Hereford having received the 100 acres, by a deed, T. 31 (C. DCXLIV), he granted to Margam Abbey all his lands in the arable district of Kenefec, as he held it of William Earl of Gloucester, for the souls of his lord and others, in pure and perpetual almoign. The Abbot, in view of the necessity of the granter and his devotion, lends Hugh ten marks, to be repaid when he has prevailed on his heirs to assent to the agreement between himself and the Abbot. Hugh consents, if he dies before the monks get peaceable possession of the land, that he will bequeath five marks, the moiety of the loan, by way of alms to the Abbey. The other five he shall have who restores the sealed letter which the Abbot delivered to Hugh as a basis of the transaction. The Abbot will give no more, whether Hugh be alive or dead, until he has a valid title.[1]

Hugh evidently had difficulty with his heirs; they clearly did not emulate his devotion, and were averse to handing over the land to the monks.

Hugh, full of devotion to the Church, made another

---

[1] Hugh de Hereford's seal, a sword erect. ✠ S I G I L L : H VGONIS: DE H EREFORD.

grant, T. 33 (C. DCXLVI). In this deed he granted
in frank almoign to Margam Abbey thirty acres of
land on the west of Corneli from the old cemetery to
the boundary of the land of Walter Luvel ; then to
the land of Joaf, son of Herebert, then as far as the
highway, coming from the chapel of Corneli, belonging to Walter Luvel towards the water ; also the
moorland adjacent to the other land on the water.
The charter was offered on the altar at Margam for
the soul of his lord, William Earl of Gloucester, and
others.

Hugh seems to have got into difficulties—perhaps
he took sides against his lord—and he again appeals to
the monks of Margam for help. T. 34 (C. DXXXI)
is an acquittance by Hugh to the Abbot and Convent
of Margam, for nine marks of silver which they had
lent him to obtain his redemption from his lord,
William Earl of Gloucester, who had imprisoned him ;
for which sum he had pledged all his land in Corneli
except that which he had given to the Abbey as
above.   Of the nine marks, three were delivered
at the Michaelmas after King Henry II. took the
cross for going to Jerusalem, the remaining six to
be paid in twelve years at half a mark yearly,
because the land is very sterile.   Date *circa* A.D.
1187–1188.

Taking the cross meant going to the Holy Land to
fight under the banner of the Cross for the deliverance
of the country in which the Saviour died from the
polluting presence of the infidel Turk.   Giraldus
Cambrensis, who went through Wales with Archbishop
Baldwin preaching the Crusades, tells us " the same

evening, Malgo, son of Cadwallon, prince of Melenia, after a short but efficacious exhortation from the Archbishop, and not without the tears and lamentations of his friends, was marked with the sign of the cross."

Spenser gives a picture of the knight, full of devotion to his Lord and Master, going forth to win back the Holy Land :—

> "Upon his breast a bloodie Cross he bore,
> The deare remembrance of his dying Lord,
> For whose sweet sake that glorious badge he wore,
> And dead, as living, ever Him adored ;
> Upon his shield the like was also scored,
> For sovereign hope which in His help he had."

Extraordinary enthusiasm was displayed at this time in the cause by kings, princes, and knights, and even bishops took the Cross and went to Palestine. Jocelin of Brakelond, monk of St. Edmundsbury, tells us that his abbot wished to go to the Holy Land .—

"21 Jan., A.D. 1188. When King Henry had taken the cross and was come less than a month later that he might pray among us, the Abbot secretly made for himself a cross of linen cloth. Then, holding in one hand the cross and a needle and thread, he sought leave from the King that he might take the cross. But leave was refused him, for John bishop of Norwich opposed it, and said that it was not well for the land, nor safe for the counties of Norfolk and Suffolk, that the bishop of Norwich, and the abbot of St. Edmund's should go away at the same time." It is strange to us in

these days to think that at one time it was considered unsafe for two counties to be without the
presence of a bishop and an abbot. "Tempora
mutantur, nos et mutamur in illis."

Of course the reason is that the bishop and abbot
had temporal duties and rights—hanging felons, for
example, etc. In fact, justices and judges.

Hugh makes yet another gift, T. 35 (C. DCXVIII),
to Margam Abbey of land at Corneli, and the deed
is interesting as showing, as mentioned before, that
Margam comprised a much larger area than it does
to-day, and included in its district Kenfig and Corneli.
The reference to Welsh lands in this deed and in
others to English and French shows the country
to have been parcelled out among Welsh, English,
and French.

This deed is a grant to the Abbey of all the
land which Hugh de Hereford holds of the Earl
of Gloucester in *Margam*, namely, thirteen acres
and a half, measuring 27 perches along the Welsh
lands on the west, and 80 perches along the land
of Walter Luvel towards the moor; and his
meadow to be theirs and any place where they
can find marl to belong to them, with a wayleave
for carrying marl to their land. He also grants
common of pasture throughout all his lands,
meadows, and crops.

In a Bull of Pope Urban III.—Harley Charter,
75, A. 1 (C. DCXXX)—directed to the Abbot and
Brethren of Margam, in response to their request,
taking them under the protection of St. Peter and
the Pope and ordaining various matters, he confirms

to them various grants, and among them is the gift of arable land by Hugh de Hereford at Kenfig. The deed is ratified by the Pope and twelve Cardinals. Verona, 18 Nov., A.D. 1186.

Mr. Clark, in his " Cartae de Glamorgan," gives a deed (C. XXXIX) containing letters of John Earl of Mortagne,[1] afterwards King John of England, to his men and friends, French, English, and Welsh, notifying his confirmation to Margam Abbey of the lands in Kenfig given to it by the burgesses of Kenfig in frank almoign ; and also his grant to the Abbey of the service of Hugh de Hereford for his land as far as belongs to the Earl, provided Hugh is willing to grant it—that is, exchange lords. The land was held, as in this case, in return for military service, and as Margam Abbey became the owner the military service due from it would pass to the Abbey. The Abbeys held their lands in return for so many knights' fees, viz., each Abbey had to find so many knights for the King for his wars in return for its holdings. Dated at Cardiff, Tuesday before the Feast of St. Hilary, A.D. 1193.

T. 72. (C. DCCVLI) is a quit-claim by Ivor Vaghan and his sons Madoc, Leukin, Waleueð,[2] and

---

[1] John, King Henry II.'s second son, was adopted by Earl William as his heir in A.D. 1176. He married one of the Earl's daughters and succeeded him as Earl of Gloucester and lord of Glamorgan. John divorced the heiress and gave up her estates, though, Mr. Clark says, with a very bad grace. John's marriage was opposed by Archbishop Baldwin, as both were descended from Henry I., and the marriage was within the forbidden degrees. On his accession to the throne he divorced her.

[2] ð stands for dh.

Gneithur,[1] to the Abbey of a right to twelve acres of land in the fee of Kenefeg, between Sturmy Moor, Cornelidune, and the valley of Mey. Stormy Moor and Corneli Down are well known. The valley of Mey (Deumay), as before mentioned, lies between the road which passes Marlas and the Avon Fach.

A Bull of Pope Innocent III. to Gilibert, Abbot of Margam, dated at Anagni, 20 Nov., A.D. 1203 confirms to the monastery the grants and gifts made to it by various benefactors, among whom are the burgesses of Kenefeg and free Welshmen ; one hundred acres of arable land in Kenefeg given by Kederec, or Ketherech, and a similar quantity by Hugh de Hereford.

I hope my readers will not lay to my pen the vagaries in spelling. They are due to the monks, who not knowing Welsh, had to trust to the sounds as the words were pronounced ; one may sympathise with a testy or partly deaf monk grappling with a rough countryman shouting into his ear the difficult Welsh names.

The family, distinguished by the name Du, "black," were landowners possessing much property, which they freely gave to Margam Abbey. The Du family were also connected by marriage with the sons of Herbert, son of Godwinet, and also with the lords of Afan, Gwenllian daughter of Morgan ap Caradoc, married Yoruard—or Yorwerth, as it would be spelled to-day—son of Espus Du. One branch of the Du family started from John Du, the earliest

---

[1] Sometimes Cnaithur, Knaitho, and Cnaytho.

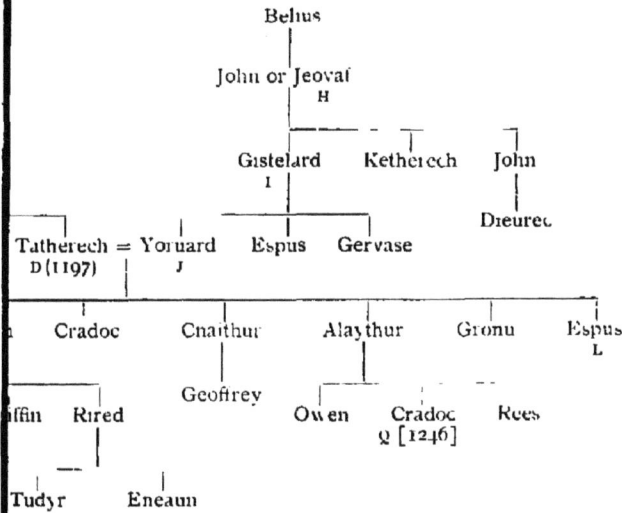

Belius
|
John or Jeovaf
H
|
Gistelard — Ketherech — John
I | |
| Dreurec
Tatherech = Yoruard   Espus   Gervase
D (1197)   J

Cradoc   Cnaithur   Alaythur   Gronu   Espus
                                        L
         Geofrey   Owen   Cradoc   Rees
ffin   Rired   Q [1246]
         |
Tudyr   Eneaun

at Cwm

ieli (x) to

had be-

near Tor

II. I believe this is Jouaf Trwyn gain (crooked nose) who gave lands at Pwll-y-gath to the Abbey.

I. Gave lands near Kenfig river.

L. The brothers quit claimed Perteuin to the Abbey, their mother's land.

[Insert between pp. 142, 143.

PEDIGREE OF THE FAMILIES OF DU, BELIUS AND HERBERT

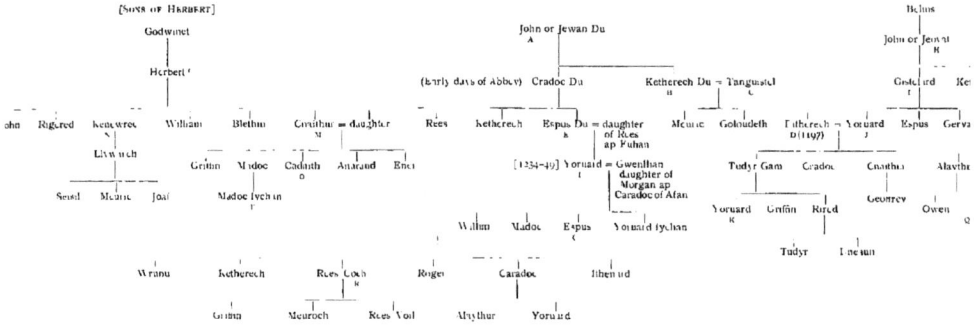

[SONS OF HERBERT]

Godwine

Herbert

John Rigered Kenwerec William Blethin Cruithin = daughter Rees ketherech Espus Du = daughter Meuric Goludeth Latherech = Yoruard Espus Gerva
Llwnich   of Rees   D (1197)
                                                                          ap Fuhan

John or Jewan Du
A

(early days of Abbey) Cradoc Du   Ketherech Du = Tangwisiel

Belius

John or Jewan
H

Gislard Ke

Griffin Madoc Cadnith Anaraud Enci   [1234-49] Yoruard = Gwenllian   Tudyr Gam Cradoc Cnathu Alaythe
                                                          daughter of
Seisil Meurie Joaf   Morgan ap   Yoruard Griffin Rired   Geoffrey
Madoc Ivch in   Caradoc of Afan   Owen
                                                          Willim Madoc Espus Yoruard fychan   Tudyr Ineian

Wranu Ketherech Rees Coch Rogen Caradoc Ithen ud

Gruffu Meuroch Rees Voil Ahythur Yoru ard

a Herbert gave lands near Llangewydd and Stormy to
   Margam Abbey
b Gave lands at Rhonellt river to Margam Abbey
c Gave lands at Halodbeuing to Margam Abbey
d Gave lands at Gullwern and lands on the river Firwdwellt
   to Margam Abbey
e Gave lands at Tre y gadd, Mynydd Buden, to Margam
   Abbey. Ha made, Enci, same
u Gave lands at Cornel Pentum to Margam Abbey
        Willam Kilhenehel = Angarat
        (kinsman of Cruythin, son of Herbert)

   Walaneth Ketherech Ivo Weinvill

A John Du owned lands at Cwm Cerwn and
   Ffrwdwellt. he gave land at Pelteum to
   Margam Abbey.
B Gave lands at Pentum to Margam Abbey.
c Owner of Ty Langlwys gave it to Margam
   Abbey
D Granted all her father's land at Pelteum to
   Margam Abbey
E Gave Cornell (b) and Pentum, which belonged
   to Caradoc Du to Margam Abbey
F Confirmed his father's gifts. Gave lands at
   Cwm Cerwn and Llangemor,

G Confirmed his father's gift of land at Cwm
   Cerwn and Ffrwdwellt
J Gave land at Pwll y gath and Cornell (s) to
   Abbey
K Granted lands at Newcastle which had be
   longed to Ketherech Du (a)
g Granted lands in Avan Marsh and near Lor
   Crumenna to Abbey

H I believe this is Joan
   neser who gave lan
   Abbey
I Gave lands near Kenfi
L The brothers quit claim
   their mother's land

member known to us, and the other from Belius.
The Du family owned land at Corneli, near Kenfig
river, Pyle, Newcastle, Bridgend, at Cwmkerwn and
Ffrwdwyllt. Their kinsmen, the sons of Herbert,
owned land near Stormi, Baiden, Hafod-heuloug,
Gallt-y-cwm, and land near Llangynwyd and other
places. Ketherech Du married Tanguistel, and so
became owner of Ty Tanglwys land; the name
appears as Tangistellond for a long time after.

The pedigree discloses how great in numbers and in
influence the related families became. They possessed
lands reaching from Resolven to Llangeinor. These
families were also connected by marriage with the
family of Cradoc ap Jestyn, lords of Afan, as mentioned
above. Owen Cradoc and Rees bore a banner-flag
charged with four chevrons. The pedigree could be
extended considerably, but so many of the descendants bore the same name that it would be unreliable,
and I forbear from risking it further. Some of the
members of the families became monks of Margam
Abbey.

Mr. Clark gives a pedigree of the Du family in
"Cartae," etc., vol. iii. p. 127.

We have seen that King John, formerly Earl of
Gloucester and lord of Glamorgan, divorced his wife,
Countess Isabel. Subsequently she married Geoffrey
de Mandeville about the end of A.D. 1213, and he
was made Earl of Gloucester and lord of Glamorgan,
owning with his wife Kenfig Castle and lands.
Geoffrey was fourth Earl of Gloucester, and was also
Earl of Essex.

Isabel, the Countess, with consent of her lord,

Geoffrey de Mandeville, the Earl of Gloucester, grants, T. 113 (C. DCCCXVIII), to Margam Abbey various lands in the fee of Kenefeg, viz., the land of Peitheuin, the land of Hugh de Hereford, that of the Welsh, one burgage in Kenfig town, the grant of Gillebert Gramus, which we shall come to later, and the grant of the burgesses of Kenefeg, in the town and outside, amongst other grants. This means probably a confirmation of various grants. It is, however, curious that in large grants of lands like the grant of Margam to the monks of Clairvaux, referred to before, a number of landowners possessed land in the area given. We see this in the Du family and the Herberts ; they owned land in various parts of Margam in the area given to the monks of Clairvaux.

CHAPTER VII

THE PORT AND TOWN OF KENFIG

I THINK, after reading so many dry and musty documents, it will be pleasant to have a break and turn our attention to the town, little as we may know of it. We have seen how often the town was burnt; to avoid monotony I have kept one burning back, and that occurred on the 18th of May, A.D. 1227. The town was set fire to by lightning and a horse was killed. The buildings at that time were built of wood and easily fired. I believe the buildings were in great part of wood when the first besanding took place, and this accounts for the lack of ruins. The material of the later stone-built houses was no doubt carted away.

Rees Meyrick wrote in A.D. 1578 : " This William [1] caused to be rebuilded a Towne for Marchandize upon the Sea banks of Kynfege which he retayned, with certain parcell of land thereto belonging in his own possession."

Kenfig was a town of trading importance in addition to being one of the residences of the

[1] William Earl of Gloucester, son of Robert Earl of Gloucester.

lords of Glamorgan. It is clear from the above that the town was re-built at the instance of William the Earl for *sea-trading*, and therefore it possessed a port. In A.D. 1147 the Earl succeeded his father Earl Robert, who is also said to have re-built Kenfig in A.D. 1129.

We find in the Magnus Rotulus Pipae,[1] or the Great Roll of the Pipe, an entry which refers to Kenfig as a port. The date is the 31st year of Henry II., A.D. 1184–1185. Earl William died on the anniversary of his birth, 23 Nov., A.D. 1183, and the lordship of Glamorgan fell into the custody of the Crown hence the reason for the accounts of Glamorgan appearing in the Great Roll.

The entry is: "And in delivery of 24 ships which bore the king's timber from Striguil [Chepstow] for the work of the Castle of Kenefeg £14 8sh. 3d., by the King's writ."

The inference from this is that the timber was sent by sea for the reason that Chepstow and Kenfig were seaports on the water-way, the Severn Sea.

In the *inspeximus*[2] by Thomas le Despenser, lord of Glamorgan, on the 16 Feb., A.D. 1397, of the confirmation of Edward his father, to the burgesses of Kenfig we read: "We have granted also to our aforesaid burgesses that of all merchandise coming to or passing through the aforesaid town as well by land *as by water* [italics are mine] an inspection shall first be made by our aforesaid con-

---

[1] Clark's " Cartae et alia Munimenta de Glamorgan "
[2] " We have inspected "

stable or the provost of the town before any thereof be sold, under a suitable penalty."

If goods were not brought to the town from the sea the words "by water" would be meaningless. I think these quotations show us that Kenfig had a shipping trade and therefore possessed a harbour.

Pondering on this question while walking along Kenfig river, I was struck by the canal-like appearance of the river where it passes through land not covered with sand, such as it would be like when Kenfig was built ; with a little clearing out, small vessels— "shiplettes," as Leland calls them—could pass along the river at this point. He wrote of Neath river "there cummith up shipplettes almost onto the Toun of Neth from the Severn." Of course, in those far-off days, the vessels would be very small, something from twenty to forty tons. Phillips writes that when King Charles I. desired the county of Glamorgan to supply a vessel of thirty tons, the reply was, "there was not a vessel of that tonnage in the county."

I have no doubt the flatness of the land through which the Kenfig river flows was the reason of its depth and suitability then for small craft to ascend. The river runs very slowly ; it ran in former days with little haste, because its course was through smiling meadow-land right to Severn Sea, the banks of the river being as they are now where no sand is. The water in parts is deep still ; it was several feet deep, eight or more, at the time of my visit, and the tide had then fallen 3 feet from its highest level.

We have reason to believe, judging from the situation of the grange or homestead of the Hermitage of

Theodoric, two miles north-west of Kenfig river, now
in a desolate waste of sand-hills, that the land around
it was in remote times a fertile tract of land, or the
farm would not be established there, and so it would
be at Kenfig.

In the time when merchandise came to Kenfig
by sea, the vessels would ascend the river a mile
or more, judging by levels of a few years ago, but
it is possible that the river was navigable to the
town itself. To show the continual process of the
filling up by sand of the river, in the Ordnance Survey
of 1876 ordinary tides reached inland four-fifths of a
mile. In the revision of the Survey in 1897 the
highest point reached by ordinary tides is only two
hundred and sixty yards.

So serious had the besanding become in this neighbourhood that the attention of the authorities was
directed to it, as I have before mentioned. The
former Act of Henry VIII. and the Act of A.D. 1554
gave the Commissioners full power to act " for the
withstanding and avoiding of the outrageous course
and rage of the Sea, or other Waters."

For a great part of the seven hundred and fifty
years or thereabouts since William Earl of Gloucester
caused Kenfig to be re-built the sand has been piling
itself up and doing its utmost to prevent the Kenfig
river from reaching the sea, but " even the weariest
river winds somewhere safe to sea." So does the
Kenfig to-day.

It is not possible to form any clear idea of the size
of the town of Kenfig ; we have faint glimpses of it in
the monastic deeds of Margam, and also in the Account

of John Giffard of Brymmesfeld, custodian of the lands
and tenements which belonged to Gilbert de Clare,
Earl of Gloucester and Hertford, deceased, being in
the hands of the King, in Glamorgan and Morgannoc,
dated in the ninth year of King Edward II. (A.D.
1316).

We find in it a reference to burgages in Kenfig and
those untenanted by reason of war ; the number would
indicate that even at that time the town was of considerable size.

The entry is under the head : " The Vill of Kenefeg
with the Castle."

" Rent of Assize. The same (Brymmesfeld) answers
for 71 shillings received of rent of assize of one
hundred burgages of the town of Kenefeg at the
terms of St. John Baptist and St. Michael. And
no more because forty-two burgages which were
accustomed to render for the same time 21s. were
burnt in the war and the tenants went away and the
burgages remain empty. And for 4s. 6d. of rent of
small cottagers[1] there at the term of St. Michael.

" And for 6s. 5d. received of certain rent for castle
ward at the term of Hokeday,[2] and for 35s. of the
rent of eight free tenants there at the terms St. John
Baptist, St. James, and St. Michael."

We have in this document some indication as to the
size of the town at that date. Rent is received for
one hundred burgages, and forty-two more untenanted ;
this gives a total of one hundred and forty-two
burgages. Eight tenants, called free tenants, although

---

[1] *Coterellorum.*
[2] Second Tuesday after Easter.

they paid rent, apparently lived in the castle-bailey, raising the number of tenements to one hundred and fifty, without counting the small cottages.

If we take the number of persons occupying each house as we do at the present day the number of the population would be about seven hundred and eighty-seven. But by A.D. 1316 I believe the sand had already made considerable encroachment, and probably many of the houses had been at this time besanded. In fact, in the same documents as I have mentioned elsewhere only part of the rent for a meadow called Conynger was received, the great part having been covered by sand.

When we consider the population of Cardiff in A.D. 1801 was only 1,870, the population of Kenfig at the early date of 1316 marks it as a town of considerable importance.

By the deed T. 386 (C. MXV.) William the chaplain, son of Ketherek, grants to John Peruat and Alice his wife a messuage and land in the town of Kenefeg near Monk's-street, between the Abbey grange and Thomas Gramus's land. Rent 2d. to the lord of the fee, one man's work for one day in autumn and 20s. beforehand. It was customary for tenants to pay rent and also to find labour at certain seasons. As, for example, at Ibstone, Oxon (thirteenth century), Henry Perys held half a virgate in fee by deed; he paid a rent of 5s. 6d. per annum and three capons at the Feast of St. Thomas Apostle, and had to find a man to reap for three days in autumn at his own costs, with other services.[1] Witnesses: Wm. Terry, Henry

---

[1] "The Manor," by N. J. Hone.

Willoc, Adam Harding, W. Magor, Nicholas Rotarius,
or wheelwright, and others.

Alice Peruath, relict of John Peruath, by a deed,
T. 199 (C. MCVI.), quit-claimed to the Abbey and
Convent of Margam a messuage and curtilage in
the town of Kenefeg, next Monk's-street, between the
grange of the Abbot and Convent of Margam and the
land of William Ketherek; and another messuage in
the same street, between the grange and Thomas
Gramus's land, which Alice and John had of William
the chaplain, son of Ketherek. The Abbot and
Convent, in return, grant "by a letter" to the said
Alice, for life, one conventual loaf and a gallon of beer
daily.

Seal of the burgesses of Kenefeg and Alice's.

Witnesses: John Luvel, W. de Cornely, and others.
Margam, 15 February, A.D. 1320 for 1321.

(Seal, a star of   ✠ s'. A L I C I E . P' V A (T).
eight points.)

In Mr. Clark's "Cartae" I find a Kenfig
document of about A.D. 1325. This document
(C. MCXXVI.) gives us the name of another
street, Esstreet.

It is a grant by Nicholas, son of John Nichol,
to William and Johanna Terri of one messuage
in the vill of Kenefeg and four virgates (120 acres)
of land, of which one end of the said messuage
extends to the messuage which Adam Herdig
formerly held on the west, and the other end
reaches in length to the road which leads outside
the town on the east, and stretches in width to

the road called Esstreet on the north and the
well which Helena Meleward formerly held on the
south.   Paying to the said Nicholas his heirs and
assigns 4d. at the four terms of the year—that is to
say, at the feast of St. Michael a penny, at the feast
of St. Andrew a penny, at Palm Sunday a penny,
likewise at the Feast of St. John Baptist a penny
for every service and secular exaction and demand.

"And I the said Nicholas and my heirs and assigns
will find to the aforesaid William and his heirs and
assigns a road to the aforesaid Well and to the aforesaid
four Virgates of land at whichever time they shall
please.

"And I the said Nicholas and my heirs or assigns
shall warrant acquit and defend the said messuage
and four Virgates of land to the said William and his
heirs and assigns against all men and women for ever ;
moreover for this my gift grant and confirmation of
my present charter the said William Terri has given
to me beforehand ten shillings sterling.   And that this
my gift grant and confirmation of my present charter
may remain for ever sure and stable I have confirmed
this present charter with the impression of my seal.
These being witnesses : Wm. Ailleward, John [son ?] of
Alexander, Henry Willoc, Thomas Gramus (this name
is sometimes spelled Grammus, but I shall adhere to
Gramus), John Cohz (Coch probably), and many
others.

One of the Margam MS. gives us yet another street.
Robert de Magour grants by T. 2011 to William,
son of Master Nicholas, of the place of a house with a
curtilage in the town of Kenefec, between the land of

Nicholas Le Welar on the south, and that lately held
by Adam Herding[1] on the north, and extending from
Monekin-street to the land of John Hugelot. Also of
two and a half acres of arable land ; one between the
land of Thomas Gramus on the east and land lately
held by John Peruat on the west ; land lately held by
Helena Jordan and Kenefec water, *i.e.*, river; the other
between John Herberd's land on the south, that of
John Ruthin's on the north ; the high-road to Corneli ;
and the meadow of John Faber ; the half acre between
Philip Gramus' land on the south ; that of John
Hugelot on the north ; the meadows of John Faber,
and that of Henry Vot. Rent to the Abbey 2s. yearly,
a suit of court, half a mark consideration money
beforehand.

(Seal, a quatrefoil.) ✠ s' R O B E R T I : M A G O R.

In the ordinance of Kenfig is mentioned the usual
High-street. I say usual, for almost every town has
its High-street. High-street must have been the fine
street of Kenefig, for great care seems to have been
exercised with its keeping. The ordinance states :
" Item it is ordained that no butchers shall cast noe
heads, feet, nor none other garbage in the High street
nor in other place," &c. ; and there was to be no tennis-
playing within the High street."

The town boasted, of course, of its Guildhall, and so
proud of it were the townspeople that the ordinance
ordains that " noe stranger shall have free prison in the
Guildhall above but in the lower prison, unless he be
a burgess giving, yielding, and paying within the said

[1] Probably the Adam Herdig of the previous deed.

town according to charter." The burgesses only were to enjoy free prison in the upper storey of the Guild-hall, strangers were probably placed in a cell under the hall.

It is interesting to learn that the town had its hospital. It is mentioned in a deed of the late twelfth or early thirteenth century. Richard de Dunster grants, T. 79, 289, 21 (C. DCCCII), with counsel and consent of his wife (prudent man !) and heirs, to Margam Abbey his burgage with land adjacent to the castle and one acre outside the town near the Maladeria, or Hospital.

As I have said, the town lay on the seaward side of the castle. On the south of the castle moat, close to it, was the cemetery of St. James's Church. This we find from the deed, already mentioned in the reference to the castle-bailey, granting a messuage within the bailey on the east, near the wall of the cemetery.

The town continued along the moat on the seaward side and along the cemetery wall towards the south, and then followed along the south wall of the cemetery to the east; thus T. 153 (C. MIII) is a grant by Philip, son of Robert Palmer, or le Palmer, to Margam Abbey, with consent of Amabilia his wife, of a messuage in the town of Kenefeg which appertains to his burgage, *on the south* of the cemetery, having on the east the messuage of Hugh, son of John the priest, and on the west that of Osbern le Hopar. Among the witnesses is Walter Luvel, who occurs as a witness to a large number of deeds. Walter Luvel was constable of Llangewydd.

No part of the town existed on the eastern side of the castle moat and cemetery ; it was confined to the seaward side and south of the cemetery.   This we find from a deed T. 105 (C. MCCCCIX).   This is a grant by Gillebert Gramus to God, Blessed Mary of Margam, and to the monks, with consent of his wife Aliz, of ten acres of his land, beginning at the Kenfig river, then along the old cemetery to the south.   This land apparently lay along the castle moat and continued along the east side of the cemetery southward

The following is an interesting deed, as showing the methods adopted by the monks to obtain houses and lands in the town and without, by giving certain benefits to the owners in return.

T. 200 (C. MCXXIV.) is a quit claim by John, son of John Nichol of Kenefig, to Margam Abbey, of the right in all his lands, burgages, messuages, and other liberties in the town of Kenefeg and without, on condition of receiving daily one conventual loaf, two loaves called " Liuersouns," [1] and a gallon of beer, half a mark silver for wages, four pairs of shoes, price 12d., a quarter of oats, and pasture for two beasts, and he is to perform the service of a free sergeant. [2] Under seal of the borough of Kenfeg.   Attested by

[1] Liuersouns.   Dr. Birch says the word is from the French *livraison*, a book ; the bread being made in thin leaves and resembled our "parliament cakes."   Probably they resembled our oatmeal cakes called " blawd ceirch."

[2] Free Serjeant. Probably his duties were serving the abbot's writs, or holding his courts. There was a grand serjeantry, a little serjeantry, and a free serjeantry : grand sergeantry implied military service ; little serjeantry, feeding the lord's dogs, mewing his hawks, and furnishing him with bows and arrows.

John Luvel, or Lovel; Philip Stiward, David Marescal, W. Terry, Henry Colyn. Margam, Day of St. Donat, Bishop and Martyr. 7 Aug., A.D. 1325.

I give here the Kenfeg Ordinances, fourth year of Edward III , 1330.

KENFFEG VILLA.

A good set of ordinances for the government of the town considering the remote period in which they were drawn up.

Copy Kenffeg Ordinances, fourth year of Edward III. or 1330.

KENFFEG VILLA.

" The ancient, true and laudable Ordinances of the said town newly drawn by the consent of the portreeve and aldermen thereof whose names are hereunder written, word by word and agreeable to the old decayed roule, with other more ordinances added thereunto, for the good government of the said town and libertys. Dated the twentyeth day of May and the fourth year of Edward the Third after the Conquest.

1. "First it is ordained by the portreeve and his brethren the aldermen of the said town that every baker licensed by the said portreeve, from time to time shall bake good and sufficient bread to be sold as well to all burgesses, chencers, inhabitants and strangers, keeping such true size as shall be limitted unto them by the portreeve, weighing according to the

rate of the corn sold in the markett, on pain of a grievious amerciament at the portreeve's pleasure, and further punishments and penalties provided [by] his Majesty's laws and statutes for such heinous and intollerable offences.

2. "Also it is ordained by the said portreeve and aldermen that every oven-keeper within the said town shall keep true and lawfull weights, and the same deliver to him or them bakeing bread to be sold, whether they be burgesses, chencers, inhabitants or strangers, upon pain of a grievious amerciament.

3. "Item it is ordained by the said portreeve that noe manner of person shall buy wheat nor noe other corn in the markett for to make their mault upon pain of amerciament.

4. "Item it is ordained by the said portreeve that noe baker nor brewer shall buy noe manner of corn in the markett before xii of the clock in the summer and xi of the clock in the winter, upon pain of a grievous amerciament.

5. "Item it is ordained by the said portreeve that all brewers shall brew good and wholesome ale, third drink and small drink, as well to strangers as burgesses, chencers and inhabitants of the town upon pain of amerciament.

6. "Item it is ordained that no tapster shall wern her ale to selling to burgesses, chencers and inhabitants of the said town by gallon, pottle or quart, if she hath above three pottles in her house, upon pain of a grievious amerciament.

7. "Item it is ordained that all brawlers and fighters that draweth blood the one upon the other, shall pay

iij*s.* and iiij*d.* for the bloodshed, and for the fray such amerciament as shall please the portreeve.

8. " It is ordained that noe butcher shall not hold noe open shop on a Sunday, nor on that day sell noe flesh openly, upon pain of amerciament.

9. " It is ordained that noe butcher shall not slay any manner of victuall neither make any scalding in the high street, upon pain of amerciament. Also that noe butcher being burgess shall sell flesh but under the shambles, upon pain of amerciament. And also that all butchers, strangers, shall sell noe flesh within the said town but upon Frydays and Saturdays, upon pain of amerciament.

10. " Item it is ordained that noe manner of burgess shall buy noe manner of merchandizes that shall happen to come to the said town, but such men as shall be appointed by the said portreeve and aldermen, upon pain of xl*s.* ; and all such merchandizes to be divided amongst all the burgesses, every man according to his ability.

11. " Item it is ordained that noe butchers shall cast noe heads, feet, nor none other garbage in the High Street, nor in noe other place, to the annoyance of his neighbour, upon pain of amerciament of xij*d.* at every time he is so found or taken.

12. "Item it is ordained that if any burgess have any wrong, and may be (by the portreeve thereof) remedied, and will make any other suit against the portreeve or Councell, unto the Lord or his deputy, that burgess soe doing to be discommoned by the portreeve and Councell for evermore without any gainsaying, and a grievious amerciament at the

pleasure of the portreeve, if he be found guilty, by III of the Councell and III of the com'ons.

13. "Item it is ordained that noe burgess, chencer nor inhabitant, nor their servants, shall buy within the gates nor without the gates noe manner of thing coming into the markett, untill the time it be brought unto the place accustomed ; and all those that be taken up or put up for that forestalling or regrateing to be amerced in xs. at every time that any of them be found faulty, unless it be the portreeve or any of his brethren for their own house ; and all chencers or strangers that selleth any fish until the time it be brought unto the place accustomed, shall pay amerciament at the portreeve his pleasure.

14. "Item it is ordained that noe chencer nor inhabitant or resciant shall say noe unfitting words which should be rebukefull or spitefull to the portreeve or to any of the Councell, or will gainsay the good rule and ordinances of the said town which is made and ordained by the said portreeve and aldermen, upon pain of imprisonment and amerciament of xs., the one half thereof to the lord, and the other half to him that the rebuke is given ; and the third fault to be discommoned, if he be found guilty by three of the aldermen and three of the burgesses.

15. " Item it is ordained that noe burgess, chencer, nor inhabitant of the said town shall take noe part against the portreeve and aldermen with noe burgess, chencer, nor noe other person, upon pain of xs. ; and if he be a burgess, to pay the penalty forthwith, and to be discom'oned, and his body to prison ; and if he be a chencer, to pay the said penalty, and his body to

prison, there to remain untill the portreeve and the Councell doe commune together.

16. " Item it is ordained that noe burgess be made or received into the Guildhall except he be admitted by the portreeve, aldermen and burgesses, soe that he may be ruled by the portreeve of the said town ; and he or they soe admitted and received, shall take noe maintenance, upon pain of discomyneing, if he be found guilty by three of the aldermen and three of the burgesses, and amerced at the portreeve's pleasure.

17. " Item it is ordained that noe burgess, chencer nor inhabitant of the said town shall buy neither cheese, butter, eggs, capons, henns, chickens, nor noe other manner of victualls coming to the said town to be sold, untill it come to the common markett of old time used, upon pain of amerciament of vj*d.* at every time that any of them be found guilty or faulty.

18. " It is ordained that noe taverner keep noe open tavern in the annoyance after x of the clock at night, noe tapster after ix, upon pain of amercia-ment.

19. " Item it is ordained that noe manner of person shall play at dice, cards, bowles, nor no other unlaw-full games within the said town nor the franchise of the same, upon pain of amerciament of xij*d.* upon him that owneth the house that such play is kept in, and the players to be brought to prison, and an amercia-ment at the portreeve's pleasure ; and also there be noe tennis playing within the High Street, upon pain of v*s.* to be levied upon every of them that playeth.

20. "Item it is ordained that noe burgess, chencer, nor inhabitant of the said town shall not suffer any stranger within his house privily nor openly to buy nor to sell any manner of merchandizes against the royaltys of the said town and the freedom thereof, upon pain of xx*s*.

21. "Item it is ordained that noe ostler shall hold noe ostrey without a sign at his door, upon pain of amerciament of xx*s*., and that noe ostler shall werne noe lodging nor harbour noe strangers comeing to the said town on horseback or on foot upon pain of amerciament of xij*d*. at every default.

22. "Item it is ordained that noe stranger shall have free prison in the Guildhall above, but in the lower prison, unless he be a burgess giveing, yielding and paying within the said town according to the charter ; and he to find suretys to save the serjeant harmless.

23. "Item it is ordained that noe manner of person shall make noe foraigne nor piggestye to the annoyance of his neighbour upon pain of five shillings, unless and except it be in his garden within the walls of the said town.

24. "Item it is ordained that noe manner of person or persons shall cast noe dust, dung nor other filth in the streets nor in the town ditches, nor within fifty foot of any of the gates of the said town or any part of the walls thereof, upon pain of amerciament at the pleasure of the portreeve.

25. "Item it is ordained that noe burgess nor chencer shall goe out of the franchise and libertys of the said town to the wedding ale of any person

or persons whatsoever, upon pain of five shillings at every default.

26. "Item it is ordained that if any woman be found guilty [by six men] of scolding or railing any burgess or their wives or any other of their neighbours, then she to be brought at the first fault to the cucking-stool there to sit one hour, and the second fault two hours, and third fault to lett slippe, or else a high fyne at the portreeve his pleasure.

27. "Item it is ordained that noe manner of person shall hold nor open shop to cutt carne or trawntrey or ostrey hold, unless he be a burgess yielding and paying by the appointment of the portreeve, upon pain of a grievous amerciament.

28. "Item it is ordained that noe manner of person shall have any swine goeing within the town walls upon pain (if a complaint be made) of twelve pence amerciament at every time that they be found faulty; and if any swine be found about the Cross, the Cross keeper is to have for every swine so found four pence; and further, if any complaint be made by the hay-warden or by any other person of any swine going upon the common unringed, the owners of the said swine to pay and forfeit for every such default two shillings and six pence.

29. "Item it is ordained that all such persons as have burgages or any houses within the town or franchise of the same shall take no tenants into their houses but such as will and may be allowed and admitted by the portreeve and aldermen and other officers of the said town, and not to hurt the libertys and franchises of the same, upon pain of discomyneing

(if he be a freeman) and ten shillings amerciament; and if he be not a burgess, ten shillings amerciament and his body to prison.

30. "Item it is ordained that noe burgess shall not merchandize with noe strangers goods to their singular advantage and for to inhance merchandizes and for to imbeazle the lords royaltys, dutys and customs, upon pain of high amerciament at the portreeve's pleasure.

31. "Item it is ordained that noe burgess, chencer nor inhabitant of the said town doe not say against the royalties and libertys of the same, nor of the charter, upon pain of amerciament.

32. "Item it is ordained that noe chencer nor stranger shall buy any corn within the markett nor within the franchise of the said town, to be sold again, upon pain of amerciament.

33. "Item it is ordained that noe chencer shall sell bread, ale, nor noe other victualls, nor hold noe open ostrey by night nor by day within the said franchise of the said town, but through license from the portreeve for the time being, upon pain of amerciament.

34. "Item it is ordained that noe stranger shall buy any corn in the markett untill the portreeve, aldermen and burgesses be served, except gentlemen for their own household, upon pain of amerciament.

35. "Item it is ordained that noe stranger shall walke by night after nine of the clock, without a reasonable cause, or fire in his hand, upon pain of amerciament of twelve pence, and his body to prison, at the portreeve's pleasure there to remain.

36. "Item it is ordained that noe burgess shall

discover the Councell of his brethren burgesses of the said town, upon pain of discom'oning without gainsaying, and a grievous amerciament at the pleasure of the portreeve.

37. "Item it is ordained that every burgess, tenant and resciant dwelling within the town walls where the pavements or causeways hath been, shall and doe keep them clean from dung and other filth, upon pain of twelve pence at every fault; and where the streets be unpav'd, every man to pave the same, upon pain of amerciament, before his door.

38. "Item it is ordained that no man nor woman shall milke any kine within the High Street, within the town walls, nor none shall suffer their beasts to abide in the High Street nor in noe other street by night nor by day, but only going and comeing to and from their pastures, upon pain of amerciament of twelve pence at every such fault.

39. "Item it is ordained that noe burgess shall buy noe manner of wares as boards, lathes, tyles, nor noe other chaffre for any strangers, whereby the libertys and freedom of the said town may be hurt and hindered to the annoyance of any other burgess, upon pain of three shillings and four pence at every fault and offence comitted therein.

40. "Item it is ordained that every tanner using the mystery of tanning shall sell their leather well and sufficiently tanned accordingly, upon pain of forfeiture of his said leather or a fyne.

41. "Item it is ordained that noe burgess nor chencer shall buy noe manner of hides or skinns (comeing to the markett) of any beasts or cattle what-

soever or wool but only in the com'on markett place of old accustomed, upon pain of amerciament.

42. " Item it is ordained that all butchers, as well strangers as burgesses and chencers, shall bring unto the markett good and wholesome and sufficient victuals unblown not raised upon the kidney or otherwise abused contrary to his highnesses laws, upon pain of a greivious amerciament. And all strange butchers that bringeth beef, mutton, or other victual to be sold shall bring with them the hides and skinns thereof, upon pain of forfeiture of their victualls.

43. " Item it is ordained that no burgess of the said town shall sue, arrest, trouble, or vex any other burgess at any court, shire, or franchise, or any other court if out of the said town, upon pain of discomyne-ing and amerciament if such his plaint and action be and may be determinable within the court of the said town.

44. " Item it is ordained that noe manner of burgess, chencer, nor inhabitant of the said town shall keep noe licentious naughtipacks, bawdrey, or suspected harlotts, vagabonds, nor loyterers in their houses, upon pain of ten shillings amerciament.

45. " Item it is ordained that noe manner of person or persons whatsoever, burgess, chencer, nor inhabi-tant of the said town, shall make noe mixions in any place within the franchise and libertys of the said town to the annoyance of any man nor to the inconvenience of any of the streets of the said town, upon pain of ten shillings on every of them so doeing.

46. " Item it is ordained that noe burgess nor

burgesses be admitted to be putt in election for portreeve, nor in the councell of the said town, nor in any other office with the said burrough except he or they be dwellers therein.

47. "Item it is ordained that noe burgess or burgesses shall have liberty for his or their cattle or cattles to pasture (in any place) upon our common and freedom except he be a dweller within the said town.

48. "Item it is ordained that noe burgess or burgesses shall take upon any condition noe manner of cattle or cattles of any person or persons whatsoever thereby to overpasture our com'on and freedom but such number as is reasonable and fitt, and that noe burgesses shall take noe manner of cattle or cattles under three years, upon pain of amerciament at the pleasure of the portreeve.

49. "Item it is ordained that noe aldermen burgesses that have been portreeves shall appear in a jury between party and party. And those who are elected and chosen for election portreeves are also to be free from being in the said jury for the present year in which they are elected.

50. "Item it is ordained that the hayward shall dayly make a diligent view and survey over our com'on and freedom, and thereby to see that no strangers cattle nor cattles doe pasture upon our freedom. And also to see that noe manner of person or persons whatsoever doe reap any sedges, neither draw nor pull any rootes, nor cutt any furzes in any place whatsoever, nor do any other thing that may be to the ruin, destruction, and overthrow of the said

burrough nor the inhabitants thereof, upon pain of five shillings for every default.

51. "Item it is ordained that noe burgess nor burgesses stranger nor inhabitant shall reap or pluck any sedges nor any other rootes (in any place upon) the said burrough to the annoyance ruin and overthrow of the same. But only such person or persons as the portreeve and councell shall admitt, and in such place upon the said burrough as the said portreeve and councell shall appoint, upon pain of two shillings and six pence for the first fault, for the second fault five shillings, and for the third fault to be discomyned and disfranchised.

52. "To all to whom these presents shall come to be seen read heard or understood that where as the Lords of Glamorgan and Morgannog of old antiquity of their meer clemency and mercy and by their goodness and freewill and by their several charters have given and granted to the burrough and town of Kenfegg their libertys and franchises with the freedom appertaining to the same with many goodly and Godly comoditys for the preserving of the government and profitts of the com'onwealth of the burrough and town corporate of Kenfegg and to the burgesses of the same as in the said severall charters under their hands and seales more att large may and doth appear. And amongst divers other gifts and grants the said Lords of Glamorgan and Morgannog in their several charters and letters patents have given granted and fully confirmed to the burrough and town corporate of Kenfegg and burgesses of the same and to their

successors for ever as well certain parcells of free
com'ons sett lyeing and being at Kevencribor between
the lands of the Lord of Newcastle on the east part
and the lands of the late dissolved monastery of
Margam on the north-west and south as alsoe many
other parcells and quilletts of lands with free libertys
and freedoms within the franchises aforesaid as in
their severall charters is mentioned Know ye
further for good and reasonable considerations us
moveing and alsoe for a com'onwealth and comodity
of our burgesses and successors for ever and according to the tenor and purport of the said severall
charters to us severally granted by the said Lords
of Glamorgan and Morgannog wee the burgesses
aforesaid have consulted ourselves together and to
and thereupon concluded and agreed within ourselves for because wee have and yett doe yearly
fall in arrearages and losses the which is to the
portreeve's great charges by reason of the overthrow
blowing and choaking up of sand in drowning of our
town and church with a number of acres of free lands
besides all the burgages of ground within the said
libertys except three for the which burgages so lost
by the said overthrow yett nevertheless the rent
thereof is and hath allways been paid to the lords
receivers to the portreeve's great losse and hinderance
yearly in making of auditt Therefore it is con-
discended concluded assented and fully agreed between all the burgesses of the said town that the said
portreeve shall call twelve before him and of them to
name of the most substantial honest and the best
freeholders of the said town eight and they shall

yearly make their ordinances for any com'onweale to
stand and remain for their comodities amongst them
their heirs successors and assignes and soe being once
substantially made to continue for ever   And thereupon Evan Griffith portreeve of the same called these
eight burgesses to him to make this present order or
composition videlicet William Thomas Aylward Gent.,
John Morgan Gent., Rees Thomas Melen, William
ap William, Rees Thomas Ievan, Thomas Jenkin,
Llewellyn Pritchard, and Robert John.   The said
portreeve and the eight beforesaid have stablished
this for com'onweale profitts and comodity of our said
burgesses and to their heirs successors and assigns and
to every of them for ever for the inclosing parking
and ditching in part of the aforesaid free comon at
Kevencribor for and towards some help of the loss
of their burgages of lands by the overthrow aforesaid
and that the same be and shall bee inclosed parked
and ditched in by the burgesses on this side and
before the twenty fourth day of Aprill next comeing
after the date hereof and soe from thenceforth shall
stand and remain to every of the said twenty-nine
burgesses and to their heirs successors and assignes
and to every of them for ever every one his part
as to the chances by lotts none shall challenge otherwise and they shall begin on the eastern part to ditch
at Clawdd-y-ffin [1] and soe westward under the hill to
Trod Rhyw Yr Glo' and from thence downwards
to Rhyd Yorath Goch   To have and to hold the
aforesaid parcells of free com'on to every one of
the twenty-nine burgesses hereon indorsed and to

---

[1] Clawdd-y-ffin, the boundary hedge.

their heirs and assigns for ever without any lett
interruption molestation or vexation of the burgesses
inhabiting or dwelling within the said libertys or of
any person or persons in their behalfs or steads
Item wee order that the same parcell of free comon
shall be fenced and put into hayne on the twenty
fourth of March and shall not be depastured untill the
feast of Saint Matthew before Michaelmas And alsoe
then there shall none of the said twenty-nine burgesses
pasture or grass the same but by the Oyfri.[1] Item wee
doe order that none shall rent his or their part nor sell
the same to any stranger if there will be any of the
burgesses that will buy or rent the same upon pain
of forfeiture of his or their libertys within the same
parcell of meadow   Also if any burgess doe rent his
or their part to any other burgess he shall have it
for three shillings and fourpence the acre and not
above Item wee doe order that noe one burgess
of one part or parcell in the said free comon meadow
shall not by inheritance challenge two parts or more
so that allways the portreeve and other eight burgesses
shall by their discretion devide the same as they shall
seeme good and convenient to maintain allways the
twenty-nine within the same   Item wee doe order
for the better establishinge of these our ordinances
by us the portreeve and the other eight of the twelve
for the performance of every point and article that
shall bee broken or discontinued wee do bind us and
every of us each to the other in the sum of five
pounds of good and lawful money of England apiece

---

[1] Oyfri ; this is probably a mistake for Cyfrif, an account or
reckoning—a register.

and that it shall be levied upon our goods and lands without any delay or wager of law. In witneese whereof we the portreeve and the other eight have thereunto put our seales and signes the twentyth day of January in the thirteenth year of the reign of our sovereign lady Elizabeth by the grace of God of England France and Ireland Queen Defender of the Faith etc. Annoque Domini 1572 [1571].

53. "Item it is ordained that every widow shall enjoy the priviledge of her husband dureing her widowhood except the heir apparent bee sworne burgess to doe service within the said town thereby to have the peice of hay within the aforesaid meadow if soe it bee that the said heir apparent doth challenge and claim his right to it the said peice of hay and provided that noe manner of person nor persons whatsoever doe interrupt the said widow of her priviledge as long as she liveth and dwelleth within the said burrough and town.

54. "Item it is ordained that noe burgesses nor burgess shall sell any peice nor parcell of hay at Kimley Meade or Kevencribor to any burgess being an outdweller from the said burrough nor to any stranger nor foreigner upon pain of discomyneing.

55. "Item it is ordained that noe burgess nor burgesses shall rent any peice nor parcell of hay at the foresaid meadow to any burgess nor burgesses being outdwellers from the said town and burrough nor to any other person or persons whatsoever if it be necessary to any burgess or burgesses dwelling in the said burrough to have the said parcel of hay for and that noe burgess nor burgesses shall rent any

parcell of the said hay before he or they do publickly on a court day offer the same parcel of hay
to a burgess and burgesses dwelling in the said
burrough   And alsoe that noe burgess nor burgesses
shall henceforth rent any peice or parcell of the said
hay above three shillings and four pence per acre
upon pain of forfeiture of his or their libertys in the
said parcells of hay as aforesaid.

56. "Item it is ordained that if any burgess happen
to dye without any lawfull heir within the said town
and burrough to enjoy the said dece'dent burgess his
parcell of hay within the said free com'on meadow the
portreeve for the said year in which he happeneth to
dye shall have and enjoy the benefitt and profitt
of the said parcell of hay for one whole year after
his decease and after one year the said parcell of
hay to be by the portreeve and the eight burgesses
settled to a burgess that hath not a parcell of
hay paying therefore twenty shillings per acre to
the treasury of the said town for the maintenance
allways of the comonweale of the said town and
burrough.

57. "Item it is ordained if any difference shall
happen to arise between any of the said burgesses in
claiming any right or title in any of the said parcells
of hay within the said free comon meadow the
portreeve and the eight elected burgesses shall try
and decide the same debate and difference without
any delay or wager of law.

58. "Item it is ordained that noe burgess nor
burgesses shall rent any parcell of fernes att Kenfeg
Down to any burgess nor burgesses dwelling out of

the said burrough nor to any stranger nor foreigner before he publickly on a court-day held for the said town offer the same parcell of ferns to a burgess or burgesses dwelling within the said town and burrough And also that noe burgess nor burgesses shall rent out any of the said parcells of ferns above eight pence per parcell yearly upon forfeiture of his or their libertys within the said parcell of ferns at the said down.

1773.

59. "Item it is ordained that no manner of person or persons whosoever dwelling within the said borough town or their franchise thereof shall be admitted and sworn burgess or burgesses except such as gain legall settlement in the same wherein he or they then resides.

"[*Endorsement.*]—These blotts or lotts shall begin on the east part next to Clawdd y ffin. Every man's hit shall chance by the said lotts.

"Imprimis.—1, Llewelyn ap Richard; 2, Robert John Richard; 3, Rees Thomas Melen; 4, William ap William; 5, John Morgan; 6, Thomas Jenkin; 7, William Thomas Ayleward; 8, Rees Thomas Bevan; 9, Evan Griffith; 10, Thomas ap Thomas; 11, Rees ap Ievan John; 12, Llewelyn Griffith; 13, Watkin Thomas; 14, David John Ayleward; 15, David John Goch; 16, Howell ap Howell; 17, Evan ap Morgan; 18, Jenkin ap Ievan; 19, Jonnett Verch Evan; 20, John Jenkin; 21, Dennis Verch John; 22, Catherine Verch Fforath; 23, Thomas Griffith; 24, Amy Verch John; 25, John Thomas

Llewellyn; 26, Howell Thomas; 27, Johan Verch Ievan; 28, John Hortton; 29, Morgan Evan.

"Copia vera nominorum."

Some of the ordinances are curious; for instance, "all butchers, strangers, shall sell noe flesh within the said town but upon Frydays and Saturdays upon pain of amerciament."[1]

Pigstyes were not to be made to the annoyance of a neighbour, unless and except it be in his own garden within the walls of the town.

Item 6 refers to tapster as being a woman. Tapster means a bar-*maid*, here it means a woman holding a small ale-house. The tapster was not to wern her ale to selling to burgesses, etc., that is, she was not to refuse to sell. Wern to refuse, to forbid ("Halliwell's Dictionary of Archaic and Provincial Words").

No. 13 provides that nothing was to be bought except in the market, and 17 is to the same effect as regards cheese, butter, eggs, capons, hens, chickens, or other victuals.

Resciant, in No. 14, means a resident.

No. 18 the taverner, or public-house keeper, was to close at 10 p.m., the tapster at 9 p.m.

No. 21. Ostler, from the old French *hostelier*, an inn-keeper; Ostrey, from old French *hostellerie* (in this case clearly different from the tavern), a place where persons could stay at, a small hotel. The ostler was not to werne lodging or harbour to strangers; he was not to refuse them lodging. "Withey's Dictionary" mentions that taverns which

[1] Amerciament = punishment.

existed in England as early as the thirteenth century at first sold only wines and liquors.

Item 24 shows that the town was walled and provided with entrance gates.

Item 25 is very severe : it allows no burgess or chencer to go to the wedding ale of any person or persons outside the franchise and liberties of the town, upon pain of 5s. at every default.

A chencer is, I believe, a dweller in the town having no burgage rights, a simple householder (Chencer, 1535, Act 27, Henry VIII., "Yerely tributours or chensers ").

No. 26 shows us how women with wilful tongues were to be dealt with. If six men find any woman guilty of scolding or railing at any burgess or his wife or neighbours, she is to sit in the cucking-stool [1] one hour, and for the second fault two hours, and for the third fault to let slippe, or else a high fyne at the portreeve's pleasure.

No. 27. To cut carne : This means probably to cut meat up and display for sale. Trawntrey : This word may be from Traunter, a pedlar, or it may mean Taverntry.

No. 28 deals with pigs wandering within the town

[1] Cucking-stool, for ducking scolds. The stool which is chucked or let down into the water; to "let slippe" meant that the woman was let down into the water. From the archaic word cuck—to chuck or throw

"Now if our cucking-stool was for each scold,
  Some town, I fear, would not their numbers hold."

("Poor Robin," 1746).—Dr. E. C. Brewer, "Dict. of Phrase and Fable."

walls and also with pigs found about the Cross, the Cross-keeper to have the fine for every swine so found.   I am not sure if this Cross is what is found in almost all mediæval towns and known as the Market Cross, or if it is the cross known as the Groes-y-dadl, to which I shall refer hereafter.   Whichever cross is referred to, it was carefully guarded by an officer specially detailed for the purpose.

No tenants to be taken into the houses except by permission of the town officials.

They were early bedgoers in those days, for " noe stranger shall walke by night after nine of the clock, without a reasonable cause, or fire [a lantern] in his hand," upon payment of a fine or imprisonment.

The streets must have had a curious chess-board-like appearance, for "where the streets be unpav'd, every man to pave the same, upon pain of amerciament, before his door."   Mixion mentioned in No. 45 probably means mixon, or midden, an ash-pit, a refuse-heap.

Tanning was regarded as a handicraft.   Mystery is derived from the old French *mestier*, a trade or handicraft.

Naughtipack, a woman of bad character, or a wicked or dissolute man (" Murray's Dictionary ").

No. 50 mentions an official called the Hayward, who is to see to the common land of the borough, to distrain cattle trespassing, and to see that the sedges binding the sand together were not to be reaped nor plucked up by the roots, neither were furzes to be cut " that may be to the ruin, destruction and overthrow of the said burrough nor the inhabitants thereof." This indicates that trouble was threatening the town in the shape of drifting sand. At Aberavon there were formerly four haywards.

No. 51 modifies the above, and the portreeve and council may allow persons to pluck sedges and other " rootes."

No. 52 was added in A.D. 1572, and, as I have already mentioned, it discloses a sad condition of things. It mentions the late dissolved monastery of Margam, the dissolution having taken place thirty-five years before ; many of the burgesses whose names are appended doubtless remembered the Abbey before the end came.

ᐧIt goes on to relate that, whereas the Lords of Glamorgan and Morgannog of old antiquity of their meer clemency and mercy and by their goodness and free will have given and granted to the burrough and town of Kenffeg for ever certain parcells of free com'ons at Kevencriber between the lands of the Lord of Newcastle on the east and the lands of the late dissolved monastery at Margam on the north-west and south : Know ye further for good and reasonable considerations according to the tenor and purport of the severall charters granted by the said Lords of Glamorgan and Morgannog wee the burgesses have consulted ourselves together and agreed within ourselves for because wee have and do yet yearly fall in arrearages and losses by reason of the overthrow blowing and choaking up of sand in drowning of our town and church with a number of acres of free lands besides all the burgages of

12

ground *except three;* it was agreed to call twelve
of the most substantial honest and best freeholders of
the said town and of them to name eight who shall
arrange for the inclosing and ditching of part of the
aforesaid free comon at Kefncribor as some help for
the loss of the overflow aforesaid : the lands so
inclosed to be allotted among twenty-nine burgesses.
None of the new allotments are to be sold save at
a fixed price and none to a stranger to the exclusion
of a burgess.   Other regulations with regard to the
allotments are numerous.   Dated 20 Jan., 13 Elizabeth,
A.D. 1572 [1571].

CHAPTER VIII

KENFIG POOL; THE GROES-Y-DADL AND TYN-Y-SELER

AFTER puzzling over the strange words in the ordinances of Kenfig it is refreshing to stand on the shore of Kenfig Pool.

Restful is the great pool to-day, and you are impressed with the peaceful aspect; "smooth-faced peace" is surely here. No sound breaks the stillness save the lowing of cattle in the adjacent fields which rise in gentle slope from the water on the landward side. On the other, the seaward side, the great waste of sand, having won its way right up to the pool, seems now at rest. The string of cattle, wending its way to refreshing coolness, comes with laggard, lazy steps. The houses along the ridge seem in the drowsy sunshine to have no dwellers. Yet in the dim and distant past this pleasant spot echoed with the shouts and clang of fights, red war close by, and the pool shone ruddy with the lurid glare of burning Kenfig reflected from the skies. People, blenched with fear, sought safety in the church from double foe—man drunk with lust of blood, and fire with keen and lapping tongue.

The pool embraces an area of 68 acres at the present time: in the year A.D. 1814[1] the area was 83½ acres, and in A.D. 1876 the Ordnance Survey gives the area as 75½ acres. The configuration of the water-line next the sand-hills changes from time to time with the moods of the drifting sand; the distance to high-water from the pool is 1,100 yards, all sand-dunes. The water is fresh, and is mainly from springs on the landward side and the rainfall. Its greatest depth is 12 feet as measured by Mr. R. W. Llewellyn, of Baglan Hall.

The pool is locked in on all sides by sand-hills, except along its eastern side; from here the grassland rises to the ridge, which varies from 90 to 100 feet above the sea-level, along which are the houses of Lower Kenfig, or Ton Kenfig, as it is variously named. It is curious, but no outlet or overflow can be seen, and yet outlet there must be. It seems clear to me, from the words of the charter of Thomas le Despenser, that a stream formerly flowed from the pool to the River Kenfig. The part of the charter referring to it is as follows : " Et tales sunt bunde libertatis eorum Videlicet inter locum vocatum Newditch et Taddulcrosse et quandam divisam ducentem de Newditch usque Taddulcrosse inter terram Abbathie de Margan et terram Abbathie de Teokesburie in parte orientali et quendam rivulum vocatum Blaklaak qui solebat currere de aqua australi usque aquam borialem de Kenfig in parte occidentali, etc."

---

[1] "The Borough of Kenfig," R. W. Llewellyn, Esq. (*Arch. Camb.*, 1898).

("And these are the bounds of their liberty, namely, between a place called Newditch and Taddulcrosse and a certain boundary leading from Newditch to Taddulcrosse between the land of the Abbey of Margan and the land of the Abbey of Teokesburie [Tewkesbury], on the east; and a certain stream called Blaklaak [*i.e.*, Black river] *which used to run from the southern water [i.e., the Kenfig pool] to the northern water of Kenefeg* on the west, &c.")

This, I think, is evidence of the existence at one time of a stream flowing from the pool to Kenfig river.

The Rev. Thomas Howell tells me that when he was at school in Kenfig, he with the other boys used to bathe in the pool, and the schoolmaster always warned them to avoid the Gwtter-du, or Black ditch, in the pool. This seems to recall the Black River of the charters.

At the north-west corner of the castle-bailey, at the point where the moat joined the river, a strong spring or stream of water issues—the Ffynon Lygad (the eye-spring). It is still resorted to, Mrs. Yorath, of the "Prince of Wales," tells me, by persons who have eye troubles. This stream is, possibly, part of the overflow from Kenfig Pool. The water thus apparently flowing from the ancient moat would show that a stream had been brought into the moat at its point nearest the pool, as the water would be required as an auxiliary to the River Kenfig in dry weather for filling the moat.

The river, referred to elsewhere as the Black river,

must have been considerably west of the town. It doubtless was the natural outlet for the waters of the pool.

The only mention of Kenfig Pool in the Margam MSS. is in T. 231 (C. MCLXXXVII): a mandate by the Rector of Coytiff [1] and the Rural Dean of Gronyth, [2] Special Commissaries to Thomas Lovel or Louel, clerk, to cite John Philip of Kenefeg, Rees ap Gruff' Gethyn of Avan, Hoel ap Gruff' Hagur and others to attend in Kenfig Church in the suit of Margam Abbey against them for unlawful fishing in Kenfig Pool and Avan waters. Dated at Coytiff, 2nd Nov., A.D. 1365.

It is endorsed with a certificate of the due citation of the above defendants, who are called Hoel' ap Gruff Hagir, [3] Rees ap Gruff' Gethyn, Jevan ap Philipot, Rees ap . . . ap . . ., Thomas de Browneswolde of Avan. 11 Nov., A.D. 1365, at Kenfig.

In T. 232 (C. MCLXXXVIII), we have the record of the proceedings before the Dean in Kenfig Church, in the case between the Abbot and Rees ap Gruff' Gethyn, Hoel' Du ap Gruff' Hagur, Jevan ap Philipot, Rees ap Wylym, Thomas Browneswold of Avan, John Philip, W. Steward, John Thomas, Philip Walsche, W. Marle, John Doyle, John Day, W. Hauker, and Henry Prowting of Kenfeg, defendants.

Kenfig Pool is called in the mandate " Kenefeeg is

[1] Coity.
[2] Groneath.
[3] Probably Hagr—ugly, unseemly.

Poil "; when I first saw it I did not realise it meant Kenfig Pool.

Rees confessed that he took fish in the Avan river, but took them justly, and thus had fallen under sentence of excommunication. He was ordered to prove his right at Newcastle Church on the following Monday.

John Philipot and the others confess to having fished in the water and fishery of Kenfig and Avan and are left to the grace and absolution of the abbot.

At Kenfig the defendant Rees delivered in his defence that his ancestors had forfeited their jurisdiction in their courts, and the abbot exhibited deeds of appropriation, confirmation, and agreement to prove their right. Then the defendant admitted and confessed that after Robert Fitzhaymon had conquered the hereditary land of him (the said Rees) and others, with the water and fishery in dispute, two hundred and seventeen years past—*i.e.*, A.D. 1148—he, the said Robert, gave the said fishery to Margam Abbey in recompense for injuries it had sustained at the hands of his (Rees') ancestors.

6 Nov., A.D. 1365.

* S' DE (CAN) ATV (S.) DE . GR ONYTH.

In T. 232 (C. MCXC) we have the record of an Assize of Novel-dissein before a jury of twelve men in the Glamorgan County Court, held at Cardiff, taken before Sir Edward de Stratelyng, Knt., Sheriff of Glamorgan and Morgan, whereby John, Abbot of

Margam, recovers with 40s. damages his fishery o. salmons, gyllyngs,[1] suwyngs,[2] and several other fish in the water of Avene, from the head thereof down to the place where it goes into the sea (worth £10 yearly), against Rees, son of Gruffin Gethyn, and Howel, son of Griffin' Hager, each of whom is fined 3d. damages. 40 Ed. III., Monday before Midsummer Day, A.D. 1366.

T. 234 (C. MCLXXXIX) is a mandate issued the same day by Edward de Stratelyng to Wm. Wynchestre, bailiff of the county, or to Nicholas Cantelo, sub-bailiff, to deliver seisin to Abbot John of the several fishery of Auene which he has thus recovered.

By order of Lord Edward le Despenser. Cardiff, Monday, St. Alban's Day, 22 June, A.D. 1366.

On the margin of the pool is found the spearwort [3] bright with intense yellow. But the glory of the pool is the water-lily,[4] which grows in abundance on the seaward side.

---

[1] Gyllyng. A salmon on its second return from the sea is sometimes called a gilling in the Severn District (1880, Buckland, 19 Report Salmon Fish). The Salmon growes by their degrees and ages, viz., 1. a pinke , 2. a botcher ; 3. a salmon trout , 4. a gillinge ; 5. a salmon (1640, J Smith, Hundred of Berkeley : an extract from the "Oxford Dictionary," 1901).

[2] The Sewin. Many writers maintain that this fish is a distinct species ; others, as Dr. Günther, regard it as a trout. Aflalo writes, " The Peal, Sewin, or Bull-Trout, is also regarded by most writers as a species, though not admitted by Smitt as more than a variety of the Sea-Trout." *Salmo cambricus* Dr. Gunther terms the Sewin of Wales.

[3] Ranunculus lingua.

[4] Nymphœa alba

THE GROES-Y-DADL.

The Kenfig river and Goylake brook run parallel for some distance and not far apart, as if too coy to join fortunes, but a high hill causes them to join and go together to greet the sea. On top of this high hill, a quarter of a mile west of the junction, stands the base of a cross, the Groes-y-dadl as it is known to-day, but correctly the Groes-y-dadleu—the cross of contention, of dispute, of debating; this is the "Taddulcrosse" of the charter of Thomas le Despenser to the burgesses of A.D. 1397.

The Groes-y-dadl, to use the name now in use, marked a celebrated spot in the life of ancient Kenfig, for here came the townspeople to settle, or try to settle, by debate, and perhaps by stronger measures, their grievances and disputes. What a quiet spot it is to-day! No cries rend the air, as disputants shouted to each other, the idle bystanders, as they are ever wont, adding to the confusion. All is still and peaceful as you stand by the base of the Cross; to the south-east the view is charming—no prettier scene of pastoral country can be seen; below lies Danes' Vale, with smiling fields in green and gold; further off and nearer south are the rounded hills of Old Ballas,[1] green with trees to mark their swelling pride; and snugly ensconced under them is fair Ty Tanglwys, once the home of Tanguistel, who married Ketherech Du, owner of much of Peiteuin.

Ty Tanglwys—*ty*, house; *tan*, under; *glwys*, a delectable and fair spot: a house so pleasantly

[1] Bal-las—*bo* , a belly, a rounded hill, and *glas-las*, green.

situated as to give one the feeling that it is almost a hallowed solitude.

Truly has it been named; the view is somewhat like that seen from the Groes-y-dadl, except that you are looking towards the cross to the north. It is a fair and glorious scene; on the west you look over smiling fields, and in the distance see the glittering Hafren sea and in front of you Corneli, looking fair and prosperous, as should a place dedicated to the patron saint of beeves, Saint Corneli. The background of the view is the crowning part; you see right up to the top of the valley of the Kenfig river, and all along are the Margam mountains, framing, as it were, the delightful prospect. Ty Tanglwys is a smiling solitude.

To return again to the Groes-y-dadl. Through the glorious landscape creeps the Roman highway,[1] as narrow as it was when the Second Legion passed along, and up in front it climbs, passing Ty Tanglwys, a white, narrow streak, and then we lose it just east of Old Ballas trees, for it goes to meet the pleasant breezes of Stormy Down; in winter the Roman soldiers cursed its nakedness and nearness to the clouds when it had reached the open downs. On your left is the narrow gorge, the Porth or Gate, through which the Kenfig river emerges and in which is hidden Llanfihangel Mill, as hot in that hollow to-day as Araby. On the south side of the gorge is Marlas, with goodly trees and grateful shade. Here

[1] Heol-y-sheet: this is a puzzle; what it means I cannot say, there being no "sh" sound in Welsh. It may be a corruption of Heol-y-stryd, the road of the vale, or the main road.

Thomas le Marle invented a new excuse, although it was so long ago, for taking the property of others ; he did it out of "levity of mind." A little south by east stands among noble trees and brightest meadows the Hall, where nearly eight hundred years ago Thomas Gramus lived and loved and gave his lands with lavish hand to Blessed Mary of Margan.

Dominating all is the British camp on the end of the ridge of Cefn Cribwr east from here, and one clearly sees the importance of the position of the ancient camp seated right on the point. Old "Castel Kribor" was in far-off days a noted place of defence— so important that I venture in all humility to say it gave its name to Pyle or Pylle or Pill, as it is variously spelled. Pill is a fortress, a place of defence, in Welsh.[1] Pyle lay at the feet of the camp and gladly took its name.

Turn round to look to west, and then no pleasant fields greet the eye ; the golden sands reign supreme.

We have read in the Ordinance of Kenfig of the cross and the care with which it was guarded. I do not know if it was the Groes-y-dadl , I am inclined to think it refers to the market cross. All towns and villages had their market cross, in some cases open and vaulted structures. Mr. Pope, in his "Old Stone Crosses of Dorset," says : "Often on market and fair days a preaching friar would address the people from the market-cross, reminding them of the sacredness of bargains, and telling them, both buyers and sellers, to be true and just in all their dealings, and that 'no one

---

[1] Leland : "In the Edge of a Mountaine northward standith an old Castle or Pyle, called Castle Coch."

ought to go beyond or defraud his brother in any matter.'" The same writer says: "There were Memorial Crosses, Churchyard or Preaching-Crosses, Market, and Village-Crosses, Boundary-Crosses, Weeping-Crosses, and Pilgrim-Crosses."

Although the cross was known as the Groes-y-dadl, it was erected for a different purpose from that of marking a place of contention and of disputes. The emblem of the Passion of the Saviour of the world was placed by the roadside, on mountains, and in lonely places so that passers-by might be reminded of the sufferings endured for their sake, for things and events presented to the eye are realised more vividly than when read of or spoken of. At these roadside crosses funeral processions were formerly stopped for a rest and meditation. In the words of a writer in the fifteenth century, "For this reason ben crosses by ye waye, that when folke passinge see the crosses, they sholde thynke on Hym that dyed on the Crosse, and worshyppe Hym above all thynge." [1]

The Groes-y-dadl was placed high above the surrounding country, a short distance from the then main highway and near the road leading to S. Mary Magdalene's Chapel. Here, doubtless, as funeral processions wended their way to the chapel of S. James's Church, as the sacred emblem came in sight a halt would be made—the last halt before the earthly cross.

Not far off, on the road passing Marlas Farm, is

[1] "Dives and Pauper." *Printed by Wynken de Worde* A.D. 1496. From "Forgotten Sanctuaries," by Miss Gwenllian E. F. Morgan.

tne Groes Siencyn, an incised cross with arms of
about eleven inches long on a round-headed slab; it
marks the borough boundary. The Rev. Thomas
Howell tells me it marks the spot where a man
was buried in an upright position, and great was the
fear with which he and other boys passed the cross
at night.

On the side of the turnpike road, about seven
hundred yards up the hill towards Stormy Down, is
the base of a wayside cross similar to the base of the
Groes-y-dadl.

On the boundary line of Kenfig parish south of
Groes Siencyn stood another cross, the Groes-y-gryn;
perhaps Groes-y-gryniau, the cross of groanings.

In the churchyard of St. James's at Pyle a considerable part of the churchyard cross still remains, and in
the position usually given to the cross in front of the
entrance door—one of the few remaining crosses in
our "God's acres."

In Margam parish, the Abbey MSS. tell us, a cross
existed on the roadside leading from Rhyd Blaen-y-
Cwm, at the top of Kenfig Valley, to Ton Mawr; it
was called Groes Gruffyd. Another cross stood near
Ton Grugos, at the top of the lane leading up the
mountain from Troed-y-rhiw. Cynan's Cross[1] stood
on the roadside between the top of Cwm Kenfig and
the top of Baiden. There was also a cross called
Brombil's Cross, probably the village cross, at Groes,
and which may be the reason of the village being so
named. It is probable that all the crosses remained

---

[1] Cynan may be the son of Cynwyd, patron saint of Llangynwyd.

until the Act for the demolition of crosses, passed 1643, came into force.

Ty'n-y-Seler.

A considerable part of Kenfig borough lies in Margam parish, and in this part is a farm having a name which had long puzzled me—Ty'n-y-seler;[1] on the Ordnance Survey, Ty'n-y-Cellar. It stands on the west side of the Roman road Heol-y-troedwyr, "Soldier's Lane," or, as it is now called, Water Street.

As to the origin of the name: in the monasteries it was the rule to allocate farms or other property to the offices of the various officials, with which to provide the necessary funds for carrying on the duties appertaining to them. The abbot, the cellarer, the sacrist, the almoner, the infirmarer, the tailor, the shoemaker, and others, each had lands with separate granges. In that delightful book, "The Chronicle of Jocelin of Brakelond, Monk of St. Edmundsbury," we are told, for instance, about the cellarer of St. Edmund's Abbey. "The cellarer had his messuage and barns near Scurun's well, at which place he was accustomed to exercise his jurisdiction upon robbers and to hold his court for all pleas and plaints. Also at that place he was accustomed to put his men in pledge, and to enroll them and to renew their pledges every year, and to take such profit therefor as the bailiff of the town was to take at the portman-moot. This messuage, with the adjacent garden, now in the occupation of the infirmarer (the Abbey official who

[1] Seler—cellar.

had charge of the sick), was the mansion of Beodric, who was of old time the lord of the town, and after whom also the town came to be called Beodricsworth. His demesne lands are now in the demesne of the cellarer . . . and the total amount of the holding of himself and his churls was thirty times thirty acres of land. . . ."

T. 280 (C. MCCCXVIII) is a lease for seventy years by Abbot John Gruffydd to Jevan ap David ap Jankyn and his wife of two parcels of the tithes of the sheaves at Ffynon Gattuke, one of which belongs to the "Domus Sutorum," or the shoemaker's house, of the Abbey of Margam, and the other parcel to the *subselaria* of the Abbey. Subsellaria is the sub-cellarer's house.

T. 4120 is a lease by Sir Edward Mansell of a messuage and tenement in the parish of Margam, manor of East Margam and Higher Kenfigge, called "The Cellar." This is Ty'n Seler. Dated A.D. 1692.

Here, then, we have the key to the meaning of Ty'n-y-Seler, the farm or homestead assigned to the cellarer of Margam Abbey or the homestead of the cellar, the office of the cellarer, shortened by custom into Ty'n-y-Seler. The cellarer was one of the most important of the Abbey officials, the official, in the song of "Simon the Cellarer," existed only in the imagination of the writer. The cellarer was the manager, in fact, of the monastic establishment; he was the purveyor of all foodstuffs for the community; he had to keep an eye on all stores, to see that the corn came into the granges and flour from the mills, that flesh, fish, and vegetables were ready at hand. He had to attend fairs and markets to make purchases. All the servants were under him, and he alone could engage or dismiss, and he presided at their table. He also saw to the fuel supply, repairs and purchases of all materials. The cellarer's accounts, which have come down to us, are models of carefully kept documents ; they invariably commenced with the entry of the cost of the parchment on which the account is written.

John de la Warre, cellarer of Margam Abbey, became Abbot in A.D. 1237, and Bishop of Llandaff in A.D. 1253.

Ty-yn-y-seler, Ty-yn-y-ffynnon, shortened into Ty'n-y-seler, ty'n-y-ffynnon, regarded as the house in the cellar and the house in the well, is nonsense. Properly it should be Tyddyn-y-Seler—the homestead of the cellar, and Tyddyn-y-ffynnon—the homestead of the well. " Tyddyn seems to mean a 'house-hill,' *i.e.* a place suited for a house.   *Ty*, a house—in old Welsh, *tig*—is for *tegios*, corresponding to the Greek Τέγος (a house).   From the word *tig* is partly derived the word *tyddyn*, plural *tyddynau*.   In modern Welsh place-names *tyddyn* is reduced to *tyn*, as *Ty'n yr onnen* for Tyddyn yr onnen ; *Ty'n Siarlas* for Tyddyn Siarlas (Charles's tenement)." [1]

Lewis, in the " Ancient Laws of Wales," writes :— " Tyddyn : this word also denoted an acre of land with the homestead on it. The Venedotian Code gives maenor (in place of the trev) = 4 trevs = 16 rhandirs (sharelands) = 64 gavaels = 256 tyddyns = 1,024 erws.   The erw was the unit of occupied land, and

[1] " The Welsh People," Rhys and Jones

it was measured with the plough." The same author
says : " The measure of a lawful acre, *i.e.* erw, is a
rod of the length of the tallest man in the vill, with
the length of his arm ; sixty lengths of that rod are to
be the length of the erw ; its breadth is the length of
that rod on either side of the driver, with the length of
his arm, he holding the middle of the middle yoke in
the plough."

The Maenhîr at Ty'n-y-Seler.

Standing in a field, near Ty'n-y-seler, is a large
monolith or maenhîr 8 feet high, 5½ feet wide, and
3 feet thick. Miss Emily David, Maesgwyn, informed
me that it is said in the neighbourhood this huge
stone goes each Christmas morning before cockcrow,
to drink in the sea.

When we look at this great solitary stone we are
apt to wonder, as probably did the Romans fifteen
hundred years ago, and ask—many have asked me—
What is the meaning of it ; for what purpose was it
placed there ? It has no inscription on it, nothing to
indicate to us the reason for its standing there ; grim
and impassive it stands.

We must look to other parts, where knowledge has
been gained regarding these monoliths, for the key
with which to unlock the secret.

The Rev. S. Baring-Gould, in a book on Brittany,
writes : " The *menhir* is an upright stone, standing
alone; but one cannot be certain that it is not a solitary
stone spared from a row that has been destroyed.   In
England, this is nearly always the case.   Sometimes

13

these upright stones have hollows worked in them—
cup marks—that have been objects of much specula-
tion.   Councils of the Church in Gaul expressly
forbade the anointing of obelisks, and to the present
day peasants still daub them with honey, wax, or
oil. . . .

"The *alignment* is a series of parallel rows of
upright stones, erected in honour of a dead chief,
each household contributing a stone. . . . On Dart-
moor, where there are over a quarter of a hundred of
these stone-rows, all without exception start from a
tomb.   In one instance, where three bodies had been
buried in as many stone boxes in one cairn, three
rows start from the same mound. . . . The custom
was never wholly discontinued.   With the advent
of the Britons,[1] menhirs continued to be set up,
and were called *lechs*,[2] some bearing inscriptions, but
many without.   Indeed, it was usual for a saint when
he travelled to take his *lech* with him, ready to be
planted at his head when he died.   A great number
of these remain."

I pity the poor saint who may have carried the
Ty'n-y-Seler *lech* about with him!

In Brittany there are immense maenhirs.   One at
Dol is twenty-eight feet above the surface, and sixteen
feet of it is embedded below.   The Men-er-H'roech

[1] The Iberian, Ivernian, or Silurian race—the race which
underlies the population of all Western Europe.   It came from
Asia, and crossing Europe, reached and spread over Britain and
also Ireland.   This is the race which left these maenhirs and
other monuments.   Later, the Gauls conquered these people.
Then came the Roman domination.

[2] Welsh *llech*, a stone.

MAENHIR AT TY'N-Y-SELER.

at Locmariaquer was sixty-four feet high before it was shattered by lightning.

Mr. Bertram Windle, in "Remains of the Pre-historic Age in England," writes : "The menhir or standing-stone is as ancient an institution as it is world-wide, and, in the shape of obelisks and monuments, persistent. Such stones . . . are some-times met with in conjunction with other varieties of megaliths. Sometimes, as at the Tingle-stone barrow, the menhir is on the mound ; sometimes as at Ablington, it is inside the chamber of burial ; sometimes it is embedded in the substance of the mound itself. Again, the menhir may be quite isolated and independent of other ancient remains. Perhaps this is the most common occurrence."

It is possible, therefore, that the Ty'n-y-Seler maenhir may be the only remaining stone of a row of others, or it may be an independent standing-stone marking the burial-place of a great chief of prehistoric days. I am inclined to think it always stood alone. If it means little to us to-day, it was an important object to those who lived long, long before us ; it was placed there as a memorial of a man looked up to by his people.[1]

[1] Mr. Evan John, of Ty'n-y-Seler, recently told me of a large stone lying on Margam Moors, and of the tradition in the neigh-bourhood about it, that Samson threw it from near the "Pound" at Margam, to where it lies, five-sixths of a mile away. I found it to be a maenhir lying on the ground, partly covered with earth and over-grown by a thorn-bush. Having regard to its position it may have had some relation to the maenhir at Ty'n-y-Seler, from which it stands north-west about one and an eighth mile, and half a mile outside of Kenfig Borough boundary to

What an interesting district is this! Here we have a monument of prehistoric times, a highway of Roman times, and a mediæval castle all within a small area.

Now, after this long digression, I hope my readers will not think it amiss if I return to dry manuscripts—dry to some, maybe, but delightful to me.

the north, in Margam Parish. The stone measures nine feet in length, six feet in width, and one foot in thickness, but a large flake of stone near had evidently been split off it, so that it was formerly much thicker. It probably weighed nearly four tons originally and must have been an imposing monument when upright. When the ditch was made near the stone, in the time of the monks, it was carried partly round it, and I have no doubt the digging of the ditch caused the fall of the stone.

This maenhir stood in a peculiar position, for at high-water of spring tides, before the first of the sea walls was constructed, it would be surrounded by the tidal waters.

CHAPTER IX

THE GRAMUS FAMILY AND OTHER LANDOWNERS

I CANNOT write of Kenfig without mentioning an important family of landowners, and to make the account more interesting, I am able to tell you the names of the wives of some of them.

Thomas Gramus, or Grammus, as the name is variously spelled, lived in The Hall at Corneli, and he and his family owned part of the lands near there, and also in other parts. They, from time to time, parted with their lands to Margam Abbey, and so it is that we know of them through the ancient MSS. of the monastery.

Gillebert Gramus,[1] as we have seen in the chapter on the town, page 155, gave to Margam Abbey ten acres of land beginning at Kenfig River and then along the ancient cemetery. Aliz, his wife, gave her consent. Gilbert, Abbot of Margam, one of the witnesses, occurs A.D. 1203–1213. Ernald, constable of Kenfig, another, occurs in the time of Morgan ap Caradoc.

I may say of the first of the family nothing is

[1] Gillebert Gramus's charters were confirmed by Pope Innocent III. in A.D. 1203.

known, beyond the name of his son, Richard, who appears as a witness in early deeds; the relationship of Gillebert to Richard is not ascertainable.

Gillebert's son Roger married Agnes, and had four sons and a daughter : (1) Thomas, heir, occurs in A.D. 1245-1264—he married Ysota (Yseud, Ysoud, or Isota) the sister of William Luvel, and had a son Philip; (2) Hugh, had a son Thomas ; (3) Roger, occurs in A.D. 1245—his wife was Alice. (4) Maurice, occurs in A.D. 1253-1261—he married Johanna, daughter of Philip ap David of Kenfig; (5) Alice, married Roger Palmer. William Gramus seems to have been the last of the family ; he was a witness to a deed in A.D. 1312.

Roger Gramus, senior, by *Harley Charter* 75, C. 3 (C. DCCIII), leases for ten years from Christmas, A.D. 1202, to the monks of Margam his part of the land between Kenfig and Goilache, Afon fach, for ten marks paid beforehand, with power to the monks to renew the lease. Pledged in the hands of Osmer : " Et sciendum quod affidavi in manu Osmeri me hoc totum servare sine omni dolo et sine omni malo ingenio." This phrase "affidavi in manu" occurs frequently in the Margam deeds, and relates to the practice mentioned by Giraldus Cambrensis[1] in the chapter on the Welsh nation, "and so lightly do they esteem the covenant of faith, held so inviolable by other nations, that it is usual to sacrifice their faith for nothing, by holding forth the right hand, not only in serious and important matters, but even on every

[1] "Itinerary through Wales," by Giraldus Cambrensis. A.D. 1188.

trifling occasion, and for the confirmation of almost every common assertion." Mr. J. H. Round says in *Geoffrey de Mandeville* that the custom survives in some places.

Thomas, chaplain of Kenefeg; Walter Luvel; Thomas the miller, and others, are witnesses to Roger's deed.

Roger, by *Harley Charter* 75, C. 5, grants, with assent of his wife Agnes, and Thomas his son and Isota his wife, to Hugh his son, for his homage, two and a half acres of land near that of Maurice Gramus on the west, and the stream called Goyelake on the north and south; rent yearly, three halfpence. Eight shillings premium to the grantor and five shillings to Thomas.

Witnesses: Walter Luvel; W. de Corneli;[1] Wasmer,[2] and others.

The bearing on the ✠ S ROGERI: GRAMUS seal is a fleur-de-lis. ✠ SIGIL'. THOME. GRAMUS.

Hugh Gramus, soon after, parted with his two and a half acres of land to the Abbot of Margam, as we find from the next deed.

Harley Charter 75, C. 6 (C. DCCV), is a confirmation by Roger and his son Thomas Gramus, his heir, to the monks of two and a half acres of arable land which Hugh Gramus held, and gave to the Abbey by charter, paying yearly therefor to Roger and

---

[1] Occurs in A.D. 1245.

[2] Wasmer, derived from *was, gwas,* "a servant," *mer=mair* Mary; the servant of Mary, probably the servant of St. Mary's Church, Margam.

Thomas 2½d., and to the House of St. John of Jerusalem 1d. Witnesses : Walter Luvel ; Richard the clerk, and others.

T. 289, 25 is a confirmation by Roger, son of Gille Gramus, of the gift to the Abbey of his free tenement adjacent to the water of Kenefeg. Witnesses': William de Lichesfield, William Punchardun, monks ; William de Bordeslée, Richard Cnitth, conversi ; Tomas de Corneli ; Gille Gramus ; Adam Gramus, and others.

The *conversi* were lay brethren, who, according to Cistercian custom, worked on the farms or granges.

Roger Gramus, by a deed dated A.D. 1203, T. 289, 27 (C. DCCIV), granted to Margam Abbey all the land from the Great Stone, directly opposite Cohilake, Afon fach, on the east, and on the south of the highway leading towards Castle-Kibur, in fee farm for half a mark. Ten years' rent paid beforehand. The witnesses are the same as in the previous deed.

Cohilake is another variant of Goylake. Castle Kibur is the British encampment on the west end of Cefn Cribwr ; a farm near it is called Pen Castell. I believe all earthwork camps which were used later by the Normans were afterwards known as castles. I do not know of the Great Stone. Probably it has been broken up for road mending, as is often the case.

In another deed, T. 289, 26, Roger confirmed to the Abbey the land between the high-road from Kenfig to Castle Kibur and the water of Kenefeg, which his father gave to the monks, also marl from his marl-pit. Walter Luvel and Ernald, the constable of Kenefeg, are among the witnesses.

I have already, in the reference to the highway and Pont Felin Newydd, or Kenfig bridge, mentioned a deed by Thomas Gramus, Roger's son and heir.

Harley Charter 75, C. 12 (C. DCCCLXXXVIII), is a confirmation by Thomas Gramus, with assent of Ysota his wife, to his brother Maurice of four and a half acres of land, two of which lie near the land of Henry Baret on the east side, two near the land of Hugh Juvenis on the west side, from the high-road as far as Goylake, half an acre lies between the land the monks had by gift of Hugh Gramus (see gift by Hugh Gramus *supra*) and the land of Thomas Gramus towards Goylake, at a yearly rent of 4d. at Ockeday,[1] and for three marks silver and 18d. premium. Walter Luvel and Roger Gramus are among the witnesses.

Harley Charter 75, C. 13 T. 289, 50 (C. DCCCCXCI). In this, Thomas Gramus sells to the Abbot and Convent of Margam for four shillings a rent of fivepence in which they were bound, viz. : fourpence for his brother Maurice's land and a penny for his fee. Walter Luvel is one of the witnesses.

Harley Charter 75, C. 9 (C. DCCCCXXII), is a quit claim by Thomas Gramus to Hugh, his brother, of his right to the land which their father gave to Roger Palmer, brother-in-law of the above Thomas,

[1] Dr. E. C. Brewer, in "Dictionary of Phrase and Fable," says : "Hock-day, or Hock-Tuesday, the day when the English surprised and slew the Danes, who had annoyed them for 255 years. This Tuesday was long held as a festival in England, and landlords received an annual tribute called *Hock-money* for allowing their tenants and serfs to commemorate Hock-day, which was the second Tuesday after Easter-day."

lying between the land of Adam Alberd and that of John the priest.   For this deed Richard Flandrensis, (or Fleming), constable of Kenefeg, for love of Hugh, the grantor's brother, gave him a pair of boots (*par estivalium*)[1] worth 18d., and a *sisa*[2] of beer to Ysota, the grantor's wife.   Pledged in the hand of Thomas, priest of Laniltwit.   Richard Flandrensis and Walter Luvel are among the witnesses.

Harley Charter 76, C. 8 (C. CXX.).   Thomas again, with Isud's consent, grants to Hugh, son of Hugh, two acres of arable land on the high-road to Goilake, eight rods wide, rent 2d., and 2 silver marks consideration money.   Witnesses : William de Corneli, William Cole,[3] Gilbert de Neth, Henry de Neth, William de Sancto Donato, Adekin Jurdan.

T. 289, 44 (C. DCCCCXXV).   This is a grant by Thomas to the Abbey of three acres of land in the culture of Deumay, from Goylake stream to the road leading from Kenefeg to Catteputte, two adjacent to the land of Maurice, his brother, on the east, and the third to that of Thomas Russell, also on the east.

Harley Charter 75, C. 11. T. 289, 41 (C. DCCCCXXI). By this deed Thomas Gramus, with consent of Ysota his wife, confirms the release of Roger Gramus, his father, of half a silver mark to the monks, which they were bound to pay yearly, with due recognisance of a pair of white gloves, or one penny at Easter.   The deed is attested by William de Corneli, Richard the

---

[1] Estivalia—*ocreæ, species calceorum* (boots, kind of shoes)—Du Cange.

[2] A barrel of some size.

[3] Occurs in A.D. 1244.

clerk, David Wasmeir, and others. Dated Midsummer Day, A.D. 1245.

T. 144, 289,38 (C. DCCCCXXVIII), is a quit-claim by Thomas Gramus, with assent of Ysota his wife, to Margam Abbey of a rent of threepence halfpenny due by the Abbey to him for three acres and a half of land held of the gift of his brother Hugh. He swears on the *sacrosancta* [1] that he will never sell, give, or alienate any of his land against the will of the monks, but if he is compelled to do so, the monks to have the option of acquiring it. Witnesses: Walter Luvel, David Wasmeyr, and others. Dated 1 May, A.D. 1245.

On the day of the Invention of Holy Cross, 3 May, A.D. 1254, Thomas Gramus pawns six acres of his land to the Abbot and Convent of Margam for ten pounds silver.

T. 165 (C. MCCCCXXXII) is the acquittance by the above for ten pounds silver for six acres of land with appurtenances, of which three acres lie next to the acre which the monks had of him before on the west of Thomas Russel's land, and in length extending from the stream of Goylake to the highway that leads from Kenefeg to Catteputte, *i.e.*, Pwll-y-gâth. Two of them lie in the culture called Deumay adjacent to the road which leads from his house to the highway which leads from Kenefeg to the aforesaid Catteputte, except three acres of his land lying in between; and in length extends from the said stream of Goylake as far as the

---

[1] The relics of saints and martyrs and a piece of wood of the true cross, which were contained in a cross which stood on the high altar of Margam Church.

aforesaid highway. The sixth acre lies on the south of Goylake, near the said monks' land, and extends in length from Water Luvel's land called Heuedaker, or Hevedaker, as far as the said Goylake, having his (Thomas's) lands on the west part. At a rent of 6d; the land redeemable by repayment of the ten pounds silver to the abbot and convent.

This is an interesting deed. Thomas Gramus's house is now called The Hall, at North Corneli, just east of the boundary between Kenfig and Pyle; the road he mentions as leading from his house to the highway is the path and lane still existing, they join the road east, a little, of Marlas farm, at this point a little altered by the making of the Great Western Railway. The Hall, or part of it, is therefore a very ancient dwelling.

Thus we learn the situation of Hevedaker—doubtless Hafod-decaf, the fairest summer abode—which lies between Marlas and The Hall. It is certainly a fair and sunny spot. Walter Luvel, Philip de Corneli, Wm. Frankelyn, and others are witnesses. Endorsed · " Carta Thome Gramus de X. libris."

For one reason or other the Abbot and Convent of Margam managed to get possession of the above pawned six acres of land, and they lost no time; for on Whitsunday, 31 May, A.D. 1254, Thomas gave the land to God and the Church of Blessed Mary of Margam. The situation of the land is described in the same terms as the deed of pawn. The witnesses are the same. Endorsed : " Carta Thome Gramus de sex acris terre."

✠ SIGILL'. THOME GRAMUS.

I think at this time Ysota must have been dead—
Thomas does not mention her name; had she been
alive Thomas would have been obliged to obtain her
consent. I find since writing this Ysoude was still
alive, for in A.D. 1261 Thomas asks her consent
to another gift of land.

Thomas Gramus borrows again from the monks.
T. 168, 289, 52 (C. DCCCCLXXIV) is a deed of
mortgage to Margam Abbey, for a loan of ten marks
for forty years, of all his land between Goylake on the
south and the land called Longelonde on the north
Henry Bareth's on the east, and Alice Gramus's land
on the west, except one acre which William Frankeleyn holds. A rent of fourpence yearly accruing is to
be reckoned against the Abbey, so as to reduce the
repayment to the sum of nine marks.

T. 280, 56 (C. DCCCCLXXV) is a grant by
Thomas Gramus to the Abbey of half an acre of land
which Alice Gramus formerly bought of the grantor
between Goylake and Langeland, but he redeemed it.
To be held with the land called Sculue in frank
almoign. Dated A.D. 1258. I do not know the
location of the land Sculue, or Scilwe, or La Schilue.

Thomas Gramus appears to have been an important
personage, judging from the following document :

T. 164, 289, 63 (C. DCCCCLXI) is a grant by
John Bareth, clerk, son of Henry Bareth, of Kenefeg,
with assent of *his lord*, Thomas Gramus, to the Abbey
of three acres of arable land in the culture of Deumay,
from Goylake to Langelond.

Witnesses : W. Frankeleyn, Maurice Gramus, and
others.

Thomas Gramus mortgaged by deed T. 172 (C. DCCCCLXXXIX) to the abbot an acre of arable land at Gretehulle,[1] near the monks' land on the west, and along the north from the grantor's land near Goylake as far as Walter Luvel's land, and it is five rods in width, for thirty shillings, in goods and money, and 1d. rent yearly, with power of redemption for thirty shillings, notwithstanding any prohibition of the King or the Earl.

Walter Luvel, Philip the clerk of Kenefeg, and others are witnesses. Dated A.D. 1261.

This acre of land passed to the monks soon after, for T. 167, 289, 61 (C. DCCCCXC) is a grant of it, with assent of Ysoud his wife, to Margam Abbey. The same witnesses. Dated on St. Thomas's Day, 21 Dec., 1261.

He further granted, T. 289, 62 (C. DCCCCXXVII), with assent of Yseuda his wife, to the Abbey two acres of land upon Gretehulle. Philip de Corneli and others are witnesses.

Harley Charter 75, C. 10 (C. DCCCCXXIX) is a grant by Thomas Gramus, with assent of Ysota his wife, to William Frankelain of an acre of land stretching from Goylake to Scilwe, next to the acre of Hugh Gramus on the west side, which Roger Gramus, the grantor's brother, held, at a yearly rent of 1d., and eleven shillings and ten pence consideration money beforehand.

Witnesses: Matthew the chaplain, Henry de Neth, William, Thomas, and Philip Cole, and others.

---

[1] Gretehulle, or Greathill, is the hill south of the old railway station at Pyle.

CHARTER OF WILLIAM FRANKELEIN

[To face page 207

Harley Charters 75, A. 38, 39, T. 289, 55 (C. CXXXIII) give an agreement between Margam Abbey and William Frankelein, by which William mortgaged for 30 years from St. Mark's Day, 25 April, A.D. 1258, the acre of land given him by Thomas Gramus, for one mark, with power of redemption on paying the mark, and cost of improvement; 2d. to be reckoned off the money as yearly rent.

Thomas Grammus and others witnesses.

A photograph of Harley Charter 75, A. 38 is given, and the Latin text is given in full.

Hec est conventio facta inter abbatem et conventum de Margam ex parte una recipientem et Willelmum Frankelein tradentem ex altera videlicet quod dictus Willelmus dictis abbati et conventui invadiavit unam acram terre sue cum pertinenciis tenendum et habendum a festo Sancti Marchi evangeliste anno domini MCC quinquagesimo octavo usque ad finem triginta annorum continue subsequentium pro una marca argenti sibi ab eisdem premanibus pacata que scilicet jacet inter has divisas et se extendit in longum versus GOYLAKE ex parte australi et ex parte boreali versus La Schilue et in latum jacet inter terram Henrici Vachan ipsam vicinam habens ex parte occidentali ex parte vero orientali terram dicti abbatis et conventus. Et sciendum quod si dictus Willelmus vel heredes sui dictam acram post dictum terminum acquietare voluerint; dictam marcam cum custo melioracionis ejusdem terre dictis abbati et conventui restituent. Singulis tamen annis per terminum prefatum de dicta marca nomine redditus duo denarii remittantur.

Et dictus Willelmus et heredes sui dictam acram cum pertinenciis dictis abbati et conventui per totum dicti temporis spacium contra omnes mortales warantizabunt. Hanc vero convencionem sine dolo ex utraque parte tenendam fidei caucione prestita et sigillorum suorum impressionibus presens scriptum in modum cyrographi confectum et inter se divisum alternatim munierunt. Hiis testibus Thoma grammus Philippo de corneli Mauricio grammus Thoma russel Waltero herebert et aliis.

There are two copies, the deed and counterpart. The abbot's seal is appended; an abbot standing holding a crozier and book, white wax in red, very imperfect, the other has the seal of William de Bonneville.

The Abbey soon got possession of this acre. *Harley Charter* 75, B. 47 (C. DCCCCXXXVIII) is a grant to the monks of this piece of land, in length from Goylake to Seylve, by William Frankelyn, which he had of the gift of Thomas Gramus, at a yearly rent of 1d. to the heirs of Thomas.

Witnesses : Walter Luvel, Maurice de Corneli, and others.

T. 143, 289, 39 (C. DCCCCXXIII.) is a grant by Hugh, son of Roger Gramus, to Margam Abbey of two and a half acres of land which Roger Gramus, with assent of Thomas his heir, gave to the grantor, near the land of Maurice Gramus and Goylake stream, one acre of land which Thomas his brother gave him; it begins on the south from the said stream and stretches to La Chilue (yet another spelling of the curious word), and is five rods wide; and land at

Kenefeg, which Roger, son of Roger Gramus, gave him.

Walter Luvel, Roger and Thomas Gramus, and others are witnesses.

A small seal bearing three chevronels.

✠ S I G I L L' : H V G O N I S : G R A M V S.

Thomas, the chaplain of Kenefeg, son of William de St. Donats, granted, T. 175, 289, 64 (C. DCCCCXCVII) to the Abbey one acre of arable land in the fee of Kenefeg, which he bought of Thomas Gramus, at La Marle, viz., Marlas, between the lands held by John Faber, or the blacksmith, and John le Hoppare, of the said Thomas, beginning from la Hamme, next Goylake, and extending to the land which Walter Luvel gave to Ysota, his sister, wife of Thomas Gramus, in free marriage, at the yearly rent of 1d. to Thomas Gramus.

Witnesses : D. Hugh, sheriff of Kenefeg, and others. Dated St. Luke's Day, 18 Oct. A.D. 1264.

La Hamme I am unable to locate ; it is near Goylake stream.

Roger, son of Roger Gramus, granted—*Harley Charter* 75, C. 4 (C.DCCCCXIX)—to his brother Hugh his land between that of John the priest and that which belonged to Adam Alberd, at the yearly rent of a pair of white gloves, or ½d., at St. James' fair. Premium of 40s. sterling, and a jewel worth 12d. to the grantor's wife.

Witnesses : Richard Flandrensis, constable of Kenfeg ; Walter Luvel ; John the priest, who wrote the charter, and others.

14

The following deed is another example of the manner in which the monks obtained property, giving an equivalent in food.

Harley Charter 75, C. 7, T. 289 40 (C. DCCCCXX) is a quit-claim by Roger Gramus to the Abbey of a rent of half a silver mark yearly, due of the monks to him, paying a yearly recognisance of a pair of white gloves, or 1d. at Easter; and to provide Agnes his wife with a prebend [1] for her support, viz., every week seven conventual loaves and five gallons of beer of the convent; a crannoc [2] of *gruellum* (meal), the same amount of beans, and a bushel of salt, yearly at Michaelmas.

Same witnesses as in the other deeds of this time. Dated Midsummer Day, A.D. 1245.

Maurice Gramus, of Corneli Borealis, or North Corneli, by *Harley Charter* 75, C. 16 (C. DCCCCLX), confirmed and quit claimed to the monks of Margam all the land and possessions which his ancestors gave to them.

Witnesses: John Le Boteler of Donrevyn, or Dunraven, co. Glam.; Maurice de Cornely Australi, or South Corneli; John Peruat; Walter de Magor, and others.

✠ S. MAVRICII GRAMMVS.

We have seen that Maurice Gramus married

---

[1] A prebend, I should say, is the same as a corrody.

[2] Crannock. An Irish measure, which in the time of Edward II. contained either eight or sixteen pecks (Dr. E. C. Brewer in "Dictionary of Phrase and Fable").

Crannoc.—Crynog, an ancient local measure used in the district previous to the Uniformity Act, 1826. It was equal to ten bushels "Hist. of Llangynwyd," by *Cadrawd*.

Johanna, daughter of Philip ap David ; the latter now mortgages with his son-in-law his four acres of land. In the deed Johanna is named Joan.

Harley Charter 75, B. 44 (C. DCCCCLIV); Philip, son of David, burgess of Kenefech, mortgages or impignorates with Maurice Gramus, his son-in-law, *genero meo*, four acres of land in Pollardeslade, lying between the acre of the said Maurice on the north part, "which I gave him with Joan my daughter in free marriage," and in breadth to William, son of Herbert's acre for 10 marks sterling ; with power of redemption within ten years at the same price, and a pair of gloves only every year if not redeemed within the period.

Witnesses : Walter Luvel and others.   Dated on St. Ambrose's Day, 4 April, A.D. 1253.   Seal a quatrefoil.

✠ S . P H I L I P P I : D A V I D.

The little stream, the Goylake, of which we hear so much in the deeds of the Gramus family, is now called the Avon fach—little river.   I am surprised at the loss of names in the neighbourhood.   I constantly notice brooks and lanes in Margam parish which bear no longer any distinctive names, as they did hundreds of years ago.

The Goylake commences in various springs east of the turnpike road at Pyle, one or two of them being at Stormy, the, chief spring being Ffynnon-y-Maen.   After pursuing a tranquil, independent existence, it falls into the Kenfig river at the point where the latter, as if reluctant to lose itself in the Severn Sea too quickly, turns to the north and appears to be hastening to the mountains whence it came. A small cottage, with a neighbour, each embattled round with green defence, stands just above the junction; it is called Plwerin, which perhaps is Pwll-eirin—the hollow of the plum-trees—the hollow just beneath.

The following grant brings to our notice a curious custom connected with the monastic life.

T. 2013 is a grant by Richard Norrensis, or Norreis, to the monks of Margam of one acre of land near the stream which divides the land of Pishulle, at Kenfig, from the grantor's land. The grantor, his wife and sons, *are received into the fraternity of the monastery*.

Witnesses: Maurice de Cantelo. Robert Samson, Cradoc the physician, Philip, the priest of Lambernagd. Seal, a wyvern with a human face.

It seems a little startling to read of a whole family being received into a monastic brotherhood; and it is frequently met with in the Margam MSS.; the women of the family also!

Immediately after the conclusion of the morning Mass at the Abbey the great bell was set ringing for the daily Chapter about nine in the morning; the doors were all fastened, so that no one could enter the precincts of the monastery during the time of the Chapter. All the business of the monastery was transacted at this meeting, and all faults corrected. Then arrived the time when such matters as the issuing of public letters of thanks or congratulations, etc., in the name of the community, were sanctioned, and the granting of the privilege of the fraternity of the house to benefactors or people of distinction. When the actual ceremony of conferring this favour, which was both lengthy and solemn, was to be performed, it was at this point that the *confratres* and *consorores* were introduced into the Chapter. After the ceremony the *confratres* received the kiss of peace from all the religious; the *consorores* kissed the hand of each of the monks.[1] This, then, is the meaning of the reception of Richard Norreis, wife and family, into the fraternity of the monastery of Margam.

Another instance is that of Thomas Lageles, or Lales, from whom Laleston takes its name. Lageles and his family were great benefactors of Margam Abbey, and when he made his final gift to the monks he "placed the charter on the altar, which he kissed in the presence of the convent, who received him as a brother and partaker of all its goods until the end."

The Palmer family now come upon the scene, and the following deeds are of the date of A.D. 1266, 1267.

T. 183 (C. MVII) is a grant by Thomas, son of Robert Raul, to Philip, son of Robert Palmer, or le Paumer, of Kenefec, of one acre of arable land in the manor of Kenefec, on the south part of Goielake, along from Goielake to the land that belonged to William Cole, having on the east land of Cecilia, daughter of Alexander, and on the west that of William, son of Herebert, for due service to the lords of Kenefec, for 25s. paid, in *gersuma*, beforehand. (See page 87.)

Witnesses : Symon Tinctor, William de Pola, Roger Galun, burgesses of Tetteburi,[2] and others.

---

[1] From "Monastic Life," by Abbot Gasquet.

[2] Tetbury is a market town in Gloucestershire, ten miles south-west of Cirencester.

The business of these burgesses so far from home is not stated ; probably they were either buying or selling, perhaps both.   Symon Tinctor is Symon the dyer.

Philip, son of Robert Palmer, soon after gave his acre of land, which he bought from Thomas Raul in the preceding deed, to Margam Abbey.   T. 289, 58 (C.MII) is the deed.   Under seal of Thomas Gramus, as Philip has no seal.

T. 181 (C.MIV) is an impignoration or mortgage by the said Philip Palmer, and Amabilia his wife, to the Abbey, of three and a half acres of land in the manor of Kenefeg, for ten marks paid beforehand viz., all the land which Cecilia, daughter of Alexander, gave them in free marriage, on the east of the town of Kenefeg in Portlond, near the new foss, having on all sides the monks' land ; redeemable within thirty years, but the monks are to have the croppings for the whole term, as they have undertaken to find the said Philip and his wife food and support for their lives. All Saints' Day, 1266.

T. 182 (C.MVI) is a grant by the same Philip, and Amabilia his wife, to the Abbey of the above three and a half acres of arable land at Portlond, in the fee of Kenefeg, which Cecilia, daughter of Alexander, gave them in free marriage.   Under seal of William Frankeleyn, because they have no seals.   Witnesses : the Chaplain of Kenefeg ; William, son of Alexander, and others.   Feast of SS. Philip and James, A.D. 1267.

Here we have another instance of land being first mortgaged to the monks and afterwards made over to them.

There is another grant by the same persons of the

same land to the Abbey under seal of David Wasmeir, as they have no seal, T. 154 (C. MV).

The same Philip and his wife granted a messuage to the Abbey in the town. This deed is referred to in the article on the town.

Portlond, or Portland, is the land east of St. Mary Magdelene's Chapel, and the lands along the Kenfig. The people call it Porklond, as if it were an affectation to name a thing correctly. Porth is a gate or a door, also a port or haven, but it does not in this case refer to a port or haven. We have a similar word in Hafod-y-Porth. A Bull of Alexander IV. A.D. 1261, under Margam, mentions *Hauoto portarii*—Hafod of the gate-keeper. I believe this is an error of the scribe, who was an Italian in the Papal Chancery, and stumbled over the unusual words. The narrow neck at the commencement of the Dyffryn valley near the mill being the porth or gate, for once the neck is passed the valley opens out. In like manner the porth or gorge at Llanfihangel has given the land to the east of it the name Portland—land of the gate or opening. The path leading from Llanfihangel mill to Pyle Church passes a pistle called Pystyll-y-Portland, much resorted to by persons having limbs which are healing after fractures, for its strengthening qualities. The Newditch of Thomas Le Despenser's charter and the new foss of the mortgage T. 181 by Philip Palmer is the leat conveying water to Llanfihangel mill.

Abbot Thomas demised by T. 192 (C. MLXXX) to John le Yonge, burgess of Kenefeg, for his life, land formerly belonging to the office of the master of the works of our New Church, viz., three acres of arable land lying between the land of John Peruat and that of Robert de Cantelou, on the road between Kenefeg and Cardiff, towards Corneli; and between the road near Dame Alice grove and the land of Walter Luvel. Rent 2s. and 10s. consideration money. Margam, Sunday, 25 July, A.D. 1307.

"Our New Church" refers probably to the early English part of Margam Abbey Church. Dame Alice grove I am unable to locate; probably the name is lost in obscurity.

T. 2805. This is a mortgage by the above-named John Le Yonge of Kenefeg to Thomas le Tylar of Kenefeg of two acres of arable land of his free tenement in the lordship of Kenefeg in Passeleuisfelde for 4 marks and 8d. One acre lies in length between the way from Kenefeg towards (Cornelidon?) on the S. and the way from Kenefeg towards Nothasse the N. (if this is Nottage it should be S.), and in length between the land of Walter Thomelyn on the W. and that of Elena le Yonge on the E.; the other acre lies in length between the land of John Marzhog on the E., and the way from Kenefeg to Northasse on the W., and in breadth between the land of John Norris on the S. and that of Thomas Courog on the N., for four years from Michaelmas, A.D. 1327, and so by terms of four years until payment of the said 4 marks 8d. be made; the mortgagee to have preemption if the land be sold. Witnesses: Henry Colyn and others.

Dated Kenefeg, Sunday after Feast of S. Peter in Cathedra, 22 Feb., 1327 for 1328.

T. 3052. This is a confirmation by William de Cornely, son and heir of Roger de Cornely, to the monks of St. Mary's Abbey of Neth, of two acres of arable land in the fee of Cornely which his said father gave them for food and clothing, by the boundaries according to his father's charter. He also grants them a third acre and release of 3d. yearly rent due for the above two acres, which lie between the lands of John Adam and William Kyng, and from the land called Betynges on the north to W. Kyng's and on the south, because they (the monks) treated his father honourably in food and clothing as long as he lived. He is to pay 10 marks if he cannot warrant the three acres. Witnesses · John de Creppynge, sheriff, Maurice de Cornely and others. Whitsunday, 17 May, A.D. 1293. Here we see the Abbot of Neath helping a man in his need and receiving gifts of land in return.

T. 1969 is a grant by Zewan ab Hagarath ; Knaytho, Mayhoc, David, Gwronu, Ithenard, and Wastmer, sons of Zewan ; Wurgan, Meuroch, Reis and Madoch, sons of Wurgan Du ; and Richard Gethin, to William Alexander, of thirteen acres of arable land in Kenefeg Manor, at Balles, lying on the south, between the land of the Abbot and Convent of Margam, called Tangi-stelonde, and the common pasture called Duna de Cornely on the east of the land of Philip de Corneli called the croft of Yltuit, on the west of Tangistelonde, to be held of the chief Lord of Kenefeg at a yearly rent of 19½d.—premium paid, 100s.

Sureties.—Griffin, Meuroch, Reis Voil, sons of Res Coiz ; William and Madoc, sons of Yeruard ab

Espus; Madoc Vachan, Traherne ab Reis, Madoc ab Ithenard, Leulin ab Griffith, Lewelin ab Annarod.

Witnesses.—William Scurlag, constable of Langunith, Walter Luvel and others.

Endorsed : Charter of the Welshmen in the land of Ballis exchanged with William Alexander. Late twelfth century.

This land lies south of Ty Tanglwys (Tangistelonde) at Old Ballas, between Ty Tanglwys and Corneli Down.

In the "Annales de Theokesberia" is the entry, A.D. 1227. "Gilbertus Comes Glocestrie invenit minera argenti in Wallis, ferri et plumbi ;" "Gilbert Earl of Gloucester discovered in Wales minerals of silver iron and lead."

This was probably at South Corneli, for we have interesting information in some of the Margam MSS. which shows early searching for minerals in Kenfig manor. Near Ty Coch, on the east side of the road leading from Newton Nottage to South Corneli, are some old ironstone workings. It is known that lead exists in the neighbourhood, and silver accompanies lead ore.

Philip son of William de Cornely grants, T. 289, 43 (C. DCCCCLXXVIII), with assent of Amabilia his wife, to Margam Abbey the minerals iron and lead on the east side of the highroad which leads from the new town (Newton Nottage), to the town of Walter Luvel, called Cornely, with power to supplement deficiencies by searching for minerals on all his land and a right of way for his two-wheel and four-wheel carts. Rent a pair of gloves, or 1d. so long as the mineral holds out ; 20s. beforehand.

Walter Luvel, with assent of Angarat his wife, grants by T. 289,47 (C. DCCCCLVI) to the monks all manner of iron and lead mineral throughout his land wherever it may be found, at an annual rent, as long as they use the same, of a coulter and a ploughshare for his plough yearly at Easter, with free ingress and egress with two-wheel and four-wheel carts when required. The monks gave Luvel for this grant two quarters of wheat on the Feast of St. Mary Magdalene. 22 July, A.D. 1253.

Marlas Farm is pleasantly situated on the south side of the gorge through which the Kenfig river runs. In the bottom of the gorge is Llanfihangel Mill, nearly opposite Marlas, and nearly half a mile to the south-east, is The Hall already referred to.

The house is comparatively modern, but the out-buildings are old, a doorway into the kitchen, some built up windows, and a doorway into the malthouse are parts of the ancient building of, I should say, early Tudor architecture. At the pine-end of the malthouse a chimney supported on three corbels also seems of early date. This chimney was probably added when the building was adapted for use as a malthouse for drying malt.

Marlas is derived from *marl*, the Welsh for marl, and *glas*, *las*, green. It is geologically situated on the green Keuper marl.

William de Marle, whom I now introduce to you, has a high-sounding name, and we would think his ancestors came over with the Conqueror ; not so : he took his name from the grange of Marlas, and besides, his was too mean a nature to have had knightly ancestors "sans peur et sans reproche," as the sequel will show.

He says by special favour of those religious men, the Abbot and Convent of Margam, he was allowed to pasture his oxen, cows, and other animals upon their lands in the grange of S. Michael, Llanfihangel, which pasturage out of levity of mind he had claimed as if he had a right therein. He is, however, now moved by the spirit of truth and quit-claims to the Abbey for himself, his heirs and assigns, all right to the pasture. This deed is T. 277 (C. MCLXVIII). He appends his seal, and as it is not well known to many, John Luvel's seal is also appended. Dated at Margam, Feast of John Baptist, A.D. 1344.

Gratitude was clearly not one of William de Marle's virtues ; evidently he coveted the Abbot's fat pastures. His cattle grew so sleek on those pleasant hills around the sleepy hollow in which lies Llanfihangel Grange that he thought he would claim them.

John Luvel's arms on the seal are : a saltire below four pheons. Between two wyverns

✠ S. IOHANNIS . LOVEL.

St. Michael's Grange is in Margam parish but in the borough of Kenfig, north-east of Marlas (which is in Pyle parish) nearly eight hundred yards, so that the pastures around Llanfihangel Grange were in close proximity to Marle's own lands.

I do not know why the farm or grange is called St. Michael's;[1] it may be that a chapel dedicated to St. Michael was formerly in existence at the grange for the use of the *conversi*, or lay brethren who did the farm work, and also for those working the mill close by. It was invariably the case that chapels were attached to the isolated granges for the use of the *conversi*. Thus at Hafod Farm there was a chapel only taken down within the last forty years; at Penhydd; Cwrt Farm, or the "grangia de Melis," as it is called in one of the MSS., near Port Talbot Station, had the chapel of St. Thomas; Eglwys-nunydd; Hafod heulog and other farms had jointly the chapel of Trisaint (Trissent in some deeds); Craigwyllt Farm; the grange of the Hermitage of Theodoric—all these had their small chapels.

At St. Michael's is an enormous barn 109 feet in length, 31 feet in width, and 18 feet 6 inches in height to the eaves. At first sight the great building looks like a church. In Abbey times it was a tithe-barn. Inside it is plastered to the ceiling; the openings for air and light are widely splayed inwards with quarella stone work dressed to the splay, similar to those in the centre dormer window of the grange of Theodoric's Hermitage.[2] Two great doorways open opposite each other in the centre of the building;

[1] The ancient Abbey of St. Michael has never been located; it is just possible it may have been where the grange now stands. In the "Liber Landavensis" is mentioned "Marchi filius catgen, abbas ecclesiae sancti Micaelis."

[2] See plans of building and details in "The Hermitage of Theodoric and Site of Pendar." T. Gray, Arch. Camb., April, 1903.

these are spurred at each side. The walls are all spurred at the base.

The barn was roofed with tilestones, but the roof recently fell in, the weight and the rotting of the timber-work probably causing the collapse.

The farmhouse has evidently been reconstructed on the older building, the walls showing the spurring as in the case of the barn. The upper storey is supported on massive oak beams. Each window has a label, and the jambs and mullions are stone. The reconstructed building appears to be a little before A.D. 1600.

I quote here from my notes on the Granges of Margam Abbey. " The grange of St. Michael stands at a level of 50 feet above the sea, and nearly all round it are hills of 100 feet high, which nestle close about it ; so it is no wonder the river which runs close to the house had difficulty in finding its way safe to sea and turns and twists so. As I said before, any one standing and looking at the Kenfig (Cenffig it should be, as " k " was never born in Wales), and knowing on which hand lay the Severn Sea, would think the river had turned from its saltness, and was going again towards the hills whence it had but just come."

A quarter of a mile south from the grange stood a fulling-mill—a Pandy—on the river edge. It was demolished on the construction of the Great Western Railway. This fulling-mill is mentioned in a list of the Margam Abbey possessions set out by the Abbot dated Thursday after the Octave of Easter, A.D. 1326.

As I have said, the *conversi*, or lay brethren,

worked the Abbey farms, and we have an interesting reference to them in the proceedings at the
Glamorgan County Court, before Gilbert de Elles-
feld, Sheriff of Glamorgan, T. 229 (C. MCLXXXII),
whereat Brother John . . . was indicted for robbing
David de Gower of 15d. at the Borwes—the burrows
or sand dunes—and Brother Meuric of St. Michael's
Grange was indicted for giving money and food to
John ap Griffith and Rees ap Griffith, felons and
outlaws. But the accused say they are brethren and
conversi of the Abbey of Margam, and therefore
they ought to appear before their own ordinaries (the
Bishop or the Abbot). It is asked of them if they
are clerks ordained, and if they know how to read,
and a book is given to them for that proof, but they
declare themselves "professed religious" (*i.e.* monks),
and so not bound to answer. Thereupon came Master
David ap Rees, clerk, by virtue of the Bishop of
Llandaff's commission to him, and caused the
accused to be delivered to him for trial in an
Ecclesiastical Court. The Sheriff and Master
David disputed whether the delinquents were "professed," and so entitled to their privilege of clergy.
Eventually the Sheriff admitted the plea, and made
inquest whether they were guilty or not so as to
deliver them up to Master David.

They were tried, found not guilty, and released.
Cardiff, 26 May, A.D. 1358.

The question whether for grave offences the clergy
could be tried by the King's judges was one which
had long raised bitter feelings on the one side and
the other. In 1512 the Parliament passed a law con-

fining the immunity of the clergy to those in sacred orders.

The Abbot of Winchcombe, in a sermon at St. Paul's, argued that all clerks were in Holy Orders and consequently not amenable to secular tribunals.[1]

Touching courts, we find Richard de Clare, sixth Earl of Gloucester and lord of Glamorgan, son of Gilbert de Clare, the fifth earl and first of the Clares, A.D. 1227, allowed the monks to have a court in the fee of Kenefeg.

T. 170 b. (C. DCCCLVII) is a General Confirmation by Richard de Clare, Earl of Gloucester and Hertford, to Margam Abbey of the lands and privileges granted by his predecessors, viz., the lands in the fee of Kenefeg, New Castle, the land of Peytevin, with additional grants ; and that the monks are to have a court of all pleas and forfeits in their lands but not of felony. And in felonies, the land and chattels of the felons condemned to death which may be due to the Earl are granted to the monks.

This deed explains the reason for the case above being taken to the Glamorgan County Court at Cardiff.

There was also the court called "The hundred court," and to this every man was to resort in the first instance for justice, apparently in all matters. Hundreds were granted by the Crown as lordships. It was the court of the lord of the territory. The free heads of families were the justices or members of the court. Twice a year all freemen, whether

---

[1] "Eve of the Reformation," by Abbot Gasquet.

hearthfast—that is, having hearths or (as Bracton puts it) houses and land of their own—or *folgarii*, followers or dependents of a lord, were to be assembled in their hundred.[1]

In the Margam MSS. is a late twelfth century deed which gives the names of the justices forming the Earl's Welsh hundred (court) of Margam.

T. 1985 is a deed whereby Gugan Bodewen ; Credic Correwen ; Joaf, son of Rig', the sons of Reul and their relatives, forming the Earl's Welsh hundred of Margam, abjure the lands of Margam Abbey, swear to keep the peace, to prosecute those who injure the Abbey, and make restitution for damages done within fifteen days.

Witnesses : Helyas the sheriff's chaplain, Walter the porter, Roger the cellarer, monks ; Jordan and Meiler, *conversi ;* Walter Luvel, William de Cogahan, Thomas de Corneli, Alfred, Provost of Neth. Under seal of Robert, son of Gregory, Sheriff of Cardiff.

It is a curious document, and it would seem to indicate that the members of the court were not blameless in some respects. They apparently had claimed part of the Abbey lands, and had refrained from prosecuting those who had injured the Abbey.

T. 2798 is a grant by Amabilia, daughter of Walter Molendinarius, or the miller, of Kenfig to John Peruat and Alice his wife, of an acre of land in the field called Mullemannislond, viz., Mill-man's-land, between the land of Walter de Magor and that of the grantor, reaching from the millpond to

[1] " The Ancient Laws of Wales," in substance. Herbert Lewis.

15

the meadow of Thomas Faber, or the smith, rent 1d. yearly and 20s. beforehand.

Witnesses : David Beneyt, Walter Rudoc, and others. Early fourteenth century. Alice Peruat of the preceding deed, relict of John Peruat of Kene-feg, quit-claimed to the Abbey by T. 198 (C. MCVII) the acre of the above deed given her by Amabilia the miller's daughter in Mullemannislond, between the land of Thomas Tynkare on the east, the land of Thomas Poulyn on the west, and from the mill-pond, *stagno molendini*, in length to the meadow of Henry Vot. Under the common seal of the burgesses of Kenefeg because her seal is not known. Witnesses : John Luvel and others. The adjoining owners seem to have changed.

It is curious that "u" is constantly used for "i" in the ancient MSS.—hulle for hill, mulle for mill, le Mullestrate for Mill Street, Cardiff.

T. 289. 18 (C. DCCLXXXVII).—By this deed Diurec, son of John son of Joaf, assigned to the Abbey his twelve acres of arable and two of meadow land between Corneli and St. Michael's Grange. Rent 18d., payable at Kenefeg as gavel.[1] Diurec was one of the Du family.

---

[1] In pre-Domesday times the general name for the oblation or money payment—now constituting the entire render, but then only a subordinate part—was gafol, gavol, or land gable ; land at farm was gafolland ; freehold was ungafoled—land not subject to rent The gabel, about 1d. per acre, was only a part of the price paid for the use of the land, the rest being worked out by the tenants ; when the work was light or not constant the tenants were bound in an increased oblation, which was distinguished as "mail."—"The Manor," N. J. Hone.

T. 189 (C. MXXXIV) is a mortgage for eighty years from A.D. 1283 by Helias, son of Philip Alexander, and Amabilia his wife, to Margam Abbey, of three acres of land, for 60s., of which they were in most urgent need. Two acres lie between Goylake and the road from Kenefeg to the common moor, adjacent to the land of Maurice Gramus; the third acre is held of the Hospitallers, adjoining that of John Loue, and reaching from the Cardiff road to the road which leads from Lipthete towards Cornely. There are charges of 2d. yearly to Maurice Gramus and 1½d. to the Hospitallers.

Witnesses : Adam the Baker, John Peruat, and others.

This deed of Helias, son of Philip Alexander, introduces a new name, Lipthete, and I doubt if it can be located to-day; it also shows that the Knights Hospitallers owned land at Kenfig.

Harley Charter 75, C. 17, is a mortgage for forty years by Roger le Hastare of Kenefeg to the Abbot and Convent of Margam, with assent of his wife Alice, of two acres of his land lying between that of Maurice Gramus and the Abbey's land on the east and in length from Goylake to the high road from Kenefeg to the moor, which land he acquired with his wife; for 50s. sterling, charged with a payment of 2d. to Maurice Gramus and 6d. to the said Roger yearly.

Witnesses : Hugh, vicar of Kenefeg ; Robert, his presbyter, Lewelin the tailor, and others. Dated Sunday in the Octave of Epiphany, 12 Jan., A.D. 1276.

Abbot Thomas (who came from Portskewit) leased by *Harley Charter* 75, A. 41, on St. Martin's Day, 11 Nov., A.D. 1267, to Michael Tusard, of Kenefeg, for twenty years, two-thirds of a messuage, with orchard and croft, and an acre of land, near the new ditch on the south adjacent to the land of Philip Coh, the messuage being situate between that of William Sturie and John Asceline's ; rent yearly 2s. and 10s. premium.

Witnesses : W. Frankelein, Adam Harding, and others.

By T. 289, 53 (C. DCCCLX), Alice daughter of Alexander grants to the Abbey land which Cecilia her mother gave her lying on the south of Goylake towards the land of William Cole and having on the east the land of William Albus and on the west that of Robert Roul.

Seal of Maurice Gramus, as the grantor has no seal.

A new name occurs among the witnesses—William Le Bunz.

T. 29 (C. DCCCLIX), is a grant by Alice relict of Geoffrey, son of Seware, with assent of Alice her daughter, of her house in Kenefeg between the houses of William Faber and William Bunz. Rent 12d. to the Earl (of Gloucester). Witnesses : Father Walter Hubolt, William de Kardif, William de Chipstaple, monks of Margam, and others.

T. 289, 3 (C. DCXCII), a grant by William Gillemichel to Margam Abbey of eight acres of his land in Kenefec adjacent to the boundaries of the land of Mehi [1] on the east near the highroad from

---

[1] Deumay.

Stormy to Kenfig. Among the witnesses are William the cellarer and William the porter of Margam; Angarat (Angharad, I presume) wife of William and Weirvill her daughter.

T. 289, 5 (C. DCXCIII), is a grant by Walaueth, one of the sons of William Gillemichel, to the Abbey of all the land which was his father's in the arable part of Kenefeg, and should any service for the Earl's kitchen or anything else be required from this land, it is to be paid for out of the grantor's land at Ketlialanwir.[1]

This is followed by a quit claim, T. 58 (C. DCXCV), by Ketherech and Ivor, the other sons of William Gillemichel, to Margam Abbey of their right in the land.

The following deed gives us another name which is probably unknown to-day—Flokeslade.

T. 395 (C. MCXXXIII) is a grant by Alicia Terri, widow of Richard de Ewyas, burgess of Kenefeg, to John Tudor, burgess, of two acres of land near Flokeslade, between the town of Kenefeg and South Corneli, at the yearly rent of $\frac{1}{2}$d. and 6 marks beforehand. The mark is 6s. 8d.

Witnesses : Nicholas de Sherlake, vicar of Kenefeg; Philip Stiward, Thomas Kocz, Thomas Bounce (perhaps for Le Bunz), Henry Vote, burgesses. Kenefeg, 5 May, A.D. 1329.

---

[1] Gelli-lenwr, the learned man's grove.

CHAPTER X

THE MANOR OF SKER AND SURVEY OF THE LORDSHIP OF KENFIG

WE could not spend so much time at Kenfig without seeing Sker; and besides, Sker, with North and South Corneli as sub-manors, were under the jurisdiction of the lordship of Kenfig. Sker is a corruption of Welsh ysgyr,[1] a sharp, stony projection of rocks, on the shore.

Sker rejoices in being a parish in itself, a farm of 360¼ acres, having a narrow strip of Pyle parish between it and Kenfig parish. On this strip, just outside the boundary of Sker parish, stands a large house and its outbuildings.

You seem in the sand-dunes to be isolated from humanity, far "from the madding crowd"; the hillocks seem endless, sand everywhere; it is utterly lonely, an old-world air about it; brightened, it is true, here and there by patches of bloom, and with life in the scuttling rabbit and whir of pheasant.

---

[1] Mr. Isaac Craigfryn Hughes gives in the "Merch o' Scer," ysgair, a sudden rise in the land from the flat.

SKER HOUSE

" From the valley—'Bare downs only,'
Said I, in my haste to pass,
Till I climbed, and, lying lonely,
Found soft moss and flowering grass.

So, across bleak sand-dunes riding,
Past the net-hung fisher-cots,
Found I, 'neath the rough bents hiding,
Blue, unguessed forget-me-nots.

Striving now to pierce the human
Discord, for the hidden tunes,
I can meet no man or woman,
But I mind the downs and dunes." [1]

Three-quarters of a mile south from the pool you
reach the edge of the dunes, and you stand and
wonder at the sight of a great, gloomy house so much
out of place just on the edge of the great waste of
sand, and within six hundred yards of the sea-shore,
where the jagged rocks run out to sea full of sharp,
pointed fangs like the quills of the fretful porcupine.
When you come upon the house it fills you with
wonder why it is there; it is so sad and lonely and
grey, steeped in silence and melancholy.

It stands on down-like land which gently slopes
towards the sea, all alone. The sand-hills creep
close up to it on the north side, stopped, as it were,
in full career, as if hesitating to destroy it.[2] The
only sounds it hears, apart from the birds in summer,
are the thunders of the great Atlantic waves as they

[1] " Songs from the Downs," H. Lulham (Kegan Paul.)
[2] The sand-drift stopped at this point by reason of the shore
being rocky.

surge in and, striking the rocks, leap high in the air, masses of tortured foam.

Sker House was built by the Cistercian monks— "the sour Puritans of the cloister," of Neath Abbey, and so you can understand why they chose this lonesome spot : it was in accord with their feelings. I have no doubt the monks came often here to regain their health, for although lonely, it is most healthy. Here the winds comes off the sea, pure and free from taint of land, and thus it is most bracing.

The great house, with many gables, chimneys, and windows, looks the more gaunt in that it has no friendly trees around or near it. There it stands alone, and it gives you the idea that you had dreamed too fast, you are really still in mediæval times, your dream of progress a myth, and you look to see the white-robed Cistercian monks pass in and out of the house.

Parts of the house are of pre-Reformation times, but some parts are not older than the time of Charles II. The southern part of the house is of early date, before the sixteenth century ; as will be seen in the illustrations the windows have foliage, in the spandrils of the lights under the label ; the windows in the pine-end are ancient. It seems to me that the front portion, extending from the south and old part, was reconstructed, leaving the southern part and much of the back part as they existed in the time when the house belonged to Neath Abbey. The pine-end of the Ty-yr-ychen, or Oxens' house, is all that remains of that building of pre-Reformation days.

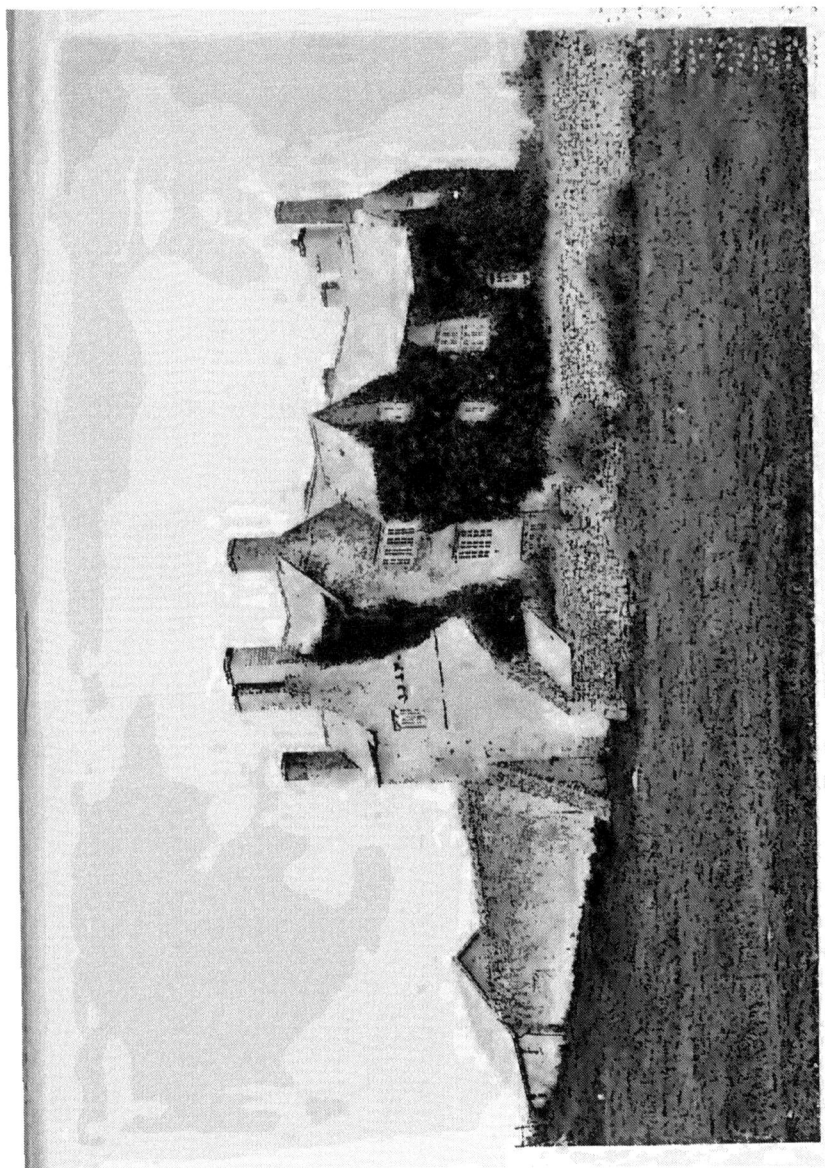

One summer's day I saw in the garden a piece
of wood from a proud ship : proud, for the legend
on the relic ran, " Nunquam non paratus " (" Never
unprepared)." One day it was unprepared. After it
had run on to the sharp fangs of Sker rocks the
little plank was all that remained with its message
of irony.

Leland tells us "There is a Manor caullid *Sker*
a 2 miles from the shore where dwellith one
Richard Loughor a gentilman." [1]

Just below Sker Grange are the rocks and little
bay, Pwll Dafan, into which came the Maid of Sker
while Davy Llewelyn was there fishing. Davy's description of the occurrence is worth repeating : " Now
as the rising sea came sliding over the coronet of
rocks, as well as through the main entrance—for even
the brim of the pool is covered at high water—I
beheld a glorious sight, stored in my remembrance
of the southern regions but not often seen at home.
The day had been hot and brilliant, with a light air
from the south ; and at sunset a haze arose and hung
as if it were an awning over the tranquil sea. First,
a gauze of golden colour as the western light came
through, and then a tissue shot with red, and now a
veil of silvery softness, as the summer moon grew
bright.

" Then the quiet waves began—as their plaited lines
rolled onwards into hills of whiteness—in the very

[1] John Leland's distances are erratic and his miles elastic
Here he has made less than half a mile into two miles. But
I have seen it suggested that the reading may have been " a
2 miles further on the shore."

curl and fall to glisten with a flitting light.   Presently,
as each puny breaker overshone the one in front, not
the crest and comb alone, but the slope behind it, and
the crossing flaws inshore, gleamed into hovering radi-
ance and soft flashes vanishing ; till, in the deepening
of the dusk, each advancing crest was sparkling with
a mane of fire, every breaking wavelet like a shaken
seam of gold.   Thence the shower of beads and
lustres lapsed into a sliding tier, moving up the sands
with light, or among the pebbles breaking into a
cataract of gems. . . . As I gazed at all this beauty,
trying not to go astray with wonder and with weari-
ness, there in the gateway of black rock, with the
offing dark behind her, and the glittering waves upon
their golden shoulders bearing her—sudden as an
apparition came a smoothly-gliding boat. . . . By
the clear moonlight I saw a wee maiden, all in white,
having neither cloak nor shawl, nor any other soft
appliance to protect or comfort her, but lying with her
little back upon the aftmost planking, with one arm
bent (as I have said before), and the other drooping
at her side, as if the baby-hand had been at work to
ease her crying ; and then when tears were tired out,
had dropped in sleep or numb despair." [1]

T. 30 (C. DCXX) sets forth the terms of a settlement between the Abbot of Neath and the Abbot of
Margam concerning a hundred acres of land at the
Grange of Skerra, which the monks of Margam had
sold to the monks of Neath, but could not guarantee
it.   Therefore the Abbot of Margam was to return
the purchase money, 12 silver marks.   But if the

---

[1] " The Maid of Sker," R. D. Blackmore.

abbot could get possession and deliver it to Neath, that abbey was to pay 20 marks instead of 12. If the Abbot of Margam failed to get possession and had to accept an exchange from the Earl of Gloucester, he is to pay to Neath Abbey 12 marks and 5 added thereto.

Witnesses: Dom Joill(enus) [1] Abbot of Savigny, and Dom Walter Abbot of Combermere, with assent of the two convents of Neath and Margam.

I have previously told you that Richard de Cardiff made claim to Sker and that I would explain this. The Earl had given Richard de Cardiff extensive grants of land at Newton (see page 132), and probably he thought Sker was included, and I believe he had reason to think so, as Sker lies within the boundaries described and is not mentioned as excluded; but he was wrong. In T. 544, 17 (C. MCCCCIII) the Earl William notifies to his Sheriff of Cardiff as to Blakescerra which is in dispute between Margam Abbey and Richard de Kardiff. The Earl states that he had given the land in question to Margam in exchange for their land of Novus-Burgus (Cardiff) long before the said Richard had any land in Wales from the said Earl, therefore he warrants it to the Abbey. Witnesses: Hawisia, the Countess of Gloucester; Master Samson; David, the chaplain. Mr. Clark says that Novus-Burgus is Newton, but Dr. Birch prefers to place it in Cardiff, and I think he is right.

Now we come to the end of the dispute.

Harley Charter 75, A. 15 (C. XXXIII), is a notifi-

---

[1] Joslenus, " Gallia Christiana," vol. xi. p. 546. He occurs A.D. 1173 and 1178.

cation by Bishop Nicholas of the canonical termination
of the suit between the Abbot of Margam and Richard
de Kardiff concerning Blakescerre.   The abbot had
proved that he held it upwards of ten years before
Richard owned any land in that district.   Judgment
was given for the abbot, and he conveyed the property
to the Abbot of Neath.

The grange was endowed by Thomas de Sanford
with a quittance of 2s. per annum on fifty acres of
land and one and a half acre upon[1] the sea at
Blakesker.   The boundary of Earl William's grant
to Richard de Kardiff is somewhat difficult to follow
in parts.

A deed of lease of Sker in possession of the Rev.
Henry Hay Knight, B.D., Rector of Neath in 1845,
was printed by Francis in his "Neath and its Abbey."
It was granted by Leysan Thomas, the last Abbot of
Neath, shortly before the Dissolution, to Gwenllyan
Turberville, widow of Watcyn Loyghor, and Richard
Loghor, her son, 8 April, 1536.   You will remember
further back John Leland mentions the Manor place
of Sker, and says Richard Loughor, a gentleman, lived
there.   Leland was there two or three years after
the date of the lease.   The lease is an interesting
document, and as it was granted before the dissolution of the monasteries I give it in full.

"This indenture made the viijt day off Aprill the
xxijt years of the reigne off o'r sov'ain Lord Kyng
Henrye the VIIjt, betwyne Lyson Thomas, Abbot of
Nethe and the Co'vent of the same place off the one
p'te and Gwenllyan Turbervill, wydoe, late wyffe of

---

[1] Upon the sea, *i.e.*, abutting on the sea.

Watkyn Loyghor and Richard Loyghor sone and
heyre apparant of the sayde Gwenllyan of that other
p'tye WYTNESSITHE that the same Abbot and Co'vent
wt one assent and consent, hathe dymysyd, grauntyd,
and to ferm lettyd and by this p'sent' dymysithe,
grauntithe and to ferm lettyth to the sayde Gwenllyan
and Richard, the Grange or Man' off Skarre wt his
singuler apportenaunce set and beyng in the Countie
off Glamorga' wt all incle'rs lands, ten'ts, medows,
lesus, and pasturis, comyns, and wast land, wt all
other comodytes and profytts belonging or p'teyning
to the same grange or man' of Skarre. Also the
sayde Abbot and Co'vent dymysyth, grauntythe and
by this p'sents to ferm lettyth to the sayde Gwenllyan
and Richard iiij closys wt ther p'tynences sett and
lyyng et the sayde grange or man' off Skarre, whereoff
one close is callyd the Abbots close, a nother callyd
the new P'kes, the thyrd called the Barbor is land, and
the fowrthe close callyd John Lloyd is close, to have
and to hold the sayde grange or man' off Skarre and
iiij closis wt, all other the p'miss wt, ther p'tynences
to the saide Gwenllyan and Richard ther ex'ers and
assignis from the fest off the Ann'cyac'n off o'r Lady
last past untyll the full end and term of iiij^{xx} xix
years[1] then next folowing, and fully to be completyd,
yelding and paying yerely therefore to the sayde
Abbot and Co'vent and to their successors vij marks
sterling at the fest off All the Saynts wt. vs. yerely
to the Lord off Glamorgan, and yelding and paying
yerely for the saide iiij Closis xxxjs. viijd. at the fest
of All saynts In lykewyse wt. xxs. in name off a

---

[1] Four score and nineteen, or ninety-nine years.

heryot after ev'y decesse, and at the fest of the
Natyvyte off o'r Lord one cople of pure and clene
capons yerely, and yff hit hapen the saide rent of vij
marks or xxxjs. viijd. and one cople of capons or any
p'cell therof, to be unpayde by xv days after any of the
sayde fests in whiche hit ow't to be payde and of no
suffyant suretys there to be found, that then hit shalbe
lawfull unto the sayde Abbot and Co'vent and ther
successors to reenter into the sayde grange off Skarre
and man' wt' other the p'miss' as in ther pristynat
estate, this Indenture notwithstanding, also the sayde
Gwenllyan and Richarde, the executors and assignis,
shall repare, uphold, and maynteyn the sayde grange
or man' wt. other the p'miss' in all things, and at the
end of the sayde term to leve and delyv' it sufficialy
reparid, and wee the sayde Abbot and Co'vent and o'r
successors the sayde grange or man' off Skarr and
other p'miss' to the sayde Gwenllya' and Richard,
ther executors and assignis during the sayde term
in man' and forme aforesaid shall warant and defend
by this o'r p'sents In Wyttness hereoff to thes present Indenturis the p'ties abovesayd interchangeable
have set ther seale, yeven the day and yere above
specyfyed."

In the "Survey and Presentment" of 1660 it is stated
that Kenfig Down was granted (time out of mind) to
the monks of the Abbey of Neath, as owners of Sker
doubtless.

A lease is among the Margam MSS. by King
Henry VIII. as lord of Glamorgan to Walter Log-
hour, probably son of Watkin Loughor, and John ap
Thomas ap Howell, of the Cornmill of Kenfegge, and

the suit[1] for grindings of Newton Notashe, with two acres of land at Grameshill (so called from the Gramus family) between the high-road on the north and Goy-lake on the south, with liberty to appoint a miller, an easement to the mill, and a site on the mill-stream for the mill if required, for 99 years, rent 20s. yearly ; with clause for repair by the lessees, to whom wood is to be allowed for " wyndyngs " and poles for the weir. The tenants of Newton Notashe are to grind at the mill under penalty of a fine.

Dated Chancery of Cardiff, 29 April, A.D. 1526.

The parish of Kenfig contains 2,996.4 acres, of which more than half consists of drift sands. The lordship of Kenfig contains Kenfig parish, or Lower Kenfig, Upper Kenfig, and part of Trisant in the parish of Margam, and its jurisdiction extended over the sub-manors of North and South Corneli and Sker.

I now give the Survey and Presentment of 1660, which I copy from Mr. Clark's " Kenfig," as being ready to hand :—

Survey and Presentment of 1660.

The presentment here printed is that of a jury of burgesses, given in the usual form, and in reply to the usual questions issued on such occasions. Such documents, of the reigns of Elizabeth, James, and Charles, are not uncommon in this county, and are usually the

---

[1] " And John Banty, a tenant according to the custom of the Manor, hath not made his continuous suit at the lord's mill as he is bound by custom of his lordship, therefore he is in mercy 12d. He had not taken his corn to be ground at the lord's mill."— " The Manor," by N. J. Hone.

earliest and best evidence for boundaries and local
rights.   There are extant two rolls of this presentment,
of which one, though not original (that is, not signed by
the jurors), is yet probably of original date, and is that
here followed.   The other is a later copy, made probably in 1773.   It is to be observed the jurors and
steward are all Welsh.[1]

" *The Lordship, Mannor, Town and Burrough of Kenfigg.*

"A presentment in answer unto certain articles
given in charge for and on the behalf of the Right
Honourable Phillip Earl of Pembroke and Montgomery lord of the said lordship mannor town or
burrough unto a jury of survey sworn and impannelled
(by Robert Williams Esquire steward of the said lordship or mannor and Constable of the Castle of the
said town and burrough) the eleventh day of January
in the twelveth year of our Soverign Lord Charles the
Second by the grace of God of England Scotland
France and Ireland King Defender of the Faith &c.
annoq. Domini 1660.

"By the oathes of

Thomas Bevan	Morgan Evan Yorath
David Thomas Howell	Henry Lyddon
Thomas Morgan	Hopkin Edward
Evan Thomas	Jenkin Griffith
Thomas Hopkin Thomas	Nicholas Morgan
Thomas Hopkin Pritchard	Thomas Prichard
Jenkin William	George Thomas, Jurors.

[1] Clark's " Kenfig Charters."

" 1. To the first article they present and say that
ie mannor town or burrough of Kenfigg is a particu-
ir and distinct lordship except only the intermixture
f certain lands of other lordshipps as shall be
ientioned in answer to the second article And the
ounds and meares of the said lordship doe extend
'om a place called Gutter y furlong on the south
art unto half the race or current of Kenfigg water or
ver on the north 'part and from the Rugge or the
irdship of Coyty on the east part unto the sea on
ie west part And that the meares and bounds of
ie said town burrough or corporation doe extend
'om the sea by a house called Ty yr Ychan in
kerre unto a stone lyeing in the highway leading
om Kenfigg to Notage and from thence by a stone
'eing in a close belonging to Rees Thomas Matthew
alled Y Kae Issha unto another stone lyeing on
Ieol y Broome on the south part and from thence
y a stone lyeing at Groes y gryn unto another stone
'eing in Kae Pwll y Kyffylau and from that stone on
ie eastern side of Marlas House unto a cross called
:roes Jenkin on the east part and from thence by a
:oss lyeing in Kae Garw unto a stone by Notch
:oarton lyeing in the highway leading from Kenfigg
) Margam on the north part and from thence directly
nto the sea And as for the compass length and
readth thereof they referr it to the said apparent
ieares and marks.

" 2. To the second article they present and say that
he lordship of Pile in Kenfig alias Kenfigg and Pile
eing the lordships and mannors of S'r Edward
Iansel Barronet and that the mannor of North

Cornely holden by John Turberville Esquire and the mannor of South Cornely holden by William Herbert Esquire doe next adjoyn unto the said town and burrough and that part of the said severall lordships or mannors of Pile in Kenfig al's Kenfigg and Pile and North and South Cornely doe ly within the bounds or circuits of the said town and burrough of Kenfigg They further say that they know not of any person or persons that did or doe intrude or incroach in or upon the said town or burrough or any part thereof

"3. To the third article they present and say that there is within ye s'd town or burrough or under the said lordship or mannor two manners of free soccage tenure one thereof called Pascall Hall holden under the yearly rent of two pence halfpenny an acre and suit of court every month And the other free tenure under the rent in the schedule hereunto añexed specified and suit of court twice in the year (videlicett) at May and at Michaelmas

" *Paschall Hill Hould*

	s.	d.
William Herbert of Swanzey Esq. holdeth one acre and a half rent p'r ann'.	o	3¾
John Turberville Esq. holdeth one acre rent p'r ann'.	o	2½
Richard Lougher of Tithegstone Esq. holdeth eight acres rent p'r ann'.	1	8
Jenkin Griffith and Thomas James jure uxoris holdeth three acres rent p'r ann'	o	7½

	s.	d.
Richard Lewis of Kenfigg holdeth seven acres and one quarter rent p'r ann' . .	1	6
Hopkin Thomas of Kenfigg holdeth eight acres rent p'r ann'	1	8
William ap Evan infant holdeth half one acre rent p'r ann'	o	$1\frac{1}{4}$
Jenkin Howard holdeth eight acres rent p'r ann'	1	8
David Bevan of Cornely holdeth 2 acres rent p'r ann'	o	5
Gronow William of Kenfigg holdeth eleven acres rent p'r ann'	2	$3\frac{1}{2}$
Thomas Hopkin of Kenfigg holdeth one acre and a half or thereabouts rent p'r ann' .	o	4
Lewis Aylward of Kenfigg holdeth thirty-eight acres and a half rent p'r annum .	8	$0\frac{1}{2}$
Edward Morgan of Lantwit by Neath holdeth 23 acres rent p'r ann'	4	$9\frac{1}{2}$
Rees Leyson of Kenfigg holdeth one acre and 3 quarters rent p'r ann'	o	$4\frac{1}{2}$
Thos. Morgan of Kenfigg holdeth eleven acres rent p'r ann'	2	$3\frac{1}{2}$
John ap Evan of Kenfigg holdeth two acres rent p'r ann'	o	5
Nicholas Morgan of Kenfigg holdeth one acre and a half rent p'r ann'	o	$3\frac{3}{4}$
George Thomas Katherine Jenkin and Elizabeth Jenkin do hold one cottage rent p'r annum	o	1
Harry Jenkin of Kenfigg holds one cottage rent p'r ann'	o	1

"*Free Tenants*

	s.	d.
William Herbert Esquire holds the mannor of South Cornely rent	16	0
John Turberville Esq. holds the mannor of North Cornely rent p'r ann'. . .	9	10½
Thomas Turbervill of Skerre gent. holds the third part of Kenfigg Down and payeth therefore yearly at the Feast of St. James ye Apostle	5	0
The burgesses of Kenfigg doe hold the other two parts of Kenfigg Down and pay therefore yearly at the feast afores'd .	10	0
Sir Edward Mansell Barronett holds part of Marlas Farm rent.	4	4
Thomas Hopkin Pritchard holds one acre rent p'r ann'.	1	0
Jenkin Thomas holdeth one acre rent p'r annum	1	0
Wenlliam Thomas of Kenfigg Vidua holds one acre rent p'r ann'	1	0
Lewis Ayleward holds one acre rent p'r ann' .	0	5½
Gronow William holdeth three acres rent p'r ann'	0	4
David Nicholas of Margam holdeth one acre called Ball Acre rent p'r ann'. . .	0	2
Richard Lougher Esq. holdeth eight acres rent p'r ann'.	0	8
Katherine John of Margam holds 3 acres rent p'r ann'.	0	2½
David Bevan holdeth one acre rent p'r ann'.	0	0¾
Hopkin Thomas afores'd holds fifteen acres rent p'r ann'.	1	4½

" They further present and say that there are within the said lordship certain free lands of soccage tenure held from time to time part under the rent of a red rose and the other part under the rent of three pepper graines to be paid yearly at the Feast of St. John Baptist and to be fetcht with wain and oxen but how distinguished the one from the other they know not   Also suit of court twice in the year (vizt.) at the two leets   The said land holden of and by the persons following

" Rees Leyson holdeth six acres

" David Bevan holdeth thirty acres and one half

" Edward Morgan holdeth twenty acres

" Mary Sanor of Ballas widow holdeth six acres

" William Thomas of Kenfigg holdeth one acre

" Alice Evan wid'w and Evan Lydon her son doe hold five acres

" Phillip Stringer of Kenfigg holdeth half one acre

" Thomas Hopkin Thomas jure uxoris holdeth one acre

" Cecill Thomas of Kenfigg spinster holdeth two acres and three quarters

" Howell Rees of Kenfigg holdeth one acre

" John Kerry of Margam jure uxoris   Hopkin Jenkin of the same jure uxoris   Leyson Edward of Newton jure uxoris   Alice William and Ann William spinsters doe hold jointly four acres

" Gronow William of Kenfigg aforesaid holdeth three acres

" Llewelyn John of Kenfigg holdeth one acre

" David Nicholas of Margam holdeth two acres

" Lewis Nicholas of Margam holdeth half one acre

" Lewis Ayleward of Kenfigg afores'd holdeth eighteen acres

" Thomas ab Evan of Kenfigg holdeth two acres

" Richard Lougher of Tithegston Esq. holdeth forty one acres

" They also present and say that severall of their free tenants have lost their freehold (time out of mind) by reason of the choaking blowing and over-blowing up of the sands what number of acres they know not

" 4. To the fourth article they say that the said town or burrough have been incorporated (time out of mind) and by prescription time out of mind they hold monthly courts and therein hear and determine all manner of suits actions and plaints between party and party to any value whatsoever and that such courts are held from time to time (before the portreeve) under the style and name of His Ma'tys Court Leet or the Court Baron of the Right Honourable Phillip Earl of Pembroke and Montgomery &c. or both and that the burgesses of the said town doe owe suit to the same courts and other free tenants at such time or times as is specified in their answer to the third article They further say that the officers yearly changeable are the portreeve one sergeant one constable one heyward and two aletasters and that the major part of the burgesses yearly elect three of their own society whereof the constable of the Castle sweareth one to be portreeve At any time after Michaelmas Leet the rest of the said officers are to be sworn by the portreeve and as for the officers

of the said town both past and present their names
are to be seen in the records of the said town and
the yearly benefitt and profitt belonging to such
officers are both uncertain and inconsiderable

" 5. To the fifth article they say that they are not
certain what number of burgesses were and are within
the said town and who ought to perform their suit
at every court They have answered to the fourth
article and they know not of any profitt or acknowledgement due unto the lord from them as burgesses
but their yearly rent which is (besides the rent of
Kenfigg Down) the certain sum of ten shillings

" 6. To the sixth article they say that (for ought
they know) the oath of late yeares administered unto
the s'd burgesses is agreeable in substance and effect
with the oath of the burgesses time out of mind but to
declare the particulars thereof they know not

" 7. To the seventh article they say they have
one com'on called Rugge within and belonging to the
burgesses of the said town and burrough the quantity
thereof they know not It is meared in length from
the Rugge of Coyty to Cats Pit in breadth from
Kevencribor to the river And one other com'on
called Kenfiggs Down the quantity thereof they know
not meared from the lands of Richard Lougher Esq.
to the sea They further say that none of the burgesses of the said town (by their ordinances) ought to
pasture in and upon the said com'on lands but such of
the burgesses as doe dwell or inhabit within the
bounds or limits of the said town or corporation.

" 8. To the eighth article they say that the fore-
mentioned com'on called Kenfiggs Down was

granted (time out of mind) to the monks of the Abby of Neath and the burgesses of Kenfigg as they were informed by their forefathers but the most part thereof is and hath been enjoyed by the said burgesses (time out of mind) at the yearly rent specified and mentioned in the third article

" 9. To the ninth article they say that they know not of any herriott profitt or acknowledgement due unto the lord of the said burrough att the death of a burgess and that the perquisites of courts waifes estrays felons goods and many other royalties happening within the said town and burrough do (for ought they know) properly belong unto the lord of the burrough and to be accountable unto the said lord by the portreeve from time to time   The estrays (time out of mind) in manner and form following (viz't) for every estrayed sheep twelve pence and for every hairy beast five shillings and the perquisites of courts fines and amerciaments to be affeered by two of the ancientest burgesses upon oath as is accustomed time out of mind

" 10. To the tenth article they say they have specified (in answer to the foregoing articles)   In particular what and how much yearly rent is payable unto the lord and that the same is levyable by the serjeant and ale tasters and accountable by the portreeve   They further say that Thomas Lougher Gent. holdeth one messuage and one hundred and six acres of land more or less but what rent or duty he payeth or ought to pay they know not but refer themselves to his lordships terriers &c   The said Thomas Lougher payeth yearly for one acre called Erw Heol Cornely

twelve pence and for one other acre called Erw yr
Gorse Heer payeth yearly five pence halfpenny   And
the said seventeen pence halfpenny is leviable by the
serjeant and accountable unto the lord by the
portreeve   They further say that John Leyson and
David Bowen of Newton doe enjoy the benefitt and
profitts of the coales at the com'on of Rugge but what
rent they pay or ought to pay they know not but
refer themselves to his lordships terriers &c   They do
further say that after the decease of every lord dyeing
possessed or lord of this lordship or mannor there is
due unto the succeeding lord thirty three shillings and
fourpence in and under the name of mizes to be paid
in five years next after the decease of every such lord
as shall die possessed of the premises viz't six shillings
and eight pence yearly for and during the said five
years to be rated upon the tenants and burgesses and
accountable by the portreeve   They further say that
they know not of any other yearly rent or profitt due
unto the lord saveing what they have mentioned in
answer to the forgoing articles.

" 11. To the eleventh article they say that the
burgesses of the said town have time out of mind
been sworn by the portreeve and thereby admitted
burgesses and they know not of any acknowledg-
ment payable unto the lord upon their admission
And as to the number of burgesses sworn within
one or two days together they are uncertain   They
further say that (time out of mind) it hath been
their practice to swear and admitt such and so
many person or persons burgesses as the portreeve
and aldermen of the said town did think fitt to be

sworn and admitted they only agreeing and consenting thereunto

" 12. To the twelfth article they say that Evan Gronow for some late yeares was and att present is the recorder or town clerk constituted by the portreeve and for his fee it is inconsiderable and uncertain They also say that the constitution and appointment of the recorder and town clerk there and time out of mind was by the portreeve of the said town and burrough for the time being.

" 13. To the thirteenth article they say that they are not certain what messuages or dwelling houses were and are within the said burrough or corporation by reason that the sands had overcomed (time out of mind) a great number of dwellinghouses within the said burrough and town

" 14. To the fourteenth article they say that some part of the said third part of the lands granted unto the said corporation and monks of Neath now in the possession of Thomas Turbervill Gent. of Skerre hath been inclosed (time out of mind) and doth soe continue The quantity and value thereof they know not And the said Mr. Thomas Turbervill doth receive the profitt and benefitt of the said land They also say that some part of the other two parts of the said land granted as aforesaid now in the possession of the burgesses of the said town or corporation containing by estimation eighteen acres (more or less) to the value of forty shillings yearly or thereabouts hath been inclosed some seven years ago by the portreeve and aldermen of the said town and the rest of the burgesses consenting

thereunto and the same doth so continue and the said
burgesses doe receive the benefitt and profitt of the
said lands   They further say that some part of
another com'on called Rugge (belonging to the said
town or corporation) hath been inclosed time out of
mind by the burgesses of the said town and that the
same doe so continue   The quantity and value thereof
they know not   The said burgesses doe receive the
benefit and profitts of the said lands

"15. To the fifteenth and last article they say
that they know not of any sort or kind of fishes that
were (or usually have been) taken within the pool
situate within the said town and burrough but only
eels and roaches   They alsoe say that the fishing
of the said pool doth belong to the burgesses of the
said town and burrough and they know not of any
certain or considerable benefitt or profitt received
thereof by any."

The boundaries : Gutter-y-Furlong on the south
part ; I take this to be Gwter-y-Cwn on the shore at
Sker Rocks, where the boundary touches high-water
mark west-south-west of Sker House, thence along the
shore to the centre of Kenfig river.   Then from the
lordship of Coity on the east unto the sea on the west,
thus apparently including the whole of Cefn Cribwr.
Then returning to Gwter-y-Cwn, Dog's ditch, on the
sea-shore the boundary passes thence through a cattle-
shed called Ty-yr-Ychen in Sker Farm to a stone
lying in the highway from Kenfig to Notage ; this is
near Ffynon-y-Mer where the road leaves the common
and the lane begins, thence to a stone in a close called
y cae Isaf, and thence to a stone lying on Heol-y-

Broome; then to a stone at Groes-y-Gryn (I think this stood at or near the blacksmith's shop at Corneli); from here to a stone in Cae pwll y Cyffylau—the field of the Horses' pool—and from that stone on the eastern side of Marlas House unto a cross called Croes Jenkin on the east part, and from thence by a cross lying in Kae Garw unto a stone by Notch Coarton (I do not know what Notch Coarton means) lying in the highway leading from Kenffig to Margam on the north part, and from thence directly to the sea. The stone by Notch Coarton is the Roman milliary stone of Pumpeius Carantorius.

The whole of Cefn Cribwr as far as the River Ogmore appears to be in the lordship of Kenfig. Thus "the Rugge which extends in length from Catput as far as the Rugge of Coitiff"—the ridge of Coity; Coity begins on the east of the river Ogmore. "And in width from Cefn Cribwr as far as the water which runs from Lowareksmore to Kenfig." Lowarekesmore is Llywarch's moor, now Hirwaun.

Kenfig Down is stated to extend from the Earl's meadow as far as Goutesfurlong of the Abbot of Neath.

CHAPTER XI

STORMY, OR STURMI

STORMY, so called from the Sturmi family, is partly in Pyle parish, and therefore needs notice in a work on Kenfig, or, as it is termed, Pyle and Kenfig.

We have an interesting and early deed in Miss Talbot's collection of ancient MSS., and it is one which gave me a great deal of thought. It was so difficult to fix the location; some persons wished to claim the deed as applying to Pentre in the Rhondda, simply because of the words *fontem Petre*, which they considered to be Pentre, and from the mention of the old castle on the hill, this referring, they said, to "the old Caer or camp above Ystrad-y-fodwg Church, exactly opposite Fons-Pentre." These are Dr. Birch's words in a footnote in his "Margam Abbey." He also says, "Perhaps for Fons-Pentre, well of Pentre Ystrad-y-fodwg or Ffynon-Pedr, Peter's Well." Unfortunately for this theory (the Rhondda Naturalist Society were most anxious, as the Rev. John Griffith, then of Pentre, wrote me, to secure the location of the deed in their midst) the Sturmi lands were not in Rhondda, but in Pyle and Tithegstone—Stormy Farm

254 THE BURIED CITY OF KENFIG

and Stormy Down, for instance. Again, fons petre cannot by any twist of desire be turned into Pentre or Pen-tref, top or end of a village or place. Fons petræ, as it should be, the stone-well, is the Ffynon-y-maen [1] near Brombil, a little way north-east of Stormy Farm. The old castle upon the mountain, "vetus castellum super montem," is the British camp, or Castle Kribor of the monastic deeds, on the nose of Cefn Cribwr.

My pen has run away and I must stop and give the deed. It is a very old deed, and among the witnesses is Brother Meiler, the hermit of Pendar, and probably before of the Hermitage of Theodoric.

Before giving the actual deed I give a deed by which the donor became possessed of the land she gave to Margam Abbey.

T. 1981 is a charter by Roger Sturmi that he has appointed to Gunnilda, his wife, at his marriage eighty acres of arable land between the streams of the Ford of Tav and Chenewini, lying between the way which leads from the stream of the Ford of Tav to Fons Petre, or stone well, and the old castle upon the great mountain. The overplus of his land there is to be divided between his two daughters.

Witnesses: The Abbot of Margam; Walter de Cardif, monk of Margam; Thomas the priest of Villa Sturmi; Walter Luvel, and others.

The following is the actual deed :—

T. 11 (C. MCCCCVII) is a grant by Gunnilda, wife of Roger Sturmi, with assent of her husband, to Margam Abbey of the land which he gave, or rather, I presume, let, to the monks for half a mark yearly

[1] The Spring or Well of the Stone, the Stone Well.

rent; the land includes her dower-land, viz., eighty acres between the stream of the ford Taus (Dr. Birch says, *i.e.*, the ford of Tâv Pontypridd) and the stream Chenewinus, and between the way which leads from the stream of the ford Taus to the *fons petre* and the old castle on the hill.

The abbot paying 4 marks silver and some lamb-skins for making a pelisse, and twenty sheep.

Sworn as a spontaneous gift by the grantor before God and His Saints, "per nullam coactionem vel mariti vel alterius cujusdam . . . set spontanea voluntate."

Witnesses : William, Archdeacon of Llandaff ; Brother Meiler the hermit ; Matildis, wife of Baldwine; Matildis, daughter of Richard, son of Gummund ; Cecilia, wife of Robert Testard ; Christiana, wife of Walter " Blanchigernonis," or " of the white whiskers " ; Beatrice, wife of Osbert the Miller, and others. A formidable array of women witnesses.

It is to be noted that the *ford* is called *Tav*, not the stream : the stream of the Ford of Tav. I am unable to locate the ford or the Chenewini, but it is clear Gunnilda's land lies between the road passing Brombil and Ffynnon-y-maen and the British Camp on the end of Cefn Cribwr, near which is Pen-Castell Farm. The ford of Tav may be the ford on the Kenfig river, now called Rhŷd Yorath Goch. The Chenewini may be the Goylake.

T. 1978 [C. LIII] is a grant by Geoffrey Esturmi, with assent of M., his wife, R. R., and Geoffrey, his sons, and Agnes, his daughter, to the Abbey of all the land between that of Herbert, son of

Godwineth, and the River Kinithwini, as that river runs down the mountain to the moors as far as the lower water, and from that lower water to the road leading through the mountain-land, and dividing the land of the Earl from his own; both pastures, arable, and moorland. The monks give 12 silver marks to the grantor to help him to pay his debts; to each son a *cappa*, or cloak, and four *nummi*, or gold pieces, and undertake to receive him into their fraternity when he becomes infirm.

Witnesses : Eglin (de Purbica [1]), Sheriff of Glamorgan, William Pincerna,[2] and several others. This is an early deed in the history of Margam Abbey.

Geoffrey Sturmi and Roger, his son, grant to Margam Abbey by T. 1979 all the land between the Ford of Tav, Vadum Tavis, and the Stone-well, Fons-Petre, as the public way leads from the ford to the well, and as the streams descend from the ford and the well down to the junction of the streams, viz., all the land inclosed between those two streams and the public road, arable, meadow, and pasture; just as William Earl of Gloucester granted to Geoffrey permission to give some of his land for his soul's health, and chiefly to Margam Church. For three and a half marks.

Witnesses : Walter Luvel; Geoffrey *Sutor*, the cobbler; John *Niger Faber*, the blacksmith; Roger Rex; Rodbert *Sutor*, the cobbler; William *Pelli-*

---

[1] *Circa* A.D. 1147–1148.

[2] Occurs in Foundation Charter of Neath Abbey, *circa* A.D. 1129.

parius, the pelterer, and others. This seems to grant the land below Gunnilda's eighty acres.

T. 1980 is a grant by Roger Sturmi to the Abbey of all the land of his father which it holds, and of all the rest of the land which his father held of the Earl of Gloucester's fee in Margam, for the half-yearly rent of half a mark silver. Gaufridus, or Geoffrey, his brother, confirms the gift. For 6 marks, *and* 20s. *for his aid in upholding the church from claimants* (italics are mine), and remission of a debt of half a mark due by his father, and 5s. which he himself owed for a horse bought from the cellarer of the Abbey. To his wife, Gunnilda, 4 marks to bar her dower. To his three children each half a mark silver, and two cows for the nourishment of the little ones—et duas vaccas ad parvulos nutriendos.

Witnesses : Eglinus, Sheriff of Glamorgan ; Walter Luvel ; Gillebert Gramus ; William the priest, chaplain of Kenefeg, and others.

I think this deed quite closes the door to the Rhondda claim.

It seems extraordinary that persons should, as we have seen, part with their land for such seemingly inadequate recompense. Six marks at 6s. 8d. each at present value of money would be at most £40. Four marks for Gunnilda's eighty acres = £29. It is true she obtained some ecclesiastical and monastic benefits in addition.

T. 1986. This is a confirmation by Roger Sturmi the younger, son of Roger Sturmi, of the gifts of his grandfather, Geoffrey Sturmi, to the Abbey of land in Margam, also of his father's gifts with assent of his brothers, Geoffrey and William. Rent, half a mark, as provided for in the charter of his father and of William Earl of Gloucester.

We have seen in the grant, T. 1980, by Roger Sturmi that he received from the Abbey 20s. for his aid in upholding the church from claimants.

Harley Charter 75, B. 3 (C. DCXIX). Testimonial letters of William, Rural Dean of Wrenid, Groneath, to Hameline, Abbot of Gloucester, and Roger de Norwich, Prior of Llanthony, concerning the church of Sturmi, whereof there was a controversy between Roger Sturmi and Gilbert the priest of New Castle; showing that Geoffrey Sturmi, his father, built the church in his vill in the wilderness, on his land whereon no one had ever hitherto ploughed, and one Tomas, a priest, was presented thereunto by the said Geoffrey, and held it all his lifetime; adding that as a fact the said church has not received chrism[1] from New-Castle Church, but from the said Dean, and, in the days of the said Geoffrey and Roger, children were baptized and the dead interred therein.

Dr. Birch says: " It would appear by the foregoing that the priest of New-Castle had complained to his patrons, the Abbot of St. Peter's, Gloucester, and the Prior of Llanthony, of an alleged invasion of his spiritualities by the erection of the church at Sturmy within the limits of his parochial boundary."

This, then, is the reason for the grant of 20s. from

---

[1] Chrism is one of the Holy Oils, and is used in the Roman Catholic Church after Baptism, at Confirmation, at the consecration of a Bishop, and at the consecration of things set apart for Divine service. Chrism is olive oil mixed with balsam.

RUINS OF STURMI CHAPEL.

[To face page 259.

the Abbey of Margam. Roger resisted the claims of the priest of New-Castle and inferentially the Abbot of Gloucester and the Prior of Llanthony.

The ruins of the church of Sturmi are in the parish of Tythegstone Higher and lie nearly 800 yards east from Sturmi Grange and adjoin the north edge of Sturmi Down.[1]

In an inclosure having trees in and around it are a pine-end and the foundations of a small building about 35 feet in length; among the *débris* are some worked stones; one about 15 inches wide has a chamfer on each side, and it has the appearance of having formed part of a buttress. This is all that remains of Sturmi Church; near it are foundations of other buildings, probably the modest dwelling of the priest Tomas, who was presented to it by Geoffrey Sturmi.

The site of the little church is secluded, nestled close to the swelling, russet-clad side of Stormy Down, glad that it was not on the top of that cold and bleak moor. In old times one can understand what Roger Sturmi meant when he said his father built the church in his vill in the wilderness on his land whereon no one had ever hitherto ploughed.

It may be appropriate here to mention that Bishop Elias notified by a letter dated A.D. 1234, T. 293, 28

---

[1] Large blocks of Rhætic sandstones are scattered over Stormy Down, and in one of these Mr. John David discovered the impression of a great reptilian jaw. The specimen has been described by Mr. E. T. Newton as a left dentary bone of a Megalosauroid reptile, *Zanclodon cambrensis.*—"Memoirs of the Geological Survey."

(C. DCCCLXXVIII), to the clergy and laity of his diocese that he had confirmed to Margam Abbey the lands of Rossaulin, Resolven; Penhuth, Penhŷdd; Havet-haloc, Hafodheulog; Sturme and Egleskeinwir, Llangeinwir, and the *chapels* of the said places, &c., as his predecessors, Bishops William and Henry, have confirmed them (italics are mine). So Margam won its object.

Harley Charter 75, A. 9 (C. XXXVI and MCCCCI), is a notification by Earl William to his Sheriff of Glamorgan and all his barons and men, French, English, and Welsh, that he has confirmed the charters of Geoffrey Sturmi and Roger his son granting land to Margam Abbey. Also he confirms the agreement between the monks and Roger Sturmi concerning all the rest of Roger's land held of the Earl's fee in Margam, viz., that the monks hold the land of Roger in perpetual farm for half a mark silver yearly service to the said Roger, and after his death to his heirs, provided that Roger does service due, as he and his father before him did, to the Earl for the land. This agreement was confirmed at the request of Geoffrey, Roger's brother, to whom the Abbot of Margam gave a silver mark and a *pullus*, or colt, for his consent. The Earl undertakes to limit his power of distraint to the said half-mark silver yearly.

Witnesses : Hawisia, the Countess, the Earl's wife ; Hamo de Valoniis, constable of Cardiff Castle, and many others. And now I must bring to your mind, by way of remembrance, the position of William Earl of Gloucester, as it seems a long time since we saw who he was, and what his possessions were.

Earl William was the son of Robert, first Earl of Gloucester, and his wife Mabel, daughter of Sir Robert Fitzhamon. Earl William succeeded to Mabel's inheritance, and so possessed Kenfig and the hundred of Margam, a much larger district than is represented by the parish to-day; we find, for instance, that the Sturmi lands were in Margam. It would also appear that all the landowners held their lands from the Earl, and did service for them, to the Earl.

From a copy of Earl William's deed in the Margam Abbey Roll, T. 544, 15 (C. MCCCCII), we find his grant was confirmed when he, Geoffrey Sturmi, became a *frater conversus of* the Monastery; he became a lay brother, and had to perform various works under the monastic regulations.

The Abbey rolls consist of copies of the various documents on small rolls of parchment with witnesses omitted, evidently for easy transport in case of attack on the Abbey, so that should the originals be lost, copies would be available.

Roger Sturmi, the younger, by *Harley Charter* 75, D. 5 (C. DCCCLXXX), quit-claimed to the Abbey, with assent of his heirs, all the annual rent due from the monks of half-mark silver for the Sturmi lands, in perpetual almoign, charged with a recognisance of a pair of spurs or 6d. yearly. The monks give him 100s. for this quit-claim.

Witnesses: Robert de Cantilupo; Wido Wake; Henry the forester; John Croili; Roger, prior of Neth; Richard, sub-prior of the same house; Gervase and Geoffrey, monks of Neth and others. Dated 23 April, A.D. 1234.

Two deeds, *Harley Charter* 75, B. 8, 9 (C. CXVIII, DCCCLXXXII), contain the terms of (1) agreement and (2) the quit-claim of John, Res, Roger, Geoffrey, Henry, Moreduth (Meredydd), and Maurice, sons of Griffin Began, with and to Roger Sturmi, their uncle, and the monks of Margam, concerning the moiety of the rent of Sturmiestune, viz., "half a mark, which they alleged their uncle Roger had given by charter to their father, Griffin, in marriage with his sister, their mother." Sworn "in ecclesia de Landaf, super Tumbam Sancti Theliawi (St. Teilo) the Patron Saint of Llandaff, et super omnia sacrosancta ejusdem ecclesiae." In the presence of Elyas, Bishop of Llandaff; Maurice, Archdeacon; Rees, son of Griffin. The Archdeacon being proctor of the said Roger Sturmi, together with John (de Goldclive), Abbot of Margam. The witnesses to both deeds being Elias, Bishop of Llandaff, and many others.

Dated in Whit-week, A.D. 1234.

Harley Charter 75, B. 6 (C. DCCCLXXXI), is a quit-claim by Lewelin Began and his seven brethren already mentioned, to the Abbey of all their right to land at Sturmi. Sworn on the *sacrosancta* at Llandaff, with solemn promises to help the monks always. A long array of witnesses follows, among whom is the Bishop of Llandaff, Helias.

Dr. Birch says the family of Sturmi is not confined to Glamorganshire, but it is met with in the West of England. Mr. Clark says "that the transaction herein recorded, the confirmation by Earl William, given before Harley Charter 75 A. 9, of the Sturmi charters, seems to point to the retirement of the family from

the County, where they are again but once heard of."
The church of Sturmi was, however, mentioned later,
as we have seen.

Various Gifts to the Abbey.

T. 52 (C. DCXL) is a charter addressed to all the
sons of Holy Church wherein Walter, son of Ulf,
notifies that he has granted to Margam Abbey, in
frank almoign, twelve acres of land near the Grange
of St. Michael, on the west part, before the full hundred
of Kenefeg, his sons William and Alexander being
present. Walter Luvel is among the witnesses.
This land in part adjoins the land of Walter Luvel
(see page 75).

In the early years of the Abbey, as I have said, the
farms were worked by the *conversi* or lay brethren,
but a change came and the lay brethren were no
longer welcomed to the Abbey and the farms were let
to secular persons; the change took place about
A.D. 1470. The Cistercians at Margam were chiefly
sheep-farmers, and for this purpose large tracts of
mountain-land were given to them, such as Hirwaun,
near Neath, and hills extending thence as far as the
Rhondda, Llangeinor, and the moors at Cardiff,
where the Abbot had a grange, hence the name
Grangetown.

On the 13 July, A.D. 1448, Henry VI. issued a royal
charter T. 1175 to the Archbishops and public officers
of the Crown, attesting that, in token of his piety and
affection for the Virgin Mary, he had granted to St.
Mary of Margam the lordship and lands lying between
the waters of Ogmore and Garrewe, from their

confluence to Rotheney, or Rhondda, in perpetual fee farm, at an annual rent of 40s., with various privileges, such as a court every three weeks at Egliskeynwyre [1] (now Llangeinor), free fishery as far as the Oggemore extends, etc.

In A.D. 1246 the Bailiff [2] of Bristol had orders to seize all the wool purchased by the merchants of Ghent in Belgium, from the Abbot of Margam, and to hold it until further disposition was made of it. The reason for this seizure of the wool I have not been able to ascertain.

As showing the change from working their own granges to the letting to secular persons is a lease (T.527) by Abbot David to Thomas Hopkyn, of the reversion of a tenement in St. Michael's Grange called Holond, and pasture on the hills near Colbroke for 70 years, at a yearly rent of 9 cranocs of corn and a heriot. This change was a precursor of the dissolution and the monastic corporations were getting frightened about their position. Later on they made almost ruinous leases and quasi freeholds. Dated at Margam, 2 Aug., A.D. 1503.

The same abbot leased—T. 277 (C. MCCCXIII)— for 99 years to Lewelyn ap Jankyng and Griffith ap Lewelyn, his son, of the grange of Tanglus-lond [3] at the yearly rent of 12 cranocs of wheat and 4 cranocs of barley [4] and a heriot of the best beast. Endorsed

---

[1] The Church of St. Ceinwyr.

[2] Clark, " Land of Morgan," p. 109.

[3] Ty Tanglwys land.

[4] " Et quatuor cranoc ordei puri sicci et bene ventulati cum modio legale mensurati.'

Tare Tanglust, probably for Tir Tanglust. Dated at
the Chapter House of the Abbey, 13 Sept., A.D. 1516.
Seal still appended.

Abbot John Gruffydd leased T. 531 to David ap
Howell Goz, Gwenllian Verz Thomas his wife, and
others, the moiety of the grange Court-Bachan [1] at
Istormy [2] in the manor of Stormy vaghan,[3] for 70
years at a yearly rent of 7s. and 8 geese, and for the
pastures 6 bushels of wheat, with specified services.
4 Feb. A D. 1518,

The other moiety was leased—T. 279 (C.
MCCCXVII)—to Jankyn ap Phelip and Elizabeth
verz [4] Jeuan his wife. Rent 6s. 4d. and 8 geese.
6 Feb. A.D. 1518.

The seal of the Abbot and Convent is appended to
this deed. The Virgin and Child in a canopied niche
between two shields of arms ; *dex.* three clarions for
the Earls of Gloucester, founders of the Abbey ; *sin.*
three chevrons for Clare and Avene.

The same abbot leased T. 533 to Jeuan ap Lle'n
vaur, Agneta Verz Thomas his wife, and Lle'n ap
Jeuan, their son, land at Istormy, in the upper part of
lands called Can Grew, for their lives at a yearly rent
of fourteen bushels of corn, and geese at Michaelmas.
Margam, 26 Nov., A.D. 1518.

And by T. 534 land called Gweyn y Brombyll (in
Storme Vachan), for sixty years at a yearly rent of nine
cranocs of wheat, &c. Margam, 26 Nov., A.D. 1518.

It will be noticed in the two previous deeds the
word " bushel " is used.

[1] Cwrt bychan—little Court or Grange.　　[2] Stormy.
[3] Stormy fychan, Little Stormy.　　[4] Verz—verch, daughter.

The abbot evidently had a liking for geese at Michaelmas.

An extract from the Court Rolls of the Abbot at Kenefig T. 264 is the earliest brought to our notice.

In it Jeuan ap Gryffyth ap Gwelym is admitted tenant in land called Gebon ys londe, and after his death to Jovvan verze (a variant of verch) Howelle his wife, and then to Thomas his son; rent 14d.; entry 3s. 4d., suit of court, and a pair of capons for entry of the said Jovvan. The capons being by way of a fine or heriot; a service still kept up in some leases.

Before John Stradlyng, Esq., Steward, 9 Oct., 1459 A.D.

And just ten years before the Abbey fell the Abbot John Gruffydd leased the Mill.

An extract (C. MCCCXXVIII) from the Court Roll of John Abbot of Margam, at Kenfig, 15 Oct., A.D. 1527. Before Mathew Cradock, knight, then seneschal, or steward. To this court came Thomas ap David ap Howelle, Johannes ap Thomas David ap Howelle et Johannes ap Johne his son, and took from the lord the water-mill called Seynt Mizhelle is mylle (this, of course, is St. Michael's Mill), to hold it for their life. Rent 40s. and court suit, two capons or 4d. for entry.

Signet seal, dark red, $\frac{3}{8}$ in. dia., a Boar's head.

TEWKESBURY ABBEY EXCHANGES LANDS WITH MARGAM AND RETIRES FROM KENFIG.

Tewkesbury Abbey and Margam came to an agreement in A.D. 1484 and 1486 and exchanged lands. On the 12 Jan., A.D. 1485, King Richard III. granted a licence to the Abbeys of Margam and Tewkesbury to exchange certain premises.[1]

Thus Tewkesbury left Kenfig.

T. 526 (C. MCCLXXXVI) is an old English deed of an agreement between Richard the Abbot and Convent of Tewkesbury, and "Richarde Stradlynge monke ofe the monastery ofe oure Ladye ofe Morgan in byhalf of William Abbot of Morgan and the covent of the same place, by reason ofe a proxci ofe theire fulle auctoritie commyttede to the same Richarde," that Margam Abbey shall assure to Tewkesbury Abbey all Margam's lands at Salte-mershe Tokynton Olverstone and Bristow (Bristol) above a pension of 5os. to be paid yearly at Bristow by the hands of their prior of St. James, and shall warrant the same to be of the yearly value of £12 over all charges thereof deducted except tythes. The Abbot and Convent of Margam to have in exchange all such lands spiritual and temporal as they of the said Abbot and Convent of Teukesbury now have by composition and the patronage of the same. Dated at Teukesbury, Monday before Michaelmas, 2 Rich. III., A.D. 1484.

Then comes the deed of exchange.

This is T. 269 (C. MCCLXXVIII), an exchange between William, by Divine permission Abbot of the Monastery of the Blessed Mary of Morgan in the County of Glamorgan and Morgan and the convent of the same place on the one part, and Richarde by Divine permission Abbot of the Monastery of the Blessed Mary of Teukesbury in the county of

---

[1] Calendar of Patent Rolls, Part 2, m. 6.

Gloucester and the convent of the same place. The former leases to Teukesbury all the lands tenements, meadows, and pastures in Salt-merch, Hosbrugge, Tokyngton, Olverston and the town of Bristoll in the County of Gloucester, for 70 years, and an annuity of 60s.   The said Abbot and Convent of Teukesbury lease to the Abbot and Convent of Morgan, for a similar term, the tithes, lands, and advowsons of Newcastle and Kenefeke in the County of Glamorgan, with undertaking of renewals.

At the end of 60 years a new deed of lease for a fresh term of 70 years to be made.   Dated in the Chapter-houses of the aforesaid Monasteries, 27 May, A.D. 1486.

Harley Charter 75, A. 29 (C. CCCXCVII).   In this John Aston, Prior of the Priory of St. James, Bristol, acknowledges having received from Brother Richard Stradlynge, Cellarer of Margam, £3 sterling yearly pension appertaining to Tewkesbury Abbey, due at the Feast of All Saints.

Dated at Bristol 13 Oct., A.D. 1486.

Fifty-one years later the King—"Bluff King Hal"— had laid his grasp on both Abbeys by reason of his quarrel with the Pope, who would not see, as Henry came to see when he wanted a fresh wife, that he had done wrongly in marrying his brother's widow, Catherine of Aragon.   The Pope declined to sanction the divorce, and because the Abbeys were faithful to the Pope, King Henry prevailed with his Parliament to pass acts of dissolution and the monastic establishments were abolished.

CHAPTER XII

THE COMMON OF CEFN CRIBWR AND THE MANOR OF KENFIG

I PRESUME this common was allocated to certain owners of land in the vicinity. The burgesses of Kenfig were given pasturage along the ridge, viz., Cefn Cribwr, which extends from Catput to the ridge of Coity and in breadth from Cefn Cribwr to the water flowing from Lowerkesmore to Kenfig.

They are to have a Messor [1] upon their pasture; should he find other than the burgesses using the pasture, their cattle to be attached, and they presented in the hundred court of the town for fine according to the offence. This is an addition to Lord Edward le Despenser's charter by Thomas le Despenser in his charter of the 16 February (A.D. 1397).

The Earl of Pembroke retained the Manor of Kenfig until it was sold to Sir Edward Mansell, the sale of which I will refer to further on. Apparently differences arose between them, and in the answer of Sir Edward Mansel much valuable information is given in a succinct form, and although I take small

---

[1] Messor, a Hayward.

interest in the deeds of later times, I give this for the interest others may find in it.

T. 586 (C. MCCCLXXV) : Trespases supposed to be done by Sir Edward Mansell to the preiudice of the enheritance of yᵉ Right Honourable the Earl of Pembroke. In Kenfig, Avan, Newton Nottage, and Tyre y yarlle.[1]

THE OBJECTION.	THE AWNSWER
Kenfigg. The fishing in the pounde of Kenfig.	Whereto I have but prescripcon.
The taking of conies upon yᵉ sands between the borough and yᵉ sea.	I neither take nor claime any.
The inclosure of ¾ of an acre (by estimation) of meadow grownde by yᵉ castell.	Hit lieth on the Weast side of the river wᶜʰ is the meare of both.
The claiming of XL acres of marish grownde.	I claim no grownde thear wᶜʰ I have not in possession descended unto me.
The breaking of quarries in the comon.	The quarry is a peece of wast ground of myne owne.
The abbridging of yᵉ bounds of the comon. The encreaching of the same, and inclosure of some parte thereof.	I never abbridged any bounds nor ever enclosed one fote of comon of mine owne on other mens.

I presume the last two refer to Cefn Cribwr.

Avan. The bounds of Avan.	They seeke to encroach upon myne inheritance.
The fishing in the streame.	Non have any colour to pretend title to hit knowen to be mine owne inheritance as well by possession dece . . . . . as judgment.
The driving of the comon.	I never drave fote of hit.

---

[1] Tir Iarll, the Earl's land, referring to Robert Earl of Gloucester.

Newton Nottadge. The driving of the comon.	Hit was my dutie so to do in that it is mine by inheritance.
Tyre y Yarlle. The driving of some part of the manor.	I never drave fote.
The intollerable threatening of the tenaunts thear in Avan and Kenfigg.	I threatened none but to take what advauntage the lawe would geve me.
The impounding of some cattel in Tiryarll beside the detayning them in pound two whole days longer than promise.	At request of ye Earle of Pembroke's surveyers. I graunted that Morgan John should have his cattell out of pound who came not for them in two daies after nor ever would I have brought or sent them unto him.

In C. MCCCCXLIV we have a copy of " Notes touching the Lands in Question," written probably by Sir Edward Mansell :—

The Earles of Glocester, the Lords Spencers, nor the Earle of Pembroke had any lands within a mile of this medowe and lande in question in all ther times, and if that peece wear the lordes of Glam. then it was his as in his right of his lordship of Glamorgan.

On the north-west thereof lieth the manor of Havodporth late suppressed lande.

On the east lieth the manor of Newcastle.

Three miles by east [of] hit lieth the manor of Coitie.

On the south lieth the manor of Tythegstowe.

On the west lieth the manor of Pitteuin or Pile the uttermost inclosures thereof towardes the lande in question are Gramus lande and Gistle land mearinge upon Catpitt.

Iorath Couch graunted and abiured all his right which he had in the lande betwixt Cattpitt and Gramus lande and between the water of Kenfigg and the great waye that leadeth from the Rugg towards Kenfigg.

The third soune of Yeroth did abiure the same lande.

Thear is a forde at the north-east corner of Gwain y Kimney [1] called Ryde Yorath Couch [2] which fully proveth that lande to be Yorath Couch and that the forde beareth none of his lande whereon the forde lieth. (I presume Sir Edward means none of the Earl of Pembroke's land.)

Griffith and Cadrauc the sounis of Cadvant Gilla-michel did graunt all the father's lande que jacet ultra Kenfigg juxta terram Thome Stormi [which lies beyond Kenfigg adjoining the land of Thomas Stormi].

Roger Gramus graunted all his land which lieth betwine the great waye which leadeth from Kenfigg towards Castell Kribor and the water of Kenfigg.

They call the place wher the stones wear digged Witherell.[3]

Isabell repudiat of King John ladie of Glamorgan did confirme to the abbot, &c. : "totam terram inter Ellenwellake [4] et Witherell, que terra jacet pro 37 acris. Et residuum ex east parte de Witherell scilicet in terra qui tendit de vado lutoso quod dicitur Sclemilake per duas quarentenas versus orientem et aquilonem usque ad terra(m) Seith." ("All the land between Ellenwellelake and Witherell, reckoned as thirty-seven acres, and the rest on the east side of

---

[1] Waun-y-cimle.

[2] Rhŷd Yorath Goch, near Longland.

[3] Witherell is near Ystrad-fawr, near Newcastle, Bridgend. Witherell stream is now Nant Cefn-glâs.

[4] Ellenwellelake is the small stream west of Ystrad-fawr.

/itherell from the muddy ford called Sclemilake for
vo quarentenes length to the east and northwards
, the land of Seith.")

She did further release 11*js.* 1*d.* ob. which the
ɔbotes did use to paye of rent for the land of Jouaf
roingan [1] juxta Cattpitt.

Richard de Clare did confirme to the said abbotes
ıe same landes by thes wordes, " silicet terre que
cent juxta Catpite que redere nobis solebant
ınuatim 30^{den} et jacent inter alias terras monach-
:um." (" That is to say, land lying near Catpite and
ljoining other land of the monks which used to yield
ɜ 30*d.* yearly.")

He also confirmed landes in Corneliesdowne be
ıes wordes, " Videlicet terre super Corneliedowne,
ue reddere nobis solebant annuatim . . . et jacet
ıter terras monachorum." (" That is to say, land
ɔon Corneli Down which used to yield us formerly
ỳ the year . . . and it lies between land of the
ıonks.")

He confirmeth " moram que appelatur Rhedes ad
]uilonem terre Hugonis de Hereford."

" Et terram que jacet ad aquilonem ejusdem more
ıter terram Sturmy et aliam terram monachorum
:edictorum de Morgan usque ad viam juxta Catpitt
ue vadit ad Morgan."

"(The moor which is called Rhedes to the north
f Hugo de Hereford's land." And "the land which
es to the north of the same moor between the land
f Sturmy and other land of the monks, as far as
ıe road near Catpitt leading to Margam)."

[1] Jouaf Trwyngam—Jouaf of the crooked nose.

18

Laleston. Morgan the soune of Cradocke gave all the lande which he hath betwine Wetherell and Ellenwellake.

Tuder, Cradock, Knaythur, Alaythor, and Grono the sounes of Yorath ap Gislarde cosins and next heires to Youaf Troingan to Catherethdde [1] and Yoroth ap Espus Lordes of Piteuin or Pile did release ther right to Piteuin.

The grant of land by the sons of Cadraut Gilla-michell mentioned by Sir Edward is T. 1965. It is by Griffin and Cadraut, sons of Gillemichel, to Margam Abbey, of all the land which belonged to the said Cadraut Gillemichel, lying beyond Kenefeg, near the land of Roger Sturmi, with quit-claim and abjuration of all their lands within or without their boundaries. Sworn upon the *Sanctuaria* of Margam Church. Witnesses : Kedivor, son of Abraham ; Ithel, son of Breavel ; Enniaun his brother ; Artur, son of David Puignel. Early thirteenth century.

" Iorath Couch granted and abiured all his right, &c."

Morgam Gam, the Lord of Afan, witnessed a quit-claim, T. 74 (C. DCCCXI), by Yoruard Coh,[2] with advice and consent of Maurice, Lowarch, and Yoruard, his sons, to Margam Abbey of land between Cattepitt, the land of Gramus, the water of Kenefeg and the highway leading from La Rigge towards Kenefeg. Sworn on the holy reliques of Margam Church.

Witnesses : Morgan Gam ; Maurice ap Willim, constable ; Yoruard ap Espus, and others.

---

[1] Kethcrech Du.   [2] Coh—*goch*, red

This is the grant Sir Edward refers to.

The ford referred to existed until recently in the Kenfig river near Longland, and was known as Rhŷd Yorath Goch. A bridge has now, A.D. 1907, been erected at the ford.

We have already seen how the land of the Gramus family passed by degrees into the hands of the Abbey.

As Sir Edward alleges, Isabella in her free widowhood granted to Margam Abbey, among other grants, a rent of 4s. 1½d. issuing out of land that belonged to ouaf Troingam.

Sir Edward states that Richard de Clare did confirm to the said abbotes the same lande by thes wordes, that is to say the land at Catpitte for which they used to pay us 30d., lying between other lands belonging to the monks.

This, I find, is a grant by Gilbert de Clare, and not by Richard de Clare; a mistake by Sir Edward, probably.

These notes of Sir Edward Mansell are interesting and useful, indicating as they do the positions of some places which were doubtful.

On the dissolution of the monasteries, the manorial rights seem to have been retained for some time by the Crown, and King Henry VIII., as we have seen, leased, as lord of Glamorgan, the mill of St. Michael.

In A.D. 1668, 11 May, Philip Herbert, Earl of Pembroke and Montgomery, and others, sold the Manor of Kenfig to Sir Edward Mansell of Margam (A. MCCCCLV!) for £525.

" They sell to the said Sir Ewdard Mansell all that

the lordships or manors of Kenfigg alias Kenfeague in the said countie of Glamorgan with all that scite, decayed castle there, ediffices, buildings, lands, tenements, meadows, pastures, feedings, comons, wastes, heaths, moores, marshes, woodds, waters, fishings, warrens, with all courts, court leetes, court barons, view of franck pledge, perquisites of courts, releefes, heriotts, wayves, estrayes, goods, chattells, ffelons, fugitives, deodands, rents, reversions, services, with all rights, royalties, franchises, liberties, jurisdictions, rents, proffitts, comodities, and appurtenances to the said lordshipp or mannor belonging . . . and all that the libertie of digging or raiseing or disposeing of coales uppon or within a comon called Rugg."

I do not think a modern lawyer could think of any more matters ; everything seems to be included.

T. 2081 is an acquittance by Sir John Williams, Knt., Treasurer of the Court of Augmentations, to Sir Rice Maunxell, Knt., for £304 19s. 10d., in full payment of £678 1s. 6d. for the purchase of the Manor of Kenfige, &c., but the Manor did not come into the possession of Sir Rice at all. In the reign of Edward VI. the Manor of Kenfig was sold by the Crown to the Earl of Pembroke.

The common of pasture in Cefn Cribwr was claimed by Sir Edward Mansell and resisted by Mr. Gamage, as appears by the following document :—

C. MCCCCXLV is a copy of brief of instruction, with the proofs in support of the claim of Edward Mansell of common of pasture in Keven Cribwr, in the lordship of Newcastle, a claim resisted by Mr. Gamage, lord thereof.

It is a very interesting document, and so is the document giving ancient evidence as to the right to pasture in Cefn Cribwr.

Morgan ap Cradok before date granted to th' abbey of Morgan " communem pasturam totius terre mee ex est parte de Neth, etc. [" common of pasture in all my lands east of Neath "]. Leyson his soune granted the same by lyke words, etc. Richard de Clare granted " totam communem pasture inter Kenfig et Ogmore " [common of pasture between Kenfig and Ogmore]. Edward Mansell claymeth lybertee of pasture for the tenants of th' abbot of Morgan in the common of Kevencribor part of Mr. Gamage lordship of Newcastle, as well as prescripcion as by these grants.

Mr. Gamage denyeth any lybertee of pasture to pass by prescription or these words, first for that they are to(o) bare. 2. In that 'ex est parte de Neth,' is to(o) generall. 3. Because hyt appereth not that Morgan ap Cradok or Leyson hys soune weare lords of Newcastell or had auctoryte to grant lybertee of pasture in Keven-cribor. 4. Because Richard de Clare, etc., doth not by his dede prove him self lord of Newcastell.

The first is to be judged by lawe.

The second is in like sorte to be judged by lawe.

The third is proved by an other dede of the above named Morgan ap Cradock of thes words: 'Ego Morgan ap Cradok dedi famulo meo Rogero Cole, pro servicio 20 acras terre de dominico meo in feudo Novi Castelli, etc.' [" I Morgan ap Cradok have given to my servant Roger Cole for services 20 acres of land of my demesne in the fee of Newcastle "] and by a grete nomber of lyke deds as by th' originall graunt of th' said fee of Newcastell by John Erle Morton then Lord of Glamorgan and after King of Ingland, to the sayd Morgan ap Cradoc before date.

The fourth by dyvers grants in the same dede of Richarde de Clare Erle of Gloucester of divers lands in the fee of Newcastell ' et de 117 acris terre de dominico mensae meae in Novo Castello ante datum ' ['and of 117 acres of land in the demesne of my table in New Castle '].

It is also proved in that th' abbot and his tenants have tyme out of mynd enjoyed comon of pasture in th' sayd comon of Kevenkribor.

Fynally hit is proved by an inquisition taken anno 3 Edward III. whereby hit was fownd that Gilbert de Clare Erle of Gloucester did eject th' abbot of Margan out of the common of pasture by thes words, ' et de communi pastura quam cum aliis liberis illius patriae habuerunt in Kevencribor, etc., liberavit dictis abbati, etc., et pasturam de Kevencribor tenendum in seperali.'

Item the said Edward Mansell claymeth common incertam upon Kevencrybor foresaid by vertue of a deede thereof made by Richarde de Turberville Lorde of Newecastell for a certaine number of cattaile therein expressas owt of the granges of Langewith and Stormy.

Then follows " Evidence as to a Right of Common of Pasture on KevenKribwr."

(C. MCCCCXLVI): " Morgan son of Caradoc, etc., . . . I have granted and by this charter have confirmed to God and to the Church of St. Mary of Morgan and the monks serving God there in alms common of pasture in all my land on the east

)f Neath as far as my land extends in length and
n width both in wood and in plain with all
:asements, etc."

Leisan son of Morgan, etc. . . . I have given to
he Church of St. Mary of Morgan common of pasture
n all my land on the east of Neath [ex est parte de
Neath].

Richard de Clare Earl of Gloucester and Hereford ;
' I have granted, etc., to the Church of Blessed Mary
)f Morgan, etc., a burgage in New Town, etc., and
ill common of pasture between Kenfig and Ogmore
inte dated, and of 117 acres of my lordship of my
able in Newcastle."

An inquisition held at Cardiff in full County of
Glamorgan, etc., . . . in the reign of Edward III.,
:tc., before a jury of 24, consisting of Sir Henry
le Humfrevil, knt., Sir Edward Stradlinge, knt., Sir
Philip Fleminge, knt., and others. They find that the
aid Gilbert de Clare, brother of the said Alienora,
:jected the said monks of Morgan from the said
ands, that is to say, a grange in the moor near
Cardiff and common of pasture in Kevencribwr for
vhich the said Earl delivered to the same monks
Ferries grange, Moregrange, and the pasture of
Kevencribor, to be held in severalty.

This Indenture made in the 34th year of Edward
II. between Sir Richard Turberville, knt., Lord of
Coytif and the religious men, etc., of Morgan on the
)ther part Witnesseth that I the said Richard grant
o the Abbot and Convent of Margam free pasture
)n my several pastures of the Rugge called Keven-
:ribor in the fee of Newcastle with free ingress and

egress to the same to a certain number of cattle, that is to say for 50 oxen, 30 cows, 40 steers and heifers and a flock of sheep housed at the grange of Langewith, and also 60 head of cattle and a flock of sheep housed at Stormy Grange, etc., etc.

The deed (T. 2067) goes on to relate the conditions for which the above is granted ; the conditions are not quoted by Sir Edward Mansell.

On condition of their, the monks, maintaining a chaplain, monk or lay [by lay, secular is meant, I presume], to celebrate services at the Altar of St. Mary Magdalene in Margam Church for his soul, etc., the entering his name in the "Martilogium" among the founders, anniversary services to be celebrated during the Mass in the choir after his death, etc.

Dated Le Coytif (Coity), 1st Dec. (A.D. 1360), 34 Edw. III.

John Earl of Mortagne, afterwards King, to all his men and friends French and English greeting.

He grants and confirms by his charter to Morgan, son of Cradoc, for his homage and service New Castell of Ogmore to be held by him by a fourth part of a Knight's fee for all service.

Gilbert de Clare Earl of Gloucester grants the whole moor between the water of Baithan as the water of Baithan on the west and as the river called Guthelendelak[1] for the east descends from Treikic

---

[1] Guthelendelak. I do not know this stream ; probably the stream flowing from Tre-y-gedd. It looks like an attempt to write Gelli-llyn-du, the grove of the black lake— Guthelende.

; far as Hollac that they (? monks) may hold the
iid moor of us and our heirs in "perpetuam
emosinam," etc.

Apparently, then, the Abbey of Margam had
>mmon of pasture on Cefn Cribwr, and so had
so the burgesses of Kenfig.

In Sir Richard Turberville's conditions which he
iks of the monks in return for common of pasture
1 Cefn Cribwr is one, among others, that his name
e entered in the "Martilogium." Abbot Gasquet
:lls us in the daily routine of monastic life, "im-
iediately after the conclusion of the morning Mass,
ie great bell was set ringing for the daily Chapter.
)n its cessation the community left the choir and
roceeded to the chapter-room, the juniors walking
rst; this would be about nine o'clock in the morning.
1 the chapter-house all stood in their places till the
ntrance of the superior. If the abbot were present,
ll bowed as he passed through their ranks, and as
e reached his seat at the upper end of the room,
ie prior and one of the seniors from the abbot's
ide of the choir came forward to kiss his hand,
owing to him both before and after this act of
omage.

"Whilst the community and superior were coming
ito the Chapter, the junior appointed for the office
f reader in the refectory stood holding before his
reast the *Martyrology*, or book of the saints daily
ommemorated by the Church. When all had
ntered and taken their seats, the reader came
>rward, and placing the volume upon the lectern
1 the middle of the room, asked the blessing of the

president in the usual form.   This having been given,
he read the portion of the *Martyrology* which gave
the brief notices of the lives of the martyrs and other
saints commemorated on the following day.   When
mention was made of any saint whose relics were
possessed by the house, or who was specially connected with it as patron or otherwise, the community
removed their hoods and bowed down as a mark of
special reverence."

Sir Richard wished to be thus remembered as a
patron of the Abbey.

CHAPTER XIII

NEWTON NOTTAGE

ONE cannot be indifferent to the doings of one's neighbours, and so Kenfig must have felt eat interest when it became known that Margam bbey was about to exchange Resolven, near Neath. r Newton and Newton Nottage, places quite near to enfig.

Richard de Neville, Earl of Warwick, Lord Le espenser, Lord of Glamorgan, Morgan and Berveny, on the 4th May, A.D. 1452, in Cardiff Castle, anted—T. 262 (C. MCCLXIII)—to Thomas, Abbot d the Convent of Margam, the manors of Newton d Notesch,[1] in exchange for the manor of Rosoulyn.[2] nder seal of the Chancery. The parish of Newton ottage, having an area of 3,391·25 acres, adjoins :er, Pyle, and Tythygston Lower parishes. This ed recalls the charter of William Earl of Gloucester, ntioned before, in which he gave to Richard de ardif, for his services, the New-Town in Margam th all its appurtenances (see p. 132). It is eresting to note that the large district given to chard de Cardiff is stated to be in Margam, so

---

[1] Nottage [2] Resolven, near Neath.

that Margam was in those days more extensive than
Margam parish.   Margam is perhaps the part of the
county called Morgan, *i.e.*, Glamorgan and Morgan.
The charter of Robert Earl of Gloucester giving
to the monks of Clairvaux all the lands between
Kenfig river and the further bank of the Afan
river does not give this tract of land the name
Margam, but later it became confined to these
lands.

The boundaries of the land given to Richard de
Cardiff included the parish of Newton, part of Pyle
parish, Sker, and a considerable part of Kenfig. How
much is difficult to say, for the boundary from Pwll-y-
gâth to the sea I am unable to locate.   I say Sker
is included because it was not apparently excluded.
In the dispute between Margam Abbey and Richard
de Cardiff, you will remember that the Earl decided
against Richard de Cardiff's claim and notifies that he
had given Sker to Margam in exchange for their land
at Novus Burgus, long before the said Richard had
any land from the Earl.   Seeing the deed did not
mention that Sker had already been given, it is easy
to understand the claim Richard de Cardiff made, as
I have said before.

The ancient boundaries appear to me to be on
the east, somewhat as the parish boundary is to-day.

It begins at the ancient ditch which ends on
the sea-shore ; this is probably the Bwlch-y-cariad,
and if so the present boundary begins at the same
point as the ancient one.   It then leads by Dewiscumbe to the ditch from above St. Tudoc, St. Tudwg
(Dewiscumbe I had considered to be the valley in

hich is St. David's Well, a little north of Nottage,
ıt Dewiscumbe must be between the sea-shore and
ythegston). Then as far as Alweiscnappe ; this
range word I have long puzzled over, but I think
 refers to the point reached by the boundary,
wmpath-y-ddaiar, the earth mound, near the
ritish Camp on the south corner of Stormy
'own, and near Ballâs.[1] I think it is derived
om allwest, pasture, and cnap, a mound or a
mp, allwest-y-cnap, *i.e.*, the pasture of the mound,
·, as it is in Welsh, twmpath. Then to a certain
one between Alweiscnappe and Bulluchesbruhe ; the
tter, I think, means Bal-lâs, bruhe I cannot make
ıt. Bal-lâs was probably pronounced Bol-lâs, as
 was written in those days, so Bulluches is near
ıough for the Norman scribe. Thence it follows
om that point (the stone is there no longer) the
[eol-y-splot to the vale of Corneli as at present,
ıt instead of continuing to the sea, it turned
ɔ the vale of Corneli to Danes' Vale, be-
veen Marlas and The Hall, joining the present
ɔundary between Pyle and Kenfig apparently
here it touches the road from South to North
orneli. From Danes' Vale it passed to Catteshole,
wll-y-gâth, thus departing from any present boundary.

---

[1] A landowner, Wronu Bil, of Kenfig, who occurs in A.D 1219–
54, grants—T. 124 (C. DCCCXXXIII)—to Margam in frank
moign seven acres of arable land ; five of them lie on the south
ljacent to the land of William Cole, beginning at a place called
ılles and reaching towards Goylake, and the other two on the
.st near Roger Gramus' land beginning at Luelsgrove. Wit-
:sses : Sir W. Luvel, and others.

From Catteshole the boundary went direct to the sea along the bottom of the valley to Baeian, which is *in sabluno.* The last word should be evidently *in sabulo,* then it would read " to Baeian which is in the sand," *i.e.*—sand-hills. The east part of Pyle parish would seem to be excluded ; east of the road from south of South Corneli to north of North Corneli.

Richard de Cardiff owned Walton in Gloucestershire. His two daughters married Bevis and Sandford, of whom the latter held Newton. These names are perpetuated in Bevos, near Newton, and the curious Sandford Well at the same place ; the well ebbs and flows contrary to the ebb and flow of the sea, so at high-water of the tide the well is empty. In the notice on Sker, it will be remembered Thomas de Sandford endowed the grange of Sker. The Earl added to the grant of Newton to Richard de Cardiff a large tract of land between the ford of Baithan (Baiden) and the high-road leading from Langewy, Llangewydd, to Trekic, Tre-y-gedd.

The witnesses were Hawisia, "the Countess my wife"; Robert de Meisi; Symon de Sancto Laudo, or St. Loo,[1] and many others.

Richard Nevill, the " King-maker," Earl of Salisbury and Warwick and lord of Glamorgan in right of his wife, who made the exchange with Margam Abbey of Newton Nottage for Resolven, was eldest son of Richard Earl of Salisbury, by Alice, daughter and heiress of Thomas Montacute, Earl of Salisbury. He married Anne, daughter and heiress of Richard

[1] St. de St. Laudo, or St. Loo, owned Newton St Loo, near Bath.

Beauchamp, Earl of Warwick, by Isabel le Despenser, eir of her niece Anne Beauchamp, being daughter nd heiress of Henry Duke of Warwick.

Richard Nevill fell at Barnet, April, 1471 (Clark, Cartae," etc.).

Newton Nottage was in later times divided between he Earl of Pembroke, Richard Loughor, Esq., and he heir of Sir William Herbert, Knt. I again make se of a document of the seventeenth century, " The Manors of the Earl of Pembroke in the County of Glamorgan."

The area is given as 1,200 acres; it is actually ,391 : it goes on to state, in addition to the above s to the division, "that it was given, as we have lready seen, by William Earl of Gloucester (then ord of Glamorgan), unto one Sir Richard Cardiffe, who had only one daughter, that married one Sir Thomas Sandford, Knt., and had issue Sir Richard Sandford, Knt., Lord of Newton ; but how the Sandfords went from the same I could not find as et. There are three wells in this lordship, which low and ebb twice in twenty-four hours, and at very time, contrary to the sea, whereupon Sir John Stradling, Knt., Baronet, moralized." This is some- what different from what I have already stated bout Richard de Cardiff.

St. John's well at Newton Nottage has long been nown to ebb and flow in sympathy with, but not imultaneously with, the tide. It was described and he movements of the water observed by H. G. Madan, from whose pages the following account is aken.

The well is 500 yards from the shore and separated from it by sand dunes and a pebble-ridge. The sand rests on Keuper conglomerate, and this on carboniferous limestone. Between the two rocks a considerable body of water flows seaward, and bursts out on the foreshore. It is this water which is tapped in the well. The well is $13\frac{1}{2}$ feet deep, and its bottom is 8 feet above Ordnance Datum. From a number of hourly and half-hourly observations Madan ascertained that the movements of the water in the well were as regular as those of the tide, but that they lagged behind the tide almost exactly three hours.

The water contains the rather high proportion of 27·2 parts per 100,000 of sodium chloride, but shows the same proportion when at its highest as when at its lowest level.

The interpretation of these phenomena presents no serious difficulty. The water contained in the Keuper conglomerate and carboniferous limestone " is in free communication with the sea along the line where the conglomerate crops out below high-water level on the shore.

" The tidal wave, on reaching the outcrop, is taken up by the water in the permeable strata and propagated landwards, but with a greatly diminished velocity, owing to the resistance to its motion offered by the solid, though porous, stratum of conglomerate. . . . Hence we have high-water in the well three hours later than high-water in the sea." [1]

─────────

[1] " Memoirs of the Geological Survey.—Water Supply," by A. Strahan, from notes by R. H. Tiddeman.

The church of Newton is situated close to the
reat expanse of sand-dunes, known as Merthyr
Iawr Warren, which reaches from Porth-cawl to
ie mouth of the Ogmore river, and deserves some
otice.

Mr. G. E. Halliday writes : " The church consists
f a chancel, nave, western tower, and an unusually
.rge south porch, containing many good examples
f thirteenth, fourteenth, and fifteenth century work.

" There seems no evidence, however, of any
:mains belonging to the twelfth century being *in
tu;* although it appears to the writer that the
ises of the fourteenth-century porch entrance-arch
·e in reality Norman capitals turned upside down,
› suit the builders of that time.

" The tower, to which the writer more par-
:ularly wishes to draw attention, is a massive
ructure, in all about fifty-four feet high—twenty-
:ven feet from north to south, and twenty-two
et from east to west, supported at its four
›rners by six exceedingly heavy buttresses. From
; general appearance, and from the evidence of
.e early details still remaining, there is little if
ly doubt that this portion of the building, at any
te, was used for defensive purposes. The range
 eight massive corbels, projecting about two feet
›m the eastern face of the tower wall, formed in
l probability the support for a temporary wooden
atform ; while the splayed and moulded battlement
ping-stones now, laid flat, would, when placed on
eir natural bed, form a moulded and weathered
.ttlement coping to the early flat-roofed tower."

19

Mr. Halliday shows how in all probability the wooden platform was arranged, and quotes from Viollet-le-Duc, who gives several illustrations of almost identical methods of outer defence adopted in France during mediæval times.

" During the fifteenth century the defensive character of the tower appears to have been done away with. The beautiful west door with crocketed label and pinnacles was inserted, and the roof assumed the present gabled form.

" The priest's door and adjacent windows seem part of this rebuilding; there is little doubt that the circular stone pulpit, with its very rudely-carved representation of the scourging of our Lord, is of the same period." [1]

It seems difficult to imagine the necessity for having the tower of a church arranged as a place of defence, but it must be remembered that for a long period there was war to all intents and purposes between the Welsh of the hill country and the Normans of the lowlands. We know from the Margam MSS. that the men from Brechinioc and Seinghenydd frequently harried the lowlands.

At Nottage is an interesting mansion house, Nottage Court, formerly called Ty Mawr, or Great House. It was the grange, or manor-house, belonging to the Abbot of Margam, to which he would retire at times, but it was altered somewhat in Tudor times and restored later by the Rev. H. H. Knight.

[1] " Church of St. John the Baptist," G. E. Halliday, *Arch. Camb.*, April, A.D. 1904.

Disputes frequently took place between Margam
Abbey and Neath Abbey, and they were generally
referred to arbitration, in accordance with the
Cistercian rule of adjusting disputes without recourse
to extraneous aid : arranging and settling their differences among themselves, they refrained from taking
their cases to the courts as far as possible. The
following is a dispute concerning Newton.

In T. 135 (C. DCCCCXI) we have the deed
of arbitration by Roger, Abbot of Ryevallis, or
Rievaulx, in co. York; Nicholas, Abbot of Vallis
Dei, or Vaudey, co. Lincoln ; John, Abbot of
Kingswood, co. Wilts, in a cause between Neath
and Margam Abbeys; that the Abbot of Margam
had endeavoured to supplant the Abbot of Neath
in Noua-villa, or Newton Nottage ; that the Abbot
of Margam is to desist from doing so ; that the
Abbot of Neath is to be careful in his dealings
respecting the acquisition of that town ; that there
is to be an amicable joint possession of the pastures
of Neutune-dune and Corneli-dune, or a fair division,
according to the view of the Abbots of Boxley,
Buildwas, and Kingswood, so that each Abbot may
have the moiety nearest his abbey, or grange.

The unfounded claim of Neath to land and pasture
held by Margam, by the charter of Robert Earl of
Gloucester, and adjusted by an award [1] of the

---

[1] This was a settlement of a dispute, 28 May, A.D. 1208,
between the Abbeys of Margam and Neath by arbitration of the
Abbots of Boxley, Wardon, and Fountains. The dispute was
as to the pastures, &c., between the Afan river and Neath and
the head of the great Afan called Blaen-Afan, and as to
Resolven, Neath.

Abbots of Boxley, Wardon, and Fountains, is to be dismissed. The text of this agreement was settled by John, first Abbot of Boxley, co. Kent, afterwards Abbot of Citeaux, at Boxley, in the presence of the Abbots of Boxley, Stratford-Langthorne, co Essex, Vallis-Dei, and Robertsbridge, co. Sussex, before St. Agatha's Day, 5 Feb., A.D. 1237 for 1238. Four seals remain—those of the Abbots of Rievaulx, Vallis Dei, Kingswood, and Neath.

Evidently there was some intriguing going on by both abbots, Margam trying to oust Neath from Newton ; on the other hand, my lord Abbot of Neath had apparently been somewhat unscrupulous in acquiring or endeavouring to acquire Newton.

The claim of Neath Abbey was apparently a renewed claim to pastures between the Afan and Neath rivers, which had before been arbitrated upon (see page 81). Two hundred and fourteen years later Margam exchanged Resolven for Newton Nottage, and so ousted Neath from Newton. In the deed of exchange Newton and Nottage are regarded as separate manors ; a deed a little later names them as the manor of Newton Notaysshe.

The Newton Wake, or Mabsant, was held on the Decollation (Old Style), instead of the Nativity, of St. John Baptist.

Old people told the Rev. H. H. Knight, he relates in his work on Newton, that there had been a custom of kindling a fire in a small circular inclosure near Newton by Sandford's well on Midsummer Day each year, and throwing a small cheese or cake across it and then jumping over the embers. This recalls the old Celtic and Scandinavian bonfires.

As I have before remarked, Nottage Court was evidently the grange belonging to Margam Abbey— the Noche, or Noge Court, so called. A chapel also was attached to it, of which the site is known. The present building replaced the old Court in Elizabethan times, as its style of architecture shows. The tapestry in the Court was brought from Tewkesbury, having hung probably in the abbot's house.

CHAPTER XIV

TALES OF KENFIG

A TRADITION persists that the ancient town of Kenfig lies at the bottom of Kenfig Pool. I do not know the origin of this idea, but it is repeated in the following tale from the Iolo MS.

CYNFFIG.

A peasant's son loved the daughter of the Lord of Clare, and she would not have him because he was not rich, and he went to the high-road and watched for the steward of the lord of the district returning towards the castle from collecting his lord's money, and he killed him and took his money, and showed her the coin, and the lady married him. He then made a magnificent feast and invited the chief men of the country to it, and they made themselves merry to the utmost. The second night the marriage took place, and when they were merriest a voice was heard, and they listened attentively, and heard "Vengeance will come! Vengeance will come! Vengeance will come!" three times. And they asked when. "At the end of the ninth generation," said the voice. "There is no occasion for us to fear," said they; "all of us will be under the earth long before that." Nevertheless, they lived till a descendant was born of the ninth generation, and another, a descendant of the man that was killed, seeing the arrival of that period, visited Cynffig, a young man, a discreet and comely young man; and looking at the town and its wealth, without any one possessing a furrow or corner excepting the descendants of the murderer, and he himself still living, and his wife. At the crowing of the cock they heard a voice, "Vengeance is come! Vengeance is come! Vengeance is come!" "On whom is it come?" said they. "On him who slew my ancestor of the ninth generation." They rose in terror and went towards the town, and there was nothing to be seen but a large lake, and in it above the surface of the water three chimney-tops smoking, and the smoke of an offensive smell. Upon the surface of the water the gloves of the man who had been killed floating towards the feet of the young man. He took them up and saw the name and arms of the murdered man; and with the dawn there were countless voices praising God with heavenly songs. And thus it ends.

The following tale is also from the Iolo MS. It is interesting as relating an episode in the monastery of Margam, Rhys, a monk, being dismissed, and also for the mention of Kenfig Castle. Sir Mathew Cradoc was steward of Margam Abbey. In the book of Sion Bradford, the history of Twm Ieuan, the son of Rhys, is as follows:

Ieuan, the son of Rhys, was a monk in Margam,

but he was turned out of the monastery on account of being a Lollard in principles. After this he married a nun, who was turned out of some nunnery, and they lived at Cynfig; but Sir Mathew Cradock,[1] of Swansea, followed him with the law, for something probably on account of his faith, until he was compelled to leave Cynfig, and then he took a place in Merthyr Cynog, in Breconshire, where he held some land. And after some time he came back to Glamorgan, where he kept a school; he was a good poet. Ieuan, the son of Rhys, had a son called Thomas, who was Twm, the son of Ivan, the son of Rhys, the poet and prophet. He was in some office in the monastery of Margam, and was turned out from thence, and was imprisoned several times at Cynfig Castle, by Sir Mathew Cradoc, who at last gave him his liberty, and behaved liberally towards him. He held land in Margam and Llangynwyd, and many other places, until some extraordinary thoughts came into his mind, which occasioned his being imprisoned by Sir George Herbert, of Swansea, in Cynfig Castle. And after he regained his liberty, he did little more than walk about the country as a beggar, thrashing a little sometimes, and making godly songs, and prophesying many things, on which account he was called "Twm of the fair lies" (Twm Celwydd Teg). He began to prophesy before he was imprisoned by Sir George Herbert, and it is said the reason was that, after the birth of the son and heir of Sir George, a feast was held, and great rejoicing, at the christening of the child, and they shod the horses with silver, and many other costly things

[1] Sir Mathew Cradock was steward of Margam Abbey.

hey did likewise. Twm, the son of Ivan, the son of Rhys, seeing this, said, "Ha! here is parade, and great pride about the baptism of a child born to be hung by the string of his forehead-band." He was seized, and put in prison, in Cynfig Castle; and the child was placed in the care of a nurse, who was ordered to watch him narrowly and carefully night and day; this went on some time, when it was reported in the house that the nurse had the itch. Sir George and his lady sent for her to the hall to them, that they might see whether it was true or not, and when they saw that there was no itch upon her they went with her back to the chamber where the child was, and the first thing they saw was the child in his cradle, having twisted his hands under the string of his forehead-band, and entangled them in such a manner that he got choked, and died from that cause, or as it be said with truth, he hung himself in the string of his forehead-band. Then they sent in haste to liberate Twm, the son of Ivan, the son of Rhys, and to give him money. Another time he was thrashing in a barn, and a young lad went by, and addressing him as follows: "Well, Twm Celwydd Teg, what news have you to-day?" "There is news or thee," said he. "Thou shalt die three die deaths before this night." "Ha! ha!" said the youth, 'nobody can die more than one death," and he went off laughing. In the course of the day the lad went to the top of a great tree on the brink of a river, to take a kite's nest, and thrusting his hand into the nest he was wounded by an adder, brought by the kite to her young ones, as she was accustomed to do.

This causing him to lose his hold, he fell down on a great branch and broke his neck, and from there into the river, and thus he met with three deaths. To be wounded by an adder, to break his neck, and to be drowned. Twm, the son of Ivan, the son of Rhys, was a good and godly man, it is said, and a good poet, and many songs of his composition are still extant in the country, and it is said he printed some of them ; but there are few, if any, now living that ever saw them. It is said he saw written in a little manuscript book these words :—

"Love thy neighbour as thou wouldest love thyself, and suffer for him as thou wouldest suffer for thy God, and for thy dearest friend, and for thyself. "Seek after God with all thy might, and with all thy mind, and with all thy understanding, and love Him with all thy affection, and with all thy will, and with all thy heart.

"Love everything that is good, and becoming, and true, and just, as thou wouldest thy God, and thyself. "Cleave to them until thou art as much one with them as God is, and by doing so, thou shalt be as separate from every evil, and wickedness, and from all that is unseemly, and unbecoming, and unrighteous, and unjust, and from envy, fraud, and delusion, as God himself is. "Fear not any punishment, or pain, or any want, or distress, nor any suffering, even death, and be not hindered by them. "Covet nothing of the worldly goods thou seest or hearest of, or understandest ; but desire the good things of God, and the peace of His Holy Spirit, and leave to thy God to provide for thee.

" And in possessing these virtues, thou shalt have right understanding of everything in the world, and f right understanding, a right knowledge, and of ight knowledge, the comprehension of all that was, nd is, and shall be ; and of that knowledge inspira- on from God, and the power of prophecy, and then halt thou understand and show all that is to come in ie world till the day of doom, for the perception of ;od shall be in thee."

After reading this, he gave himself up to be a very oodly man, and uttered many prophecies, and would ot possess any property in the world excepting what ʹas voluntarily bestowed for the work he did, which ʹas chiefly thrashing corn.

CHAPTER XV

THE ROMAN HIGHWAY IN KENFIG. ROMAN MILLIARIA. ROMAN LEGENDS

THE Roman Highway, the Via Julia Maritima, commencing on the south-east of the united parishes of Pyle and Kenfig—for it was from the east the Romans made their way from Caerleon, or as they named it, Isca Silurum—passes through them for a distance of close upon four miles before it reaches the northern limit of the borough at the milliary stone, Pumpeius Carantorius. The commencement of the Via Julia in Pyle parish is on Stormy Down, near an ancient British camp, and near the farm Bal-lâs, to which reference has been made before. This ancient camp is situated on the edge of the down at an altitude of a little above 300 feet above sea-level; the Roman road enters the parish at an altitude of 329 feet, and this is at the point at which the diversion of the main road from the old Roman highway, on account of the trouble caused by the sand invasion, commenced. About a mile and half away to the north is the British camp on the western end of Cefn Cribwr; proud of its superior elevation, for it stands 426 feet above sea-level, and also by

eason of the title of castle which it gained in early
imes. I had not realised, until quite recently, what

commanding aspect this
ncient stronghold presents for
1any miles around. It seems
nposing, as you look at it
·om the Groes-y-dadl, for it
ises from the surrounding
inds like a huge kopje, with
:vel top, and 326 feet above
ou. Again it seems to
·own on smiling, peaceful
`y-Tanglwys, for it stands
bove it quite as high as it
; above the cross of strife.
Io more the cross of quarrel,
1e whole delightful scene,
athed in the golden sun-
1ine, seems far from aught
ut "smooth - faced peace."
`he day when Roman cohorts
·ith burnished helmet, short
word, and glittering shield,
assed gladly from the cold
f Stormy Down into the
·arm shelter of Corneli Vale
1 their way to Leucarum
_oughor, as it is misspelt
)-day), has long passed into

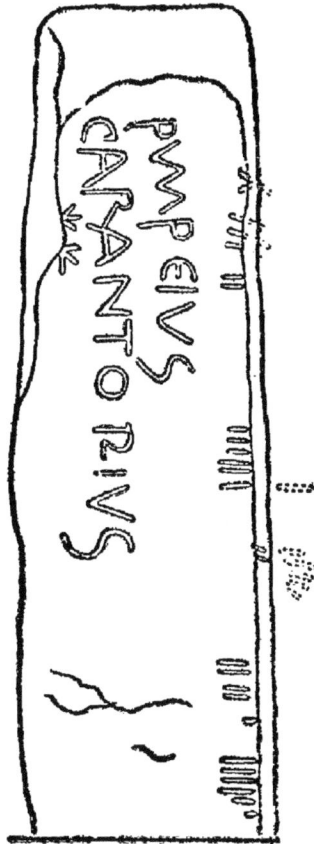

STONE OF PUMPEIUS
CARANTORIUS.

1e dim mists of ages, but the old camp still looks
)wn and bids us remember long and bitter struggles.

From Morfa Mawr, four and a half miles away to

the west on the seashore, the old castle looks more imposing still, for it is 400 feet above you, in solitary dignity. And as I looked at it, I came to wonder why it never had occurred to me before that the old stronghold must have given its name to the district it so proudly dominates. And then, as if a message from the distant past came to me, I knew it had, for it was Pill, a fortress, a place of defence. And this is the meaning of Pyle or Pill or Pyll, as it has been variously spelled, and much thought and labour have I bestowed upon it.

Away to the north-west, three miles and a half, where the hills curve round and bulge out nearer to the main road and the sea, forming from the camp on Stormy Down an amphitheatre, on one side of the entrance to Cwm Maelwg stands Mynydd Castell, a British camp.[1] On the other side, a little further west than the entrance to the valley stands another British camp, now called the Halfmoon ; perhaps because it has no further use than for pleasing lovers longing for the honeymoon at the full. It is situated at 500 feet above sea-level. Now winding up through this charming valley is a road which was the Roman vicinal way to reach the mountain-lands. And on these lonely mountain-tops much war had taken place in days gone by, for British and Roman camps and Danish too are frequent.

A Roman halting-camp stands at the very top of Cwm Kenfig near Rhŷd Blaen-y-Cwm,[2] and half a mile north-east of it is a Roman camp, having

[1] Near Margam Park Mansion.
[2] The ford of the top of the valley.

a large British, post-Roman camp circling round it. It is known as y Bwlwarcau. Just half a mile to the north from the halting-camp, and nearly half a mile north-west from the Bwlwarcau, stands Bodvoc's sepulchral stone—so old that the monks of Margam called it, eight hundred years ago, the Maen Llwyd, the venerable stone.

Around this great open plain, if I may roughly so describe it, stand, studded with entrenchments, the rounded hills, whereon the Romans found such stubborn gallant foes in a circle from the camp at Stormy to the one at Grugwallt. In this great open space stand the ruins of the Monastery of Margam.

And now we shall see what took place in this great open land sixteen hundred years ago.[1]

When Caradoc, the son of Bran, the son of Llyr Llediaith, was warring with the Romans, and slaughtering them terribly, some of those who had escaped told their Emperor that there was neither chance nor hope of overcoming Caradoc, the son of Bran, as long as the woods and thickets remained in the territories of Caradoc and his Cymry, viz., in the dominion of Essyllwg, Siluria—inasmuch as, they said, that in the woods and forests they conceal themselves like wild beasts, and it is impossible to obtain a sight or a glance of them, so that they come upon us Cæsarians unawares, as numerous as bees out of a hive in a long, hot summer day, and slaughter us in heaps. The Emperor answered, " By my great

---

[1] This account, taken from the Iolo MS., is considered by me to be fabulous ; it is as probable as narratives of other events which have come down to us from those far-off times.

name and destiny the woods in the territory of
Caradoc and his Cymry shall not long stand.   I will
despatch to that territory one hundred legions of my
best warriors with fire instead of weapons, and I will
set on fire all the woods in the territories of Caradoc."
Caradoc and his men hearing these words said, " It
is a small thing for us to defend our country, otherwise than through strength of body and heart : therefore let us burn our woods, as broad and as far as
there is a leaf of their growth, so that there may not
be found a sprig to hang a flea from the shore of
Severn to the River Towy, as broad and as long as
the territories of Siluria extend.   Then let us invite
the Cæsarians to our country and meet their army
against army upon the plain and open ground, the
same as we did on the covert ground and on the
wilds."

Then they burned all the woods from the shore of
the Severn to the extremities of the Vale of Towy,
as far as the territories of Caradoc and his Cymry
extended, without leaving a sprig upon which the
smallest gnat could alight, to rest from the heat on a
long summer day.   Then they sent messengers to
the Emperor of Rome and explained the object of
their mission.   They were the men of Caradoc who
would greatly prefer tranquillity to war, more gladly
would they feed milch kine and wool-bearing sheep
than war-horses ; more desirable to them the entertainment of their friends than slaughtering their
enemies.   Then they told the Emperor their lands
were no longer in thicket, there was no need for his
wild-fire for there was no work for it upon the face of

Vales. " Let thy men meet us army to army on open round ; two foreigners for one Cymro on plain land, nd try to win back the honour thou hast lost in the rilds ; Caradoc himself addresses thee."

The Emperor was annoyed at the protection the Cymry received from him, by the privilege of ambasadors from a foreign country, when he understood it ras no other than Caradoc who addressed him.

The Romans brought their armies into the field rheresoever the wind blew from the four quarters of he world. And Caradoc and his Cymry came against hem valiantly, slaying them in heaps. And equal rere Caradoc and his Cymry, on open ground, to rhat they before were found in the woods.

After these wars, when so many of the Cæsarians ad been killed, their bones, which had been left by he wolves, and dogs, and ravens, like a white sheet f snow, in many places covering the face of the arth ; and in the Maesmawr [1] in Wales, namely, the ountry where now is the monastery of Margam, rere found the greatest quantity of bones, on account f the great battle on the open ground, which was ought with the Romans, who were there slain.

Manawyddan, son of Llyr, caused the bones to be ollected in one heap, and also those were brought rom other parts of his dominion ; thus it came to iis mind to form a prison of the bones in which to onfine those taken prisoners in war. And a large difice was constructed, with strong walls, of those iones, mixed with lime. This was called the prison f Oeth and Annoeth, open and concealed, in memo-

[1] Maesmawr—great field.

rial of what the Cymry and Caradoc had done for their country and race, as well in the open ground as in the covert.[1]

The Cæsarians destroyed the prison, but it was always re-built; however, in course of time the bones became rotten, and the prison was taken down and the bones spread over the fields, which afterwards yielded great crops of wheat and barley.

Right over Brombil, on Margam Mountain, is a cross of raised earth and grass-grown, a conspicuous object when looked at from higher ground; it measures right across each arm one hundred and thirty feet. It was marked on the Ordnance Survey as Cross on site of Cairn. I asked the Director of the Survey whence the authority for this statement was obtained, and he said the statement was made by an aged man in this district. I then pointed out the remote period the cross would date from, and the " Site of Cairn " was abandoned. The Cross is known, traditionally, in the district of Margam, as the Soldiers' Grave. I believe the Cross marks the site of the prison of Oeth and Annoeth, and was put there many ages ago to consecrate the spot where the bones of so many soldiers had been gathered together. It evidently marks the site of some important event which can only be conjectured.

The track-way, from Bodvoc's last resting-place near the Halting Camp, crosses the mountains in a northerly direction, part of the roadway on Margam Mountain being a lane named Heol-y-Moch[2] on the

[1] The account of Caradoc (in substance) from the Iolo MS.
[2] Pig's lane.

boundary of Margam parish. The road is either a
British track or a Roman road, probably the latter,
for at one point it is pitched or paved and is raised
above the land on either side. On the way, as the
road dips down from Heol-y-Moch and in the hollow,
is the Carreg Bica,[1] or pointed stone, evidently a
direction mark necessary in the dense mists which
so often cover the mountain-tops like a pall, impenetrable and bewildering. The road, a little way
north of the Carreg Bica, climbs up on to a great
hill with precipitous side on the south. The hill

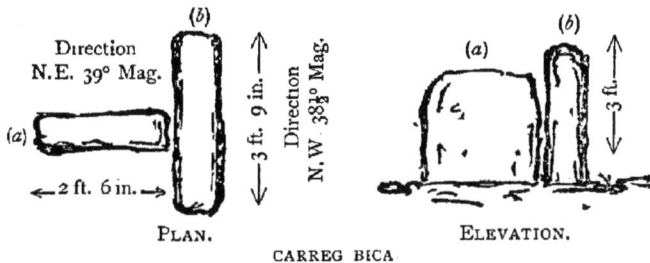

PLAN.   ELEVATION.

CARREG BICA

evidently marks the scene of fierce struggles, for it is
called the Tor-y-Cymerau—the mount of conflicts. It
is known locally as Tor-y-Cymry, but this is clearly
wrong, as we find it phonetically spelled by the
monastic scribe in the Margam MSS. as Torkemereu
or Torkemerev, the " v " standing for " u," and Toyke-

[1] Carreg Bica . I believe this to be Middlecrosse, referred
to in the Margam MSS. The pointed-stone ; the name
originally was probably pointing-stone. The two stones are not
pointed. The stone (*a*) points in the direction of the track way
as it climbs the hill Tor-y-Cymmerau after passing out of the
valley between it and the Carreg Bica.

merev; Toy being probably an error of the MSS. for
Tor.[1] Cymer, or Cymmer, is an obsolete word for con-
flict. The Ordnance Survey has it " Rhiw Tor-y-
Cymry, Site of Battle." To the west, a little north of
west, three-quarters of a mile is a tumulus called Pen
Dysgwylfa, the head or top of the watching-place :
it stands 1,191 feet above sea-level, and is the
highest point in the parish of Margam. The Rhiw
is the steep roadway leading up the side of the
Tor.

" The distances on the Roman roads were made
known to the traveller by milestones, usually called
milliaria, but sometimes *lapides*. The former term
was derived from the length of the Roman mile, which
consisted of 1,000 paces (*mille passuum*); the latter
was used in a more familiar sense, as may be gathered
from the fact that we find the phrase *ad tertium
lapidem* or *ad tertium* used to express the distance
of three miles from Rome. And a station on the
south coast, between Bittern (Clausentum), near
Southampton, and Richborough (Rutupiae), called
Ad Decimum, to denote it being ten miles from
Chichester (Regnum)."[2]

The length of the Roman mile must be considered a
moot point. Starting with the Pumpeius Carantorius
milliary stone on the north boundary of Kenfig
borough and proceeding southward, the next stone we
would come to in the borough is the Groes-y-Gryn
which formerly stood on the southern boundary at
Corneli (it is called a cross, but probably no cross ever

[1] Tor is a belly, a bulge, a boss, a belly-like hill.
[2] " Our Roman Highways," by Forbes and Burmester.

stood there). I believe this to have been a *milliarium*, or Roman milestone, but the two are two and a quarter miles apart. Starting again from the Pumpeius Carantorius Stone and proceeding north, we come to the site of a *milliarium* which formerly stood in the field near the old turnpike gate at Margam at Cefn Gwrgan lane, but on the opposite side. This stone, now in Margam Church, bears on it the inscription MAXIMINO INVICTO. The full inscription is :—

> IMPC
> FLAVA
> DMAXI or L MAXI
> MINO
> INVIC
> TOAV
> GVS.

Colonel Francis reads it :—

> IMP. C. FLA. VAL
> MAXIMINO
> INVICTO
> AVGVS(TO)

This stone was 2⅓ miles from the Pumpeius Stone. A third stone stood by the side of the tramway leading to Llewelyn's Quay on the sea side of the main road. This stone was a little under two miles from the Maximin Stone, but I am of opinion that this stone had been removed from its proper position on the main road to where it stood recently, so that probably it stood two miles from the Maximin Stone. The distance of roughly two miles in these cases is some-

what curious, and I can only think that the distance
of two miles was divided by a milliary stone which,
probably unimportant or incorporated in a wall, has
escaped notice, or it may have been removed.

On the back of the Maximinus Invictus Stone is an
inscription in debased Roman capitals with minuscule
"h," hic IACIT CANTUSUS PATER PAULINUS. The
formula *hic jacit*—"here lies" (the body of)—shows
that Cantusus was a Christian. The Latinity is
defective, for it may read, " Here lies Cantusus, whose
father was Paulinus," or "Here lies Cantusus, the father
of Paulinus," the genitive *i* being confused with the
nominative *us*. This with the Bodvoc Stone gives
us two Roman, or Roman-British, Christian sepulchral inscriptions in the parish of Margam.

The stone mentioned above as standing by the
siding tramway, described on the Ordnance Survey
as a milliary stone, is, I think, more likely to have
been a gravestone from the ancient chapel of
St. Thomas close by. It is a round-headed stone
with an incised wheel with six spokes, and on the
reverse side a cross with the upper part in a circle
and the centre line prolonged and ending with the
half-circle of an anchor.

A milliary stone was discovered several years ago
on the western side of the new cut, which was made
in A.D. 1836 to divert the water of the Afan river from
its old outlet. It had evidently served as a gravestone in the ancient burial-ground known as Platch
yr Eglwys,[1] but where it was brought from

---

[1] Platch yr Eglwys—platch means a plot of ground attached
to the church.

nothing is known. The probability is, at least so it seems to me, that the stone was placed on the highway in or near Aberavon before the town existed. In years after, some hundreds probably, as buildings came to be erected on the highway to form the High Street, the stone had to be removed, and some person thought it would make a fine headstone, and so used it in the ancient chapel burying-ground. The stone, the Rev. H. H. Knight records, was brought to Newton Nottage after being used as ballast in a pilot boat.

If I am right in thinking the position of this milliary stone was in Aberavon, then its distance from the Maximimus Invictus Stone at Cefn Gwrgan would be about two to 2¼ miles, or about the same as between the others. The inscription is, according to the Rev. H. H. Knight :

IMPC
MAGOR
DIANVS
AVG

Gordian the Third it is inscribed to. He was Emperor for six years and was treacherously put to death A.D. 244.

Colonel G. F. Francis reads the inscription on one side as —

DAEC
MAGOR
DIANVS
AVG

There are indistinct letters on the other side, as well as the following :

IMPPC

DIO

CLETI

ΛNO

MARC

VRE

OR

This inscription was to Diocletian.

Another Roman milliary stone was found near Pyle, and it is to be regretted that no record can be found as to its exact position. It is now in the Royal Institution, Swansea. Colonel Francis gives the inscription as—

IMP

MCPIλ

VONIO

VICTOR

INOλVG°

"The name of Victorinus recording one of the thirty tyrants slain A.U.C. 1019. A number of coins of Victorinus were found at Gwindy, near Llansamlet, in June, 1835 (Dillwyn's "Swansea," p. 56 ; Numism. II. i. 132). It was probably erected by the Legion which happened to be at Boverton at the time of the usurpation of Victorinus in Gaul (A.D. 265) in the time of Gallienus, whose inscriptions are of the greatest rarity and interest." [1]

[1] Westwood's " Lapidarium Walliae "

Westwood says the Pumpeius Stone bears the local name of " Bedd Morgan Morganwg," the " Sepulchre of Morgan Morganwg."

The late Mr. Leman wrote on the Roman mile : " Nothing can be clearer than that the Roman miles were not always of the same length, but differed from each other like our computed ones, or like the leagues in France ; for on measuring a space of ground where the country is perfectly level, the Roman miles differ but little from our present measured ones, but are infinitely longer than ours where the *iter* passes over a mountainous country ; for which reason I cannot help thinking that they calculated the distance between their several stations by ' horizontal miles.' "

Now, taking the Roman miles as roughly approximating to ours, the missing milliary stone between Pumpeius and Groes-y-Gryn would be between Pont Felin Newydd and the railway arch, so it is probably covered up in the sand.

Northwards of Pumpeius the missing stone would be near the ruins of Margam Abbey, for the road then passed from Beggar's Bush around by the Abbey and out by the present post-office. One can well understand a stone at this point would be in the way of building or road improvement.

Between the Maximinus Invictus Stone at Cefn Gwrgan and the stone I believe to have stood by the roadside in Aberavon, midway would be in Taibach. I think its position is approximately given us by the name of the field under Underhill and which once belonged to it, Cae Groes. It appears to me that these milliary stones came to be called crosses by the people ; thus, Groes-y-Gryn at Corneli, I believe was only a plain stone stood there. The Maximinus Invictus Stone at Cefn Gwrgan represented, I believe, what was known as Brombil's Cross ; but it was not a cross. Therefore I conclude the field in Taibach abutting on the main road was called Cae Groes from the Roman milliary stone which probably stood there.

The following is an extract from a curious letter relating to the Pumpeius Carantorius Stone. It is from Francis Godwin, Bishop of Llandaff, to Camden, the antiquary (Cotton MS., Julius F. VI., F. 297), July 14, 1603—

". . . Since my last letter, hauyng trauayled through Glamorgan Shyre I mett with a monument of right venerable antiquity which I can not but impart unto you. It is a hard stone of some 4 foote long (as I remember) about d (? demi) a foote thick and happily one foote high (? wide). Upon ye upmost edge of it are written these characters [I presume the stone was prone at that time, so the one "foote" high would be right and also the statement that the inscription was on the upmost edge]:

"PUNP EIVS
CAR AN TOPIUS

" Our Welchmen wyll needes perswade me y^t they are to be read thus 'Pimp bis *an* car an topius,' so altering ye twoo first words, and adding ye 3d

which they assure them selves to be worne out,
although there be no signe of any. And not with
standing thys alteration, rather by tradition than
y᷑ yᵉ moderne interpretation beareth it, they deliver
it signifyeth, ʻyᵉ 5 fingers of our owne freindes kins-
folks have over throwne or slayne us.' More, they
affirme it to be yᵉ monument of Morgan of whose
do . . . yᵉ whole country is thought to receave hys
name in deade it is with in one little myle of yᵉ abbey
of (Mar) gam where Sir Tho. Maunsell now dwelleth.
Viz . . . nard, neere Kenfig in yᵉ very high way.
The . . . a Roman antiquity . . . topp of a high
mountaine I take order to have it copyed ; [he refers
to the Bodvoc stone], which done I wyll also impart
it unto you, allwayes with a protestation y᷑ my self
sawe it not. As for thys & yᵉ rest ʻ Ipse vidi &
quam potui accuratissime ad archetypi exemplar
descripsi ' . . .

" Your very lo. & assured fr.

" Fʀ. Lᴀɴᴅᴀᴠᴇɴ."

There are two crosses at Margam placed in the
church for safe keeping, the Cross of Ilquici and the
Cross of Ilci ; the two formed a bridge across the
brook at Cwrt-y-defaid many years ago. The inscription, much defaced, on the Ilquici Stone, as far as can
be made out, is—

petri ilquici
acer
ef chant
t

On the Ilci Stone—

ilci.   Fecit
hanc cruce
m.   in nomin
e.   di ſummi.

" Ilci fecit hanc crucem in nomine dei summi " (" Ilci made the cross in the name of the Supreme God").

The great sculptured stone, the Cross of Ilquici, is 6 feet high, 3 feet broad, and 1 foot thick, and is ornamented on the upper part of both sides with a large plain wheel-cross with eight spokes and a raised boss in the centre, the spaces around which are filled in with irregular incised lines.   On the back the lower part has the outlines of a plain cross.

The Ilci Stone is similar, being 5½ feet high, 2 feet wide in the middle, and 34 inches wide at the top, 11 to 5 inches thick.   The upper part is occupied by a plain wheel-cross with eight spokes.

Westwood says the letters are minuscules of a more ancient form than those of Grutne [1] and Brancuf, [2] which latter he considers to be not earlier than the ninth, or later than the tenth, century.

Dr. John Jones (" Hist. of Wales," p. 331) states that the Ilquici Cross was dedicated to the Trinity by Lord Rhys ab Gryffydd, and that the Ilci Cross was erected by Alice, daughter of Richard de Clare, Earl of Gloucester, and wife of Cadwaladr ab Gryffydd ab Cynan, about A.D. 1172.   From the Abbey MSS. we find there was a Groes Gruffith (so it is spelled) on

---

[1] At Margam.   [2] At Baglan.

THE ABBEY MILL AT MARGAM

the roadside which leads from Rhŷd Blaen-y-Cwm to
Ton Grugos, probably on the west side of Moel Ton
Mawr. And from the same source that there was
a cross called Kananescros (Cynan's Cross) on the
mountain between the waters of Kenefeg and Baythan
(the latter is now Nant Craig yr Aber),[1] and near the
highway leading to Blaen Kenfig. The cross would
be, I think, about south-west from Gilfach Uchaf, on
the roadside leading to Rhŷd Blaen-y-Cwm. I find
this in a grant by Morgan, son of Owein, to Margam
Abbey of all his land of Heuedhaloc, Hafodheulog.

Dr. Jones could know nothing of there having been
a Groes Gruffydd or a Groes Cynan. It is quite
possible these stones may have been on the mountains and in the position I have assigned them, but
from their date they cannot have been put up by
Lord Rhys ab Gryffydd or Alice, daughter of
Richard de Clare.

I have said before, the ancient Roman road, "the
great high-way," as Leland terms it, runs through
the whole of Pyle and Kenfig, and through Higher
Kenfig, in Margam parish; the road in the latter is
known as Heol-troad-dwr—the road of the turning of

---

[1] I think this is a corruption of Craig-y-Abbat, colloquially it
is known as Craig-yr-apper. In Morgan's deed the brook is
called Baythan, Baiden, and it flows past a farm called Aber
Baiden. In the Margam MSS. is a warrant by Sir Ed. Mansell
to his steward, David Bennett, to make a lease to Margaret
David, wife of Robert Thomas Robert, and two others, of a
parcel of waste lands on Margam Mountain, lately enclosed—
five acres—bounded by the wood called Craig-yr-Abot on the
east and the highway from Llangonoyd Church on the south.
This I believe to refer to what is now called Craig-yr-Aber,
which seems to me to be meaningless.

the water.[1]   I have no doubt the real name is Heol-
y-Troedwyr—the road of the footmen, or infantry; but
in the course of long years, from A.D. 412, when the
Romans left this land, the name, or meaning, rather,
became lost in the mists of time.   But how did it
become to be called Heol-troad-dwr?   In this way :
before the abbey was erected, the stream from the
valleys Cwm Maelwg and Cwm Traherne went direct
to the moors, probably in the line of Smith's Lane
and near Ty'n-y-Caeau, and so to the sea by the
estuary, before the sea-walls were made.   A fulling
mill was erected by the monks at Cwrt-y-defaid,
"Sheppes Mill" as it is called in the Abbey deeds,
from its purpose—the production of the woollen
material for the monks' clothing; so the stream had
to be diverted and taken by a culvert under the
Abbey grounds and by an artificial cut at a level suitable for the stream to be utilised for the " Sheppes "
Mill.   It was continued past Eglwysnunyd and Kenfig
farms, roughly parallel with the roadway, crossing it
eventually at the modern Pont Bwrlac, near Ty'n
y-Seler, and falling into the Kenfig river near the
castle, a total distance of 2½ miles, all in an artificial stream-bed.   The turning of this stream along
the roadway, and a lingering reluctance in the old
name to pass completely away, caused people to call
it Heol-troad-dwr—the road of the turning of the
water—a name, so to speak, born of the ancient name
Heol-y-troedwyr.   At first the leat would probably
only be taken as far as Cwrt-y-defaid, just where
Water Street begins, and later the waterway was

[1] Called in English, Water Street.

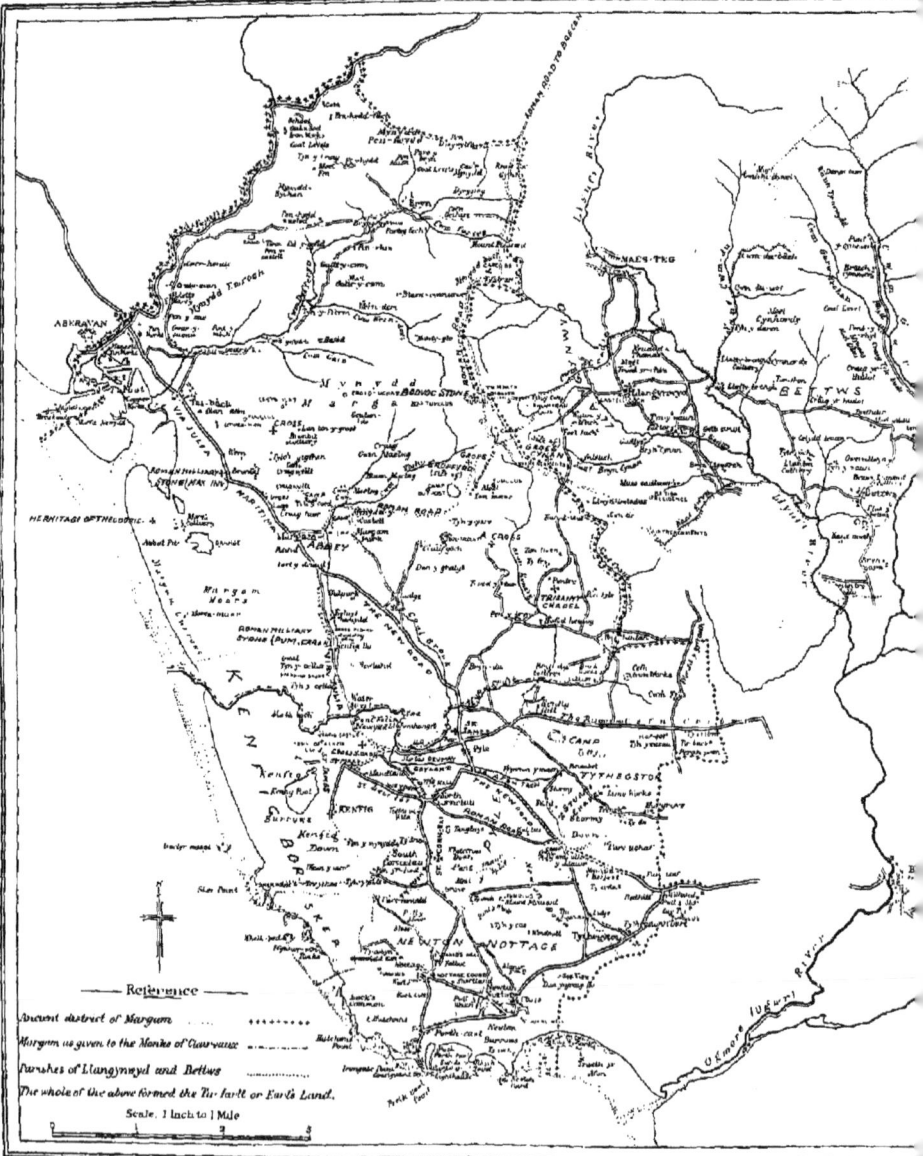

extended for the use of Eglwysnynyd and Kenfig farms.

We have already seen how Margam in ancient times comprised a much larger area than it does to-day ; probably it embraced the whole of the lands retained by Sir Robert Fitzhamon in this neighbourhood. I endeavour to show in the plan the boundaries of ancient Margam, which included in its area Kenfig, Pyle, Newton Nottage, Sker, and Margam of to-day, and probably Tythegston, or part of it.

Geoffrey of Monmouth tells us "that in very early times the Queen of Britain, Cordeilla, daughter of Levi, King of Britain, began to meet with disturbances from the two sons of her sisters, whereof one, named Margan, was born to Maglaunus, and the other, named Cunedagius, to Hennius. These, incensed to see Britain subject to a woman, raised a rebellion against the queen ; several battles were fought, and Cordeilla was captured and put in prison, where for grief she killed herself. After this they divided the island between them ; from Humber northward to Caithness fell to Margan, the other part Cunedagius's share. At the end of two years Margan began to think he should govern the whole island, his due by right of birth. He marched an army through Cunedagius's country and began to burn all before him. Cunedagius, however, met him and put him and his army to flight, till at last Margan was killed in a town of Cambria, which has been called Margan to this day. At this time Rome was built by Romulus and Remus, about the year before Christ 753."

extended for the use of Eglwysnynyd and Kenfig farms.

We have already seen how Margam in ancient times comprised a much larger area than it does to-day ; probably it embraced the whole of the lands retained by Sir Robert Fitzhamon in this neighbourhood. I endeavour to show in the plan the boundaries of ancient Margam, which included in its area Kenfig, Pyle, Newton Nottage, Sker, and Margam of to-day, and probably Tythegston, or part of it.

Geoffrey of Monmouth tells us "that in very early times the Queen of Britain, Cordeilla, daughter of Levi, King of Britain, began to meet with disturbances from the two sons of her sisters, whereof one, named Margan, was born to Maglaunus, and the other, named Cunedagius, to Hennius. These, incensed to see Britain subject to a woman, raised a rebellion against the queen ; several battles were fought, and Cordeilla was captured and put in prison, where for grief she killed herself. After this they divided the island between them ; from Humber northward to Caithness fell to Margan, the other part Cunedagius's share. At the end of two years Margan began to think he should govern the whole island, his due by right of birth. He marched an army through Cunedagius's country and began to burn all before him. Cunedagius, however, met him and put him and his army to flight, till at last Margan was killed in a town of Cambria, which has been called Margan to this day. At this time Rome was built by Romulus and Remus, about the year before Christ 753."

Iolo Morganwg's copy of Llywelyn Sion's[1] tran-
script, written probably about A.D. 1580, states that
Morgan Mwynfawr was King of Glamorgan, and
gave his name to the country ; he was a good, valiant,
and wise king. He erected a Court at Margan, a
place which he raised to a bishoprick ; which retained
that distinction during the lives of five bishops, when
it became united to Llandaff.

The following list of Bishops of Glamorgan, *alias*
Kenfigge, from Iolo's papers probably include the five
referred to. I cannot account for Glamorgan *alias*
Kenfigg.

The bishops are—

    1. Morgan, the son of Adras, Bishop and King.
    2. Ystyphan.
    3. Cattwg.
    4. Iago.
    5. Cawan.
    6. Tyfodwg.
    7. Cyfelach.
    8. Mabon.

See "Liber Land.," p. 625. But it does not
appear that they ever ranked higher than *Chore-
piscopi*, if all of them even attained that dignity.
Margam, originally *Morgan* (see Williams's " Mon."),
as well as Glamorgan, is said, with apparent reason,
to have derived its name from Morgan Mwynfawr ;
and the designation *city*, conferred on all sees of
bishops, is applied to it by former writers. (This,
of course, refers to Margam, and not the district of

    [1] Sir Edward Mansel mentions Llywelyn Sion as Llywelyn
John of Llangewydd.

Margam). In one of the Prefaces to "Cyfrinach y Beirdd," a work of surpassing erudition on Welsh Prosody, the compilation of that treatise, from old authors, is thus noticed: "Ag Edward Dafydd *o Ddinas* Margam yn Morganwg ai trefnodd, and Edward Dafydd of the *city* of Margam in Glamorgan, arranged it." [1]

So Kenfig, having been a bishopric, was equally entitled to be called a city.

Now we are drawing to a close of the early history of Kenfig. The Abbey of Margam is about to fall and its property to be sold; the old order of things is about to pass away for ever.

One of the latest deeds granted by the Abbey is a lease by David Abbot, and convent therein, to Lewis ap Thomas ap Howell, and Jankyn his son, of the Grange of Nochecourt (Nottage Court) for 99 years at a yearly rent of 30 crannocs of barley and 30 crannocs of oats, with allowance of timber for building houses on the site, &c.

Dated in the Chapter-house, Margam, 28 March, A.D. 1509.

This deed proves that the house, Nottage Court, was a grange belonging to Margam Abbey.

Very little remains to show what Kenfig was like under the rule of the lords of Glamorgan, and but little, other than deeds, to show the connection between Kenfig and the powerful Abbey. The old church, about which so much quarrelling took place, exists no longer, and all we have of ancient times are the churches of St. Mary Magdalene and St. James's,

[1] Iolo MS.

21

Pyle. True, there is a charming lane, part of the Roman highway, which leads from near Mawdlam, after passing the Groes-y-dadl, to Corneli, which remains as it was in early times ; a cart or carriage fits it so that nothing could be passed. It is pretty, and should be visited before it becomes widened and modernised.

I have nothing to say of the modern history of Kenfig, except as to the document closing the career of Kenfig as a borough town. I leave that to another pen ; it has no charm for me.

CHAPTER XVI

THE END OF THE ABBEY OF MARGAM AND ITS HOLDINGS IN KENFIG, AND THE END OF THE BOROUGH

YOU will, I fear, think I have brought Margam Abbey very much into these pages ; but if you think of it, I could only get at Kenfig's early years through the monastic deeds.

The original document, T. 359 (C. MCCCXLIV), is still extant which records the sale of the abbey, the church, bell-tower, cemetery, water-mill, the Afan fishery, the granges called Le Newe Graunge, Cwrt Newydd, Le Upper Graunge, Noge Court Graunge, Nottage Court, and White Cross Graunge, Groes Wen farm, the land called Southwose, St. Michael's Graunge, Langlond, Portland, appurtenances in Kenfegge, Tanglwst Graunge, Langewithe Graunge, Stormy Graunge, coal-mine in Kevencrebur, Brombell, tithes in Penvey, etc., to Sir Rice Manxell, Knt., to be held as the last Abbot Lodowicus Thomas held them for the twentieth part of a knight's fee. Rent for Llangewydd Grange and the tithes of Penvey 26s. 10½d., and for the site of the Abbey, &c., 27s. 5½d., the sum paid was £938 6s. 8d. This would probably be worth, in to-day's money, about £14,000.

Dated at Westminster, 22 June, A.D. 1540, 36 Hen. VIII.

A second sale to Sir Rice Manxell, T. 362 (C. MCCCLI), for £642 9s. 8d., was of the manors of Horgro, *alias* Horgrove, and Pylle,[1] *alias* Pyle, formerly belonging to the dissolved Abbey, together with various lands, mills, etc., in Margam, and in Marcrosse and Pylle, *alias* Pyle.

Dated at Terlying [Terling, Co. Essex], 5 Aug., A.D. 1543. The manor of Pyle passed into Sir Rice's hands. In A.D. 1557 Sir Rice purchased Laleston.

Sir Rice further bought the demesne of Hawode-y-Porthe, Hafod-y-porth, the manor of Kenfyge and the manor of Tethegistoo, Tythegstone, and Seynt Mychaelles Mill in the parish of Margam, lands in Kenfige, etc., for £678 1s. 7d., or about £10,000 of our money.

Dated Hampton Court, 28 Aug., A.D. 1546, 38 Henry VIII.

The manor of Kenfig, as I have remarked elsewhere, did not pass into the hands of Sir Rice. The King, later, accepted from Sir Rice £300 in lieu of £642 9s. 8d. due for the first purchase.

[1] Pyle is called Marcross and Pylle, *alias* Pyle. Margam Abbey owned a grange called Marcrosberwes, or Marcross burrows. I think the farm must have been on the edge of the sand dunes in Pyle parish, the part reaching towards Sker.

The End.

Sic transit gloria mundi.

On the 9th of September, 1886, a notice headed "Kenfig"—a dry, unsympathetic notice—was sent to the Constable of the Castle, Portreeve, and Burgesses of Kenfig, in the County of Glamorgan, dissolving the ancient Corporation. Trustees are to be appointed to manage the property of the Burgesses. They are twelve in number, and 'shall be called the Trustees of the Kenfig Corporation Property.' Four to be appointed by the persons whose names shall be on the Burgesses' Roll; four by the Rural Sanitary Authority Bridgend and Cowbridge Union; four by the Margam Local Board.

The Trustees shall stand possessed of the interest of the Corporation in Kenfig Common, referred to in the Schedule to the scheme. Upon trust as follows; that is to say :—

1. To permit the persons whose names shall be on the Burgesses' Roll as Burgesses or Burgesses' Widows, who now have, or as Burgesses' Sons or Widows who hereafter acquire, right of pasture and of cutting fern on the said Common, to exercise and enjoy the rights aforesaid as fully and effectually, and for such time, and in such manner as he or she, by any Statute, charter, byelaw, or custom of the Corporation in force at the time of passing the Municipal Corporation Act, 1883, might or could have had, acquired, or enjoyed, in case that Act had not been passed.

2. Upon the extinction of the aforesaid rights of all of the said Burgesses and Burgesses' Sons and Widows to allow all the inhabitant householders of the said place of Kenfig to exercise such rights.

3. Provides that if previous to the extinction of the said rights the number entitled to enjoy the said rights shall fall below the number of persons so entitled on the formation of the Burgesses' Roll, then the rights of pasture and cutting fern may be let at the best rent they can obtain, etc. The Trustees shall stand possessed of the income derived from the property, including rents received by the letting of rights on Kenfig Common, also any fines, fees, or sums of money paid to them subject to Manorial rents.

Upon trust to pay, etc.

1. In payment of interest, salaries, and other lawful expense and cost of administration of the scheme.

2. In recompensing existing Officers of the Corporation who, by reason of the dissolution of the Corporation, have been deprived of any emolument of pecuniary profit, etc.

3. In payment annually of 11s. to each of the Burgesses or Burgesses' Sons or Widows who represent the Burgesses who were the original holders of parcels of the Common called Gwaunycimla or Le Rugge.

4. The residue to be equally divided between the aforesaid persons.

5. Provides for the division of the said residue in case the number of persons falls short of the number

on the Roll, and a "Surplus Fund Account" to be formed.

Six articles follow, providing for the management of the scheme and the sending in of claims of persons entitled to be Burgesses or Burgesses' Sons or Widows, etc., etc.

SCHEDULE.

The Public House called the Prince of Wales Inn, now let with the plots of land next mentioned to Mrs. Yorath at a rent of £10 per annum.

A garden, a pond, and a field containing 1a. 2c. or thereabouts, known as the "Croft," and let with the said Prince of Wales Inn as aforesaid.

The interest of the Corporation in Kenfig Common or Down, containing 1,200 acres or thereabouts.

The franchise of free warren on a certain portion of the said Kenfig Common, now let at a rent of £35 10s. per annum.

Sums of £1,600 and £100 now in the custody of Christopher R. M. Talbot, Esquire, M.P., on which interest is paid to the Corporation at the rate of £5 per centum per annum.

Chattel property, including silver mace, cup, sets of weights, seal, furniture, and documents. (These are of late date—George II., I believe.)

And so, like Kenfig Borough, and maybe my readers' patience, my work has reached its close, and I have now to express my grateful thanks to Dr. Walter de Gray Birch, LL.D., F.S.A., Librarian of the Marquess of Bute at Cardiff Castle and elsewhere,

for much valuable assistance; to Mr. Godfrey Lips-
comb, of Twyn-yr-hŷdd, for much kind assistance ; to
Mr. Ed. Roberts, of Swansea, for help in elucidating
Welsh place-names ; to the Rev. D. J. Jones ; to the
Rev. Thomas Howell for information on Kenfig ; to
Mr. Voyle Morgan for sketch of altar-slabs ; also to
Mr. John Cox and Mr. E. M. Jenkins for kind assist-
ance.   My little dog I must not forget ; he willingly
sat by the menhir to give an idea of its height.
He loved the sand-dunes too, but I think rabbits had
something to do with his love.

The photographs of Sker, Kenfig Pool, Castle, and
Pyle Church are by Mr. Newark Lewis, Port Talbot ;
the font by Mr. T. W. Gray.   Some of the others
are mine.

APPENDICES

I

THE DESCENDANTS OF SIR ROBERT FITZHAMON

WE have seen a great deal about the early lords of Glamorgan and owners of the manor of Kenfig, so it may be interesting to follow the line which Fitzhamon commenced.

As we have seen, Sir Robert was succeeded by his son-in-law, Robert Earl of Gloucester, son of King Henry I.

Robert the Earl was succeeded by his son William, whose only son Robert died early in life. His daughter Amice married Richard de Clare, Earl of Hertford, and from her all the later Earls of Gloucester were descended.

The third daughter married Prince John, Earl of Mortagne, afterwards King John of England. John became the third Earl of Gloucester and lord of Glamorgan, but on becoming King he divorced his wife, who then married Geoffrey de Mandeville. Geoffrey became, by right of his wife, fourth Earl of Gloucester and lord of Glamorgan. He was killed at a tournament in London. Isabella, his widow, married a third husband, Hubert de Burgh, Earl of Kent.

Isabella's sister Mabel married Almeric de Montford, a Norman Earl who became fifth Earl of Gloucester and lord of Glamorgan ; he bore the title only for a short time before his death in 1221.

Two of the daughters of William the Earl having failed to provide a line of succession for the lands and title, both fell to the third daughter Amice, who had married Richard de Clare, Earl of Hertford, and thus it happened that the golden shield

of the Clares with the three red chevrons was first seen among
the lords of Glamorgan, and is now the heraldry of Cardiff City.
These arms were also borne by Margam Abbey.

Gilbert their son, as the lineal successor of Fitzhamon, uniting
the earldom of Gloucester with that of Hertford, became the
sixth Earl of Gloucester and lord of Glamorgan ; he married
Isabel, daughter of William Earl of Pembroke. Gilbert succeeded in 1221 ; died in 1230.

Isabel, five months after his death, married his friend Richard
Earl of Cornwall, brother of King Henry III. ; she thus became
Countess of Gloucester, Hertford, Cornwall and Poictiers She
died 1239–40. Isabel left many legacies to Tewkesbury Abbey,
among them a phial containing relics of St. Cornelius or St
Corneli.

As Richard de Clare, Gilbert's son, was only eight years old
when his father died, he became the King's ward for several
years. He succeeded in 1243. He married Maud de Lacy
after being, by the King's influence, divorced from Margaret
de Burgh. Richard took the " cross " and went to the Crusades.
He died in 1262. He was the seventh Earl of Gloucester and
lord of Glamorgan.

Gilbert de Clare, eighth Earl, was nicknamed "the red." Like
his father Richard, he was a ward of the Crown for two years
When he was nine years of age he was betrothed to Alice,
daughter of Guy, Earl of March and Angoulême, who was still
younger ; they were married in 1253, eight years after. They
were divorced twenty-three years later, and Gilbert married
Joan d'Acre, daughter of King Edward I. Their son Gilbert
was born in 1290, and was scarcely five years old when his
father died.

Joan d'Acre, almost immediately after the Red Earl's death,
married a plain esquire, Ralph de Monthermer. Her father, the
King, confiscated her lands and imprisoned her husband in
Bristol Castle, but was eventually reconciled to his daughter.
Ralph was permitted to bear the title of Earl of Gloucester until
the young Gilbert came of age. He was thus ninth Earl of
Gloucester and was also lord of Glamorgan.

In the Calendar of Patent Rolls, June 24, 1307, 35 Ed. I , is a
grant to Ralph de Monte Hermeri, Earl of Gloucester, in lieu of
a grant to him in fee simple of the Earldom of Athol and the

lands pertaining thereto in Scotland, but which the King now proposes to grant to David, son of John, sometime Earl of Athol, of 10,000 marks for him to buy land to the value of 1,000 marks a year for the maintenance of himself and his children by Joan, the King's daughter. The said David will pay 5,000 marks thereof. For the other 5,000 marks the King grants him the custody, during the minority of the heir, of all the lands in Wales without counties, which, by the death of the said Joan and by reason of the minority of Gilbert, son and heir of Gilbert de Clare, sometime Earl of Gloucester and Hertford, were taken into the King's hands. . . . Mandate to Roger du Lyt, to whom the King committed the custody of the Castle of Kennefeck to deliver the said castle to the Earl.

Gilbert de Clare was tenth Earl of Gloucester and lord of Glamorgan. He married Maud de Burgh, daughter of the Earl of Ulster. He was killed at the battle of Bannockburn, June 23, 1314, and with him the male line of the Clares came to an end; they had been lords of Glamorgan during a period of 89 years. His estates were divided among his three sisters, the honour of Gloucester going to Alianora, the eldest, who married, in 1321, Hugh le Despenser the younger, and he was created Earl of Gloucester. Thus the Despensers came to be lords of Glamorgan. Hugh was eleventh Earl of Gloucester. He had three sons—Hugh, Edward, and Gilbert. His surcoat was emblazoned with the chevrons of the Clares in the first and fourth quarters, Despenser fret in the second, and the sable bend of de ¡Chesnei in the third. He was hanged at Hereford for siding with the King, Edward II., against his wicked queen Isabel. His widow married William Lord de la Zouch.

Lord de la Zouch became lord of Glamorgan. He died in 1335. His widow retained the title of Countess of Gloucester until she died in 1337.

Margaret de Clare, sister of Alianora de Clare, married Hugh Lord de Audley, twelfth Earl of Gloucester but not lord of Glamorgan.

Hugh le Despenser, son and heir of Hugh le Despenser and Alianora, succeeded Lord de la Zouch as lord of Glamorgan. He married Elizabeth, daughter of William Montacute, Earl of Salisbury, but died childless in 1348-49. His widow married Guy de Brien, Lord of Welwyn, her third husband.

In the Calendar of Close Rolls is the entry: 1349, Apl. 30, 23 Edw. III. To Simon Basset, escheator in co. Gloucester, and to Roger de Berkerole, Order not to intermeddle further with the tenements assigned in dower to Elizabeth, late the wife of Hugh le Despenser tenant in chief, in their custody among the possessions of Hugh in Wales . . . and now the King has assigned to Elizabeth . . . the castle, manor and town of Kenfeg.

Hugh's nephew Edward, son of his brother Edward and Ann, daughter of Lord Ferrers, succeeded and became lord of Glamorgan in 1358. In the Calendar referred to above, date July 6, 1359, is the entry: To Henry de Prestwod, escheator in the co. Gloucester and the adjacent march of Wales, Order to deliver to Edward son of Edward le Despenser, kinsman and heir of Hugh le Despenser, whose homage the King has taken for the lands that the said Hugh his uncle held in chief at his death . . . the castle and manor of Kenefeg . . . taken into the King's hand by the death of Elizabeth late Hugh's wife . . . etc. He married Elizabeth, daughter of Lord de Burghersh. Edward le Despenser gave the charter dated May 14, 34 Edw. III., 1360, to Kenfig. The charter is not extant, but the text is preserved in the charter given by his son Thomas, dated 16 Feb. 1397, and preserved at Kenfig. Edward died at Cardiff Castle, 1375.

Thomas, third son of Edward, born about 1370, succeeded as lord of Glamorgan. He married Constance, daughter of Edmund of Langley, Earl of Cornwall and Duke of York, fourth son of King Edward III. Thomas, as stated above, gave a charter to Kenfig, and included in it is the *Inspeximus* of his father's charter to the burgesses. He was put to death at Bristol for siding with the King, January 15, 1399–1400.

Richard, son of Thomas, born 1396, succeeded, but he died at the age of 19 years, while still a ward of the Crown. His wife was Elizabeth, daughter of Ralph Neville, Earl of Westmoreland ; he left no children, and with him ended the line of the Despensers.

THE BEAUCHAMPS.

Richard le Despenser's sister Isabel, born at Cardiff, July 26, 1400, succeeded to his lands and rights. She married Richard Beauchamp, Earl of Worcester, who became lord of Glamorgan from 1415 to 1422. They had a daughter Elizabeth His charter is preserved at Kenfig ; it is a confirmation of Thomas le Despenser's charter Isabel's charter is also preserved at Kenfig ; it is dated 1 May, 1423. The Earl was killed at Meaux.

Isabel afterwards, Nov. 26, 1423, married her late husband's cousin, Richard de Beauchamp, Earl of Warwick, who became lord of Glamorgan. They had a son, the future Duke of Warwick. Richard died at Rouen Castle in 1439, and his son succeeded him

Henry de Beauchamp, Duke of Warwick, became lord of Glamorgan. He married Cicely, daughter of Richard Neville Earl of Salisbury He died in 1446.

By marriage, in 1449, with Anne de Beauchamp, daughter of the Countess Isabel and sister of the Duke of Warwick, Richard Neville became lord of Glamorgan. He was known as the King-maker. He it was who granted to Margam Abbey Newton Nottage in exchange for Resolven. He was killed at the battle of Barnet, April 14, 1471. His widow lived thirty years after him in poverty. They had two daughters—Isabel, who married George Duke of Clarence, and Anne, who married first Edward, son of Henry VI., and afterwards King Richard III.

George Duke of Clarence, Earl of Warwick, became lord of Glamorgan. He had two sons, Edward and Richard, and a daughter, Margaret, who became Marchioness of Salisbury, and died on the scaffold in 1541—one of the crimes of Henry VIII. George is said to have been drowned in a butt of Malmsey wine in the Tower of London in 1477.

The possessions of the Clares and the Despensers had been finally absorbed among the Crown lands long before the death of Edward, the son of George Duke of Clarence. Thus the whole of Fitzhamon's possessions and rights were lost by his descendants.

[These notes on the descendants of Sir Robert Fitz-Hamon are taken in part from "Tewkesbury Abbey," by the Rev. John Henry Blunt, M.A., F.S.A.]

Genealogical Table of the Descendants of Robert Fitz-Hamon.

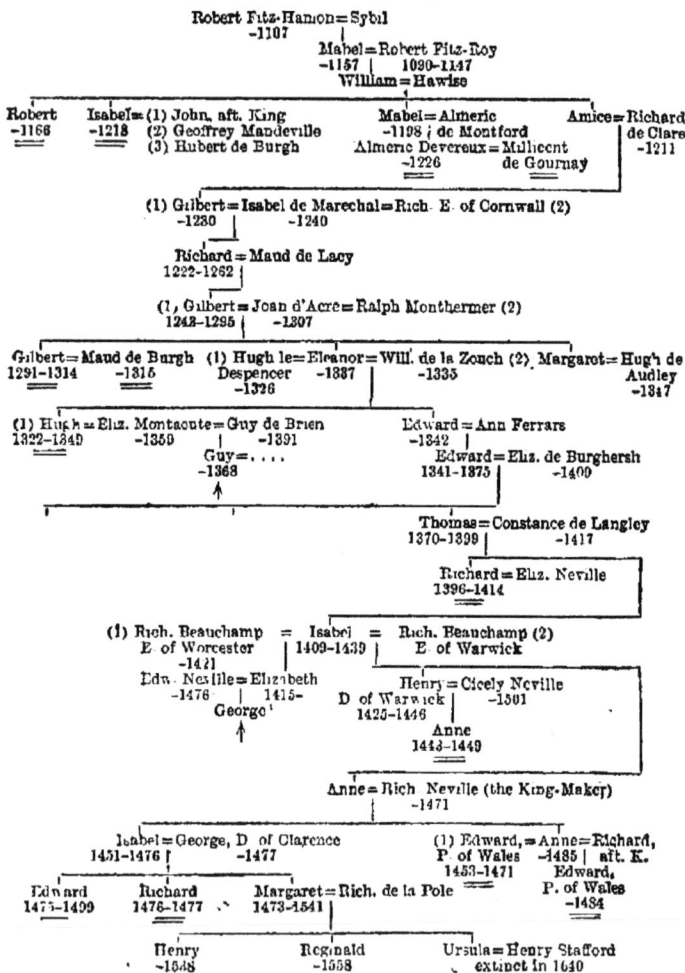

```
                    Robert Fitz-Hamon = Sybil
                           -1107
                                Mabel = Robert Fitz-Roy
                                -1157 |   1090-1147
                                William = Hawise

Robert      Isabel = (1) John, aft. King      Mabel = Almeric        Amice = Richard
-1166       -1218    (2) Geoffrey Mandeville   -1198 ; de Montford          de Clare
            ════       (3) Hubert de Burgh     Almeric Devereux = Millicent  -1211
                                               -1226          de Gournay
                                                                ═══

              (1) Gilbert = Isabel de Marechal = Rich. E. of Cornwall (2)
                  -1230         -1240

                      Richard = Maud de Lacy
                      1222-1262 |

                      (1, Gilbert = Joan d'Acre = Ralph Monthermer (2)
                      1243-1295 |    -1307

Gilbert = Maud de Burgh   (1) Hugh le = Eleanor = Will. de la Zouch (2)  Margaret = Hugh de
1291-1314   -1315           Despencer    -1337     -1335                            Audley
            ═══             -1326                                                   -1347

(1) Hugh = Eliz. Montacute = Guy de Brien     Edward = Ann Ferrars
1322-1349   -1359    |       -1391            -1342 |
                     Guy = ....                    Edward = Eliz. de Burghersh
                         -1368                      1341-1375    -1409
                          ↑

                                          Thomas = Constance de Langley
                                          1370-1399 |     -1417

                                              Richard = Eliz. Neville
                                              1396-1414

(1) Rich. Beauchamp   =   Isabel   =   Rich. Beauchamp (2)
    E. of Worcester      1409-1439    E. of Warwick
    -1421
Edw. Neville = Elizabeth            Henry = Cicely Neville
-1476    |   1415-                  D. of Warwick   -1501
   George'                          1425-1446 |
    ↑                               Anne
                                    1443-1449

                    Anne = Rich. Neville (the King-Maker)
                              -1471

       Isabel = George, D. of Clarence   (1) Edward, = Anne = Richard,
       1451-1476 |        -1477          P. of Wales  -1485 | aft. K.
                                         1453-1471         Edward,
Edward     Richard      Margaret = Rich. de la Pole  ═══   P. of Wales
1475-1499  1476-1477    1473-1541 |                        -1484

           Henry          Reginald        Ursula = Henry Stafford
           -1548          -1558             extinct in 1640
```

From whom the Earls of Abergavenney and the Barons Le Despencer are descended.

ADDITIONAL NOTES

Page 22.—Badlesmere and Brymmesfeld both appear to have been "custodes" in some manner in the year A.D. 1314, perhaps each for part of the year.

Page 38.—The year of the invasion of Glamorgan was about A D. 1090.

Page 39.—Crymlyn. I suggest Crynlyn as possibly the original name; crynu, to shake or to quake, the movement of a bog when walked on.

Page 43.—Astreville; this name no longer exists, and I have not been able to find the modern name of the town or place. Corbeil; a town on the River Seine, twenty-five miles south-south-east of Paris. Torigny; a town in the Department of La Manche in Normandy, thirty miles west-south-west of Caen. Granville; a seaport town on the west coast of La Manche in Normandy.

Page 45.—Tinchebrai; a town in the north-west of the Department of Orne in Normandy, fifty-four miles south-west of Caen. Mr. Clark says Fitzhamon was wounded at the siege of Caen and died of the wound.

Page 61.—"Calefurciis"; Mr. C. T. Martin, in the "Record Interpreter," gives Calafurcium, gallows. Ducange, in his "Glossarium," gives Calofurcium.

Page 62.—"At the command of Lewelin"; this was Llewelyn the Great, Llewelyn ap Iorwerth, Prince of Wales. He reigned from 1194 to 1240.

Page 69.—Llandaff; the Anglicised form of the Welsh Llan Dâv.

Page 84.—According to the Annales de Theokesberia Gilbert de Sullie, Vicar of Kenfig, died on August 7, A.D. 1242, and on September 4th Walter Alured was presented to the vicarage.

Page 143.—Hafodheulog; the sunny summer abode.

Page 148.—Another instance of the destruction of a port on this coast by the encroachment of the sea is mentioned by Mr.

C F. Cliffe in his " Book on South Wales." " The work of destruction," he writes, " is constantly going on. At the mouth of the Colhugh, a small stream which runs from Llantwit (Major), are vestiges of an ancient port, chiefly consisting of some piles of oak on the beach, called the ' Black-men,' an outwork of a pier. A considerable trade with Somersetshire was carried on, and vessels came here for protection in the reign of Henry VIII." With regard to Kenfig as a seaport, my friend, Mr. W. S. Powell, of Waungron, Whitland, formerly of Eglwysnunyd, tells me he was often told by old people that small ships used to use the mouth of Kenfig river, and he recollects seeing mooring-posts at the entrance a short distance from the shore. This is very interesting, and shows that up to comparatively recent times Kenfig river entrance, even after the besanding, was used as a harbour.

Page 209.—La Hamme; a plot of pasture ground, in some cases especially meadow-land, in others especially an enclosed plot, a close. Found in Old English and still in local use in the south, in some places surviving only as the name of a particular piece of ground (Murray).

Plan of site of Kenfig town, &c., is 4·20 inches to a mile.

Page 259.—A few days ago Mr. J. V. Morgan, Clerk of the Works at Margam, informed me that an ancient font had been unearthed at Sturmi Farm. As the farm is barely seven hundred yards away from the ruins of the church, I have no doubt this is the font, or part of it, which belonged to the little church It is of Sutton stone, and of somewhat rude workmanship The width is two feet nine and a half inches ; the sides are parallel for six inches, and then are splayed inwards, reducing the diameter to two feet two inches ; under the splay are two neck-rolls, the upper one two inches in depth and the lower one three inches ; the hollow is only six and a half inches in depth. This upper part originally stood on a pedestal, as an annular space ten inches in diameter and two and a half inches deep is provided for the shaft, and for further security a large dowel hole is continued for two or three inches. It is probable, if the ruins were cleared out, the base would be discovered, and thus an interesting relic of the church which Geoffrey Sturmi built " in his vill in the wilderness, on his land whereon no one had ever hitherto ploughed."

GENERAL INDEX

"Welsh People, The," Rhys and Jones, 192
Wenduin, St., 71, 75
Wern, to, 174
White Cross Down, 76
William the Chaplain, 150
Witherell stream, 272
Worcester, Earl of, 333
Wrenid, Groneath, 190, 258
Wurgan Du, 217

Y FILLDIR-AUR, "the Golden Mile," 39

Yltuit, croft of, 217
Yoruard ap Gistelard, 134
„ Coh, 274
„ son of Yoruard Coh, 274
Ystrad-fawr, near Bridgend, 272
Ystrad-y-fodwg, 253

Zancloden cambrensis, 259
Zewan ap Hagarath, 217

Lightning Source UK Ltd.
Milton Keynes UK
UKHW021151210622
404744UK00005BA/1132

9 780530 8401